Penguin Education

Ethnomethodology

Edited by Roy Turner

Penguin Modern Sociology

General Editor
Tom Burns

Ethnomethodology

Selected Readings

Edited by Roy Turner

Penguin Education

Penguin Education
Penguin Books Ltd, Harmondsworth,
Middlesex, England
Penguin Books Inc., 7110 Ambassador Road,
Baltimore, Md 21207, USA
Penguin Books Australia Ltd,
Ringwood, Victoria, Australia
Penguin Books Canada Ltd,
41 Steelcase Road West,
Markham, Ontario, Canada
Penguin Books (N.Z.) Ltd,
182–190 Wairau Road,
Auckland 10, New Zealand

First published 1974
Reprinted 1975
This selection copyright © Roy Turner, 1974
Introduction and notes copyright © Roy Turner, 1974
Copyright acknowledgements for items in
this volume will be found on page 279

Made and printed in Great Britain by
Hazell Watson & Viney Ltd,
Aylesbury, Bucks
Set in Monotype Times Roman

Contents

Introduction 7

Part One
On the Name and its Uses 13

1 Harold Garfinkel (1968)
The Origins of the Term 'Ethnomethodology' 15

Part Two
Theorizing as Practical Reasoning 19

2 Henry C. Elliot (1974)
Similarities and Differences between Science and Common Sense 21

3 Melvin Pollner (1974)
Sociological and Common-Sense Models of the Labelling Process 27

4 Dorothy Smith (1974)
Theorizing as Ideology 41

5 W. W. Sharrock (1974)
On Owning Knowledge 45

6 Michael Moerman (1968)
Accomplishing Ethnicity 54

7 Egon Bittner (1965)
The Concept of Organization 69

Part Three
Practical Reasoning in Organizational Settings 83

8 Aaron V. Cicourel (1968)
Police Practices and Official Records 85

9 Harold Garfinkel (1967)
Suicide, for all Practical Purposes 96

10 David Sudnow (1967)
Counting Deaths 102

11 Harold Garfinkel (1967)
'Good' Organizational Reasons for 'Bad' Clinic Records 109

12 Don H. Zimmerman (1969)
   Fact as a Practical Accomplishment   128

13 D. Lawrence Wieder (1974)
   Telling the Code   144

14 Kenneth Stoddart (1974)
   Pinched: Notes on the Ethnographer's Location of Argot   173

15 Robert W. Mackay (1973)
   Conceptions of Children and Models of Socialization   180

Part Four
Methodical Bases of Interaction   195

16 Roy Turner (1970)
   Words, Utterances and Activities   197

17 Harvey Sacks (1972)
   On the Analysability of Stories by Children   216

18 Emmanuel Schegloff and Harvey Sacks (1973)
   Opening Up Closings   233

19 A. Lincoln Ryave and James N. Schenkein (1974)
   Notes on the Art of Walking   265

Further Reading   275

Acknowledgements   279

Author Index   281

Subject Index   283

Introduction

This collection avoids, as far as possible, merely programmatic statements of ethnomethodology's character and directions, and focuses rather upon demonstrations and exemplars of research conducted in an ethnomethodological vein. I have attempted to represent the variety of research concerns and strategies which today pass as ethnomethodology. It is possible that some of the researchers here represented would not (or would no longer) characterize their work as ethnomethodology. The subsuming of these works under that rubric is my responsibility, and I have been guided chiefly by practical professional criteria: I think it is safe to say that all of these authors would be regarded by 'traditional' sociology – itself a gloss for a set of diverse enterprises – as practitioners of the 'school'. However, there is no guarantee that the items collected here will fit together like the pieces of a jigsaw puzzle, revealing – if only put together carefully and correctly – a picture, *the* picture, which finally makes visible 'what ethnomethodology really is'. For the truth is that the work which is thus labelled by those who are outside it demonstrates increasing diversity. Thus it would cause no dismay to most of the contributors, I believe, if what emerged for the reader was the conclusion that the work has burst whatever boundaries might have originally contained it. Garfinkel himself has called the term a shibboleth, and the vitality and fruitfulness of the endeavours it has given rise to must stand as its claim to our interest. In short, what ethnomethodology now amounts to is to be located in the research output of its practitioners, and it will be for the reader to assess the convincingness of the results to date.

These selections are to be read, then, as working papers, as a view of what is being done and what might be done by ethnomethodologists. I stress what might be done, since I have used as a selection criterion that the materials here presented should stand as exemplars and models for those who are themselves interested in working the field, whether in the form of student exercises or on a more ambitious scale.

In so far as a thread may be followed through the selections that follow, it may be thought of as a concern with *practical reasoning*. It is this abiding concern, I believe, that accounts for the standard criticisms that ethnomethodology is unclear with respect to its status as a theory, and unclear as to the methods it endorses. 'Theories' and 'methods' (in their usual sociological sense) are here regarded as socially organized and accomplished products and practices in their own right, and so regarded they are endlessly fascinating as topics. Theory and method lose their privileged position as part of the apparatus which belongs to the analyst, not themselves subject to inquiry, and take their place as phenomena whose status *vis-à-vis* other doings and accomplishments is not immediately obvious. Thus in Part Two *theorizing* is discussed, characterized and assessed not in order to yield a criterion for deciding upon the correctness or utility of any particular product – *a* theory – but as a locus for investigating instances of practical reasoning.

In this spirit, Elliot's work is a tentative beginning for a sociological investigation of 'doing science', emphasizing as it does the dependence of the accomplishment of accredited science upon the unexplicated resources that the scientist brings to his work. Elliot's aim is not to diminish science, regarded as achievement, nor is it directed to reforming scientific practice or reporting. Rather, it emphasizes that scientific reports and accounts are tied to the everyday practices of the working scientist in ways that are not captured by the idealizations of textbook or philosophy of science accounts.

Consider in this context the philosopher Caton's remarks on the 'relations between ordinary and technical language' (Caton, 1963):

[technical languages] are, of course, not related as English is to French or Swahili: one could not learn technical language as a native language, neither the technical English language of physics nor the technical French language of farming. Technical language is rather a part of some language like English or French and a part defined only by reference to some particular discipline or occupation or activity among the practitioners of which it is current. [. . .] Further, it seems clear that numerous ubiquitous words and phrases occur in technical contexts in the same senses or used in the same ways in which they are used in everyday contexts: e.g., articles, the verb 'to be', 'all', 'some', 'too', 'at least', 'there is', 'and', 'or', 'if . . . then', 'hardly', 'very', etc. For example, surely the 'are' of 'Canines are vertebrates' is the 'are' of 'Dogs are animals'. Also, most of the kinds of utterances involving technical language appear to be already found in ordinary language – I mean requests, assertions, questions, explanations of what one was referring to, etc. (p. viii).

And

There are two further relations between ordinary and technical language which I do not think have been sufficiently emphasised. First, that the clarification of what someone is saying usually is achieved by using devices which are already a part of ordinary language and which are taken over into and used in dealing with technical language. And second, that whatever technical language a person may acquire is, and, as things are, has to be acquired against the background of ordinary language (p. viii).

In a similar vein, Elliot points out the sense in which working science (accredited science – scientific undertakings honoured by the relevant colleague group as 'normal' or 'competent') is through-and-through a derivative of 'common sense'. Scientists rely upon a 'syntax' of practices and methods which are accredited as 'correct', 'sufficient to the task at hand', 'properly conducted by prevailing standards' in just those ways in which any concerted activities are warranted by a collectivity. Furthermore, the working scientist trades in objects and procedures which are not formulated in the categories of any scientific theory. This is not proposed as a limitation or defect of science – how else *could* it proceed? To follow up Elliot's hints, then, would be to undertake an investigation of the ways in which to *do* science is to employ an interpretive schema 'for constructing a sensible and intelligent environment' (Blum, 1970, p. 313). Returning to Caton, the point to be made is that the 'technical' cannot be divorced from the 'ordinary', and that their relationship invites not criticism, from either side, but empirical investigation.

The remaining discussions of theorizing as practical reasoning deal with the social sciences. Thus, Moerman provocatively remarks that 'there is ... reason to believe that the Cro-Magnon talked among themselves about culture change in much the same way as next year's journals will'. Moerman is not engaged in gratuitous insult. The issue thus raised can be formulated as querying the warrant for treating societal members' talk as containing an extractable *proto-science*.

The notion of proto-science can be explicated by reference to, for example, Homans' treatment of proverbs. Proposing that 'everyday social behaviour' is 'an intellectual chaos', Homans (1961, p. 1) argues:

Every man has thought about it, and mankind through the centuries has embodied the more satisfactory of the generalizations in proverbs and maxims about social behavior, what it is and what it ought to be. Every man has his price. You scratch my back and I'll scratch yours. Do as you would be done by. You can't eat your cake and have it too. No cross, no crown. [. . .] And so forth. What makes the subject of everyday social behavior a chaos is that each of these maxims and proverbs, while telling an important part of the truth, never tells it all, and nobody tries to put them together.

And Homans offers an excuse for the layman's failure in this regard: 'social experience is apt to come at us too fast to leave us time to grasp it as a whole' (Homans, 1961, pp. 1–2). Now it should be clear that the status of proverbs as poverty stricken is only an available characterization if we concede that they are a hurried attempt to produce 'generalizations' of a kind that a science of society would be responsible for. Under the auspices of this view, proverbial wisdom is a proto- (folk) science in much the same way as home remedies are the poor relations of a developed medical science.

There are grave problems for such a view. Homans nowhere addresses the issue of where proverbs are embedded in the everyday talk of members going about their business, nor does he treat it as a possibility that *what* proverbs do *where* they occur is a topic for sociology. Rather, proverbs are treated as extractable from their settings, and members are then held to account for what can be made of proverbs once they have been accorded the status of a folk science. Such a folk science, under these investigative auspices, stands to be corrected by a 'developed' science (in this case a scientific sociology), and members thereby stand corrected *as though they had intended to produce a science of their lives in the course of living them.*

The discussion can now be tied back to Moerman. Moerman finds the Lue, a Thai people, engaging in talk about matters which anthropologists extract and gloss as concerns about, e.g., 'culture contact', 'ethnicity', 'distinctive traits', etc. A commitment to Homans' stance (shared by many sociologists) would direct one to cull a set of propositions or models and to test their adequacy and veridicality. In this way from the talk of Thai peasants (or Cro-Magnon!) crude accounts of social life and social structure can be extracted which are subject to refinement, testing, and dispute in 'next year's journals'. But such an operation on the part of the analyst presupposes that the members are to be understood as engaged in a low-order scientific reasoning, and presupposes that the talk is not a phenomenon responsive to, consequential for, and part of, the very settings and occasions in which it is produced. The actor going about his affairs is formulated, then, as an inept scientist (in the sense that his aims roughly correspond with those of scientific sociology, though his achievements are rough and unsophisticated).

The focus on *practical* reasoning takes quite another tack. Such a focus makes problematic (which is to say, a topic for investigation and analysis) the character of members' activities in producing the action scenes and the talk embedded in and integral to those scenes – talk which *can* be made to yield extractable propositions, provided that one is not interested in the socially organized character of the world which generates, contains and is in part made up of, the talk. The focus on practical reasoning emphasizes that the talk *accomplishes* scenes and their contained activities; it emphasizes that members are – as a condition of their competence – rendering scenes intelligible, reasonable and accountable, that their world is a constant *doing and achieving*. 'Practical' actors make and find a reasonable world: their doing so is topically available for the social scientist.

Part Three presents a number of studies of members' methodical practices in a variety of organizational settings. A number of papers draw attention to record-keeping procedures, and at least in passing some attention is given to 'quantification', here treated as tied to sanctioned displays of competence by parties to organizational behaviour. (For example: what stands as a 'unit', a 'case', etc., is not determinable without reference to the socialized counting procedures which distinguish the 'experienced' agent of the relevant organization).

In Part Four, the concern with practical reasoning, with societal members' methodical and sanctioned ways of sustaining a recognizable real world, is less explicit. Nevertheless, in the study of, for example, the internal organization of conversation the emphasis is clearly upon the *speaker-hearer* as practical analyst, as practical reasoner. What warrants the student's analysis of conversational materials is his orientation to the speaker-hearer's production and recognition of interactionally consequential features of the talk. A main thrust of the research here is the finding that far from its being the case that 'social experience [comes] at us too fast' for adequate treatment, speakers and hearers, with respect to the most mundane features of talk and interaction, orient to delicate and rather complex features of the unfolding activity in what Sacks has referred to as 'utterance time' (i.e. the standard pacing of talk).

The study of the operations of practical reasoning, then, does not produce 'findings' which resemble those of traditional sociologies, and it should be abundantly clear that ethnomethodology is not an alternative 'methodology' aimed at a more effective solution of traditionally formulated problems. Focusing upon the accomplished character of action scenes, it necessarily develops a style of research and argument responsive to its elected subject matter. In noting that for members a 'real world' is indubitably *just there*, without reference to its accomplished character, the last thing it has in mind is to cast systematic doubt upon the 'existence of a real world'. On the contrary, that there is an observable 'real world' is its point of origin: its destination is a characterization of the work members do to sustain a social order in which there are 'suicides', 'ethnic groups', 'clear matters of fact', and the rest of the furniture of everyday life. Scepticism and doubt enter only in so far as for the members they are sanctioned phenomena: the conditions under which members are entitled to display scepticism, the features of the world they are warranted in doubting – these are themselves aspects of practical reasoning, and hence proper matter for the study of social order.

Ethnomethodologists, then, take as their aim (in their various ways) the description and analysis of the members' resources for finding what they find and doing what others will find them to have done. It is for the reader to decide the extent to which the research done under the auspices of this relatively new sociology has been successful. Let me close by emphasizing that this research is intendedly replicable, and let me note that quite modest observations and data collection will permit the student to replicate and/or extend the analysis of, for example, sanctioned ways in which members find phenomena to be countable (Sudnow, Reading 10); methodical ways for closing conversations with an orientation to co-participants' concerted activities (Schegloff and Sacks, Reading 18); the invocation of 'ownership' in characterizing beliefs and knowledge (Sharrock, Reading 5); or record-keeping practices in organizational settings (Cicourel, Reading 8; Zimmerman, Reading 12; Garfinkel, Reading 11).

Far from depicting a domain of established findings, the reports in this collection invite exploration and research on everyday phenomena. The horizon is an open one, for at this point in the history of the discipline the everyday world of practical activities invites investigation, discovery and analysis at every turn.

References

BLUM, A. (1970), 'Theorizing', in J. Douglas (ed.), *Understanding Everyday Life*, Aldine Press.

CATON, C. E. (ed.) (1963), *Philosophy and Ordinary Language*, University of Illinois Press.

HOMANS, G. (1961), *Social Behavior: Its Elementary Forms*, Harcourt, Brace & World.

Part One
On the Name and its Uses

The first Reading in this volume is excerpted from the transcript of a symposium which brought together some twenty sociologists for two days of informal discussion of ethnomethodology. Early in the symposium, Harold Garfinkel was invited to address a few remarks to 'the origin of the term'. In the following excerpt we have Garfinkel's extemporaneous account of how he came to coin the term in order to 'stick a label . . . for the time being' on some notions developed out of a study of jurors' practices. Ethnomethodology, Garfinkel explains, was developed as a cognate with a set of perfectly standard anthropological terms – 'ethnobotany', 'ethnomedicine', etc. Just as 'botany' in 'ethnobotany' refers to a corpus to be treated as *data*, so does 'methodology' in 'ethnomethodology' stand for a subject matter, rather than a scientific apparatus. Thus, jurors were found to have available 'methods', *qua* members of the society, for displaying, requiring and enforcing competence in the affairs of the society.

The excerpt is particularly interesting in that it reveals Garfinkel's recognition that the term has taken on a life of its own, that it has ceased to be the mnemonic 'tag' its coinage intended, and that what it is now variously made to stand for often bears little relation to the systematic studies begun in the mid-fifties by and under the influence of Garfinkel.

1 Harold Garfinkel

The Origins of the Term 'Ethnomethodology'

Excerpt from Richard J. Hill and Kathleen Stones Crittenden (eds.), *Proceedings of the Purdue Symposium on Ethnomethodology*, Institute Monograph Series no. 1, Institute for the Study of Social Change, Purdue University, 1968, pp. 5–11.

SCHUESSLER Hal, in the preliminary remarks, would you tell us a little bit about the origin of the term?

GARFINKEL Sure, I will start with that.

SCHUESSLER Also, does it have any connection with ethnoscience? This is something that puzzles me a bit.

GARFINKEL I will tell you about the origin of the term. Back in 1954, Saul Mendlovitz, who is now at the School of Law at Rutgers, was at the Chicago law school, on Fred Strodtbeck's jury project. I was between jobs, having left Ohio State on my way to UCLA, and because of bad planning I found myself without anything between roughly March and the following August. Strodtbeck said, 'You poor guy, come to Chicago and work with Mendlovitz.' Strodtbeck had 'bugged' the jury room in Wichita. He asked me to go to Wichita and listen to the tapes of the jurors. After listening to the tapes, I was to talk to the jurors. I was to see what they would say after I already knew what they had talked about. On the basis of that work, Mendlovitz and I then spent the rest of the summer and about two weeks in the fall, and some time in the fall of the following year, putting together our ideas about how the jurors knew what they were doing in doing the work of jurors. The notion was that if we used Bales' procedures we could find a lot to say from these recorded conversations. From the transcriptions we could learn a great deal about how, in their conversations, they satisfied certain characteristics of small groups. The question that we had was, 'What makes them jurors?'

On the basis of that material, Saul and I started to put together our impressions. I began preparing two papers for presentation, one at the Pacific Meetings and one at the National Meetings. It was in the course of writing these papers that the notion occurred to me of analysing the deliberations of the jurors. I was interested in such things as jurors' uses of some kind of knowledge of the way in which the organized affairs of the society operated – knowledge that they drew on easily, that they required of each other. At the time that they required it of each other, they did not seem to require this knowledge of each other in the manner of a check-out. They were not acting in their affairs as jurors as if they were scientists in the recognizable sense of scientists. However, they were concerned with such things as adequate accounts, adequate description, and adequate evidence. They wanted not to be 'common-sensical' when they used notions of 'common sensicality'. They wanted to be legal. They would talk of being legal. At the same time, they wanted to be fair. If you pressed them to provide you with what they understood to be legal, then they would immediately become deferential and say, 'Oh, well, I'm not a lawyer. I can't be really expected to know what's legal and tell you what's legal. You're a lawyer after all.' Thus, you have this interesting acceptance, so to speak, of these magnificent methodological things, if you permit me to talk that way, like 'fact' and 'fancy' and 'opinion' and 'my opinion' and 'your opinion' and 'what we're entitled to say' and 'what the evidence shows' and 'what can be demonstrated' and 'what actually he said' as compared with 'what you only think he said' or 'what he seemed to have said'. You have these notions of evidence and demonstration and of matters of relevance, of true and false, of public and private, of methodic procedure, and the rest. At the same time the whole thing was handled by all those concerned as part of the same setting in which they were used by the members, by these jurors, to get the work of deliberations done. That work for them was deadly serious. They were not about to treat those deliberations as if someone had merely set them an 'iffy' kind of task. For example, in the negligence cases they were handling up to $100,000 of somebody's business, and they were continually aware of the relevance of this.

When I was writing up these materials I dreamed up the notion underlying the term 'ethnomethodology'. You want to know where I actually got the term? I was working with the Yale cross-cultural area files. I happened to be looking down the list without the intent of finding such a term. I was looking through their taglines, if you will permit that usage, and I came to a section: ethnobotany, ethnophysiology, ethnophysics. Here I am faced with jurors who are doing methodology, but they are doing their methodology in the 'now you see it, now you don't' fashion. It is not a methodology that any of my colleagues would honor if they were attempting to staff the sociology department. They are not likely to go looking for jurors. Nevertheless, the jurors' concerns for such issues seemed to be undeniable.

Now, how to stick a label on that stuff, for the time being, to help me recall the burden of it? How to get a reminder of it? That is the way 'ethnomethodology' was used to begin with. 'Ethno' seemed to refer, somehow or other, to the availability to a member of common-sense knowledge of his society as common-sense knowledge of the 'whatever'. If it were 'ethnobotany', then it had to do somehow or other with his knowledge of and his grasp of what were for members adequate methods for dealing with botanical matters. Someone from another society, like an anthropologist in this case, would recognize the matters as botanical matters. The member would employ ethnobotany as adequate grounds of inference and action in the conduct of his own affairs in the company of others like him. It was that plain, and the notion of 'ethnomethodology' or the term 'ethnomethodology' was taken in this sense.

I encountered jurors who operated in a fashion very much like the way which the Subanun might use their ethnomedical terminology in their ethnomedical affairs. For example, a Subanun would be expected and entitled to claim to know, in terms of his ethnomedicine, certain things about the sources and the remedies for illnesses. I thought, now there is a cognate feature and that is the availability I had encountered among the jurors in their concerns for what members of the society, particularly in the situation of being jurors, came to hold each other to as what one like them would be expected to know, to deal with, and the rest where matters of fact, fancy, hypothesis, conjecture, evidence, demonstration, inquiry, ordered knowledge and the rest were a matter of practical consideration. What I mean is that it was for them a matter that somehow or other in their dealings with each other they managed, if you will permit me now to use it, to see. That is to say, in some way the good sense of somebody's inquiries was for them observable and notable. It was available, somehow or other, for that peculiar way of looking that a member has. The peculiar way of searching, of scanning, of sensing, of seeing finally but not only seeing, but seeing-reporting. It is 'observable-reportable'. It is available to observation and report. Now I need to run them together. If there was one word in the English language that would run them together, I would use it. There is not, so I have been using the term 'accounting' or 'accountable' or 'account'. When I talk about the accountable character of affairs or when I talk about accounts, I am talking about the availability to a member of any ordinary arrangement of a set of located practices. When I say located I mean situated in that setting or organizationally interesting to us as sociologists. Matters of fact and fancy and evidence and good demonstration about the affairs of everyday activities are made a matter for seeing and saying, observing for observation and report. That means then that talk is part of this. Talk is 'a constituent feature of the same setting that it is used to talk about'. It is available to a member as a resource, for his use, as well as being something that while using and counting on he also glosses. This is to say that in some important ways he ignores certain features; he does not want to make a lot of it. He wants, in fact, to remove himself from that so as to recommend in the report on a world not of his doings that which for him is now available as the thing he could put together in his account of ordinary affairs.

Having given all this about what ethnomethodology is, let me tell you the vicissitudes of the term. It has turned into a shibboleth, and I am going to tell you right now that I cannot be responsible for what persons have come to make of ethnomethodology. Here I am talking about 'ethnomethodology', because there are now quite a number of persons who, on a day-to-day basis, are doing studies of practical activities, of common-sense knowledge, of this and that, and of practical organizational reasoning. That is what ethnomethodology is concerned with. It is an organizational study of a member's knowledge of his ordinary affairs, of his own organized enterprises, where that knowledge is treated by us as part of the same setting that it also makes orderable. Now, let us say you want the term ethnomethodology to mean something. Dave Sudnow and I were thinking that one way to start this meeting would be to say, 'We've stopped using ethnomethodology. We are now going to call it "neopraxiology".' That would at least make it clear to whoever wants the term ethnomethodology, for whatever you want it for, go ahead and take it. You might as well since our studies will remain without that term. I think the term may, in fact, be a mistake. It has acquired a kind of life of its own. I now encounter persons, for example, who have a professional responsibility for methodology. They wonder what it is all about and then begin to imagine, 'Ethnomethodology must be something like this.' They talk to other persons. They have trouble getting access to the papers. They want, after all, to know and they begin to tell each other, and then the rumor mill gets under way. Pretty soon you have a machinery that is generating attitudes and questions about this work that we are now expected to take and to address ourselves to, even though these are not our attitudes and questions.

Part Two
Theorizing as Practical Reasoning

The Readings in this section all focus, in one way or another, on theory construction as a practical accomplishment. Smith (Reading 4), using Zetterburg's recommendations as example, points to one way in which theorists may ascend to formal statements via a set of cognitive operations which are made to disappear (and thus appear irrelevant) as the theorist pulls the ladder up behind him. Pollner's treatment of Becker's well-known version of labelling theory (Reading 3) argues that some forms of labelling theory can be analysed as 'scientific' renderings of lay viewpoints: this is less a critique than an attempt to illuminate ways in which 'theory' and 'common sense' mutually inform one another. Moerman's discussion of claims made by the Lue with respect to ethnic traits (Reading 6) similarly points out the by-no-means coincidental convergence of sociological 'theorizing' and societal members' accounts; while at the same time stressing that the phenomena attended to by such accounts (on the occasion of their production) may be specifically disattended by the theories which are parasitic upon them. Finally, Bittner (Reading 7) elaborates a strong argument for restoring the concept of organization, so central to much of traditional sociology, to its mundane settings, and recommends that we 'decide the meaning of the concept, and of all the terms and determinations that are made under it . . . by studying their use in real scenes of action by persons whose competence to use them is socially sanctioned'.

These Readings have it in common, then, that they propose Theory's relations to the settings about which it theorizes as a topic for empirical investigation. Though some of these pieces are critical in tone, they are most profitably read as hints and sketches at a distinctive treatment of a rich realm of data: our theories and their provenance.

2 Henry C. Elliot

Similarities and Differences between Science and Common Sense

First published in this volume.

Science and common sense: the typical philosophy of science account

Nagel (1961, ch. 1) asserts that, though there is some vagueness in how the terms are used, science and common sense refer, generally speaking, to two distinct things. Common sense refers to one set of methods and related conceptions about the nature of the world. Science refers to a quite different procedure and a quite different body of knowledge. He categorizes and contrasts both types of method and knowledge in terms of six 'important and recognizable differences'.[1] Nagel's account seems to be a reasonable account as far as it goes. Science – at least physics and biology – does seem to have the general characteristics he emphasizes, as compared to common sense. My argument with him lies in another direction. I accept his six-fold set of distinctions between science and common sense. Nagel, however, omits any discussion of how common sense may be critically involved in the actual doing of science. This matter can perhaps be best illustrated and discussed by first briefly recapitulating Nagel's distinctions and then arguing for the essential incompleteness of that account as one that adequately describes how science in fact gets done. In summary then, Nagel argues that:

1. Science has grown out of common-sense concerns of daily life, but this historical continuity does not mean that science is merely common sense organized and classified. Science seeks to provide *generalized* explanatory statements regarding disparate types of phenomena, and to provide critical tests for the relevance of the attempted explanations. The result is a deductive system whereby a few principles account for vast ranges of phenomena. This is not a fully achieved goal of science but a lot has been achieved to date (Nagel, 1961, pp. 3–5).

2. While common sense lays justifiable claims to accurate knowledge, common sense is frequently not aware of the limits to the range of validity of its beliefs or the range of success of its practices. Science seeks to examine such

1. Nagel, says (1961, pp. 2–3) that for didactic purposes he may have overdrawn the differences somewhat in places, but this consideration is not germane to my argument.

limits, to find reasons for them, and hence to remove this incompleteness (pp. 5–6).

3. Common sense entertains incompatible and inconsistent beliefs. Science, by systematic explanation, seeks to discover and exhibit logical relations between/among propositions, and hence to arrive at the sources of such conflicts. On occasion, incompatible assumptions, recognized as such, can greatly aid in the shaping up of a scientific inquiry, which, in turn, leads to a more logically coherent and unifying theory (pp. 6–7).

4. Compared with common-sense beliefs, scientific theories prevail for shorter periods of time. This is because of the vagueness of reference of common-sense terms. Science, which seeks greater precision, has greater opportunity for critical testing, and hence greater opportunity for checking on the validity of assertions. This feature of science very frequently involves counting and/or measuring. This increased precision of scientific statements gives them greater capacity for incorporation into comprehensive and clearly articulated systems of explanation. Simultaneously, this system permits the seeking out a large amount of relevant types of data for making decisions regarding the validity of the theory (pp. 7–10).

5. Common sense is largely concerned with immediate relevance for human practical concerns. Science seeks for relations between/among things irrespective of any such relevance. In so doing, it makes use of highly abstract concepts. Yet this work does have indisputable relevance for everyday concerns. However, only by invoking abstractions far removed from common-sense experience can the powerful scientific generalization be achieved. Moreover, it is not merely a matter of abstractness: common sense also has its abstractions (e.g., 'humanity' and 'mortality'). Rather it is a matter of pervasive structural properties abstracted from familiar traits manifested by limited classes of things under specialized conditions, and related to direct observation only by way of complex logical and experimental procedures. In this way science sets about developing systematic explanations for extensive ranges of diverse phenomena (pp. 10–12).

6. Implicit in the above (1–5) is science's deliberate policy of exposing its claims to knowledge to the repeated challenge of critically probative data obtained by carefully controlled experiment. Put briefly, scientific conclusions are the product of scientific method; and this method means (a) persistent criticism of arguments by tried canons of judging data-producing procedures, and (b) of assessing such evidence's probative sense.

Nagel says that these canons have been explicitly codified only in part, and mainly operate as the intellectual habits of competent investigators. But the results – the historical record of achievement, comprising dependable and systematically ordered knowledge – demonstrate that scientific procedure is superior to any known alternative (pp. 12–14).

Science and common sense: common sense as an integral part of science

Nagel's account of the relationship and differences between science and common sense is a reasonable account as far as it goes. It does, however, omit consideration of several crucial aspects of that relationship. Hence it provides a fundamentally incomplete and therefore unsatisfactory account. I will now briefly introduce and discuss the ways in which common sense is invoked by, and figures critically in, the doing of *accredited* science.[2]

1. Science inevitably starts from the experiences of everyday life as the phenomena to be investigated. Where else could it start? A well known if little considered example adequately illustrates this. Everybody knows that objects and gases (including 'air') manifest warmth or heat and variations thereof with respect to times and places. But science developed and uses an instrument, the thermometer, to measure – well, to measure *what*? First of all it was much more a matter of investigating *the thermometer* rather than making investigations *with* it (Kuhn, 1961, pp. 58–9). Gradually it *became* obvious that a thermometer measured 'degree of heat', which was to be viewed as 'a complex and equivocal phenomenon dependent upon a number of different parameters'. The point here is that not only was science introducing instrument-based precision and opening up possibilities of carefully controlled observation, it was also still dealing with a common-sensically experienced phenomenon – warmth. And the provision of adequate warmth is still a target of much science application (e.g., heating devices and controlled heat-level installations in homes, manufacturing processes, space capsules, etc.). In sum, science here started from a common-sense property of the everyday world and continually returns to it.[3]

2. The scientific investigator in fact never seriously departs from the world of everyday life. His way of perceiving his work environment clearly illustrates

2. By 'accredited science' I mean what Kuhn talks of as 'normal science'; that is, science as accepted by the scientific community at any given time (Kuhn, 1962, ch. 3).

3. Dingle, in a very interesting review article (1960), proposed a radically different account of measurement in science. He argued that one should regard measurements as *constitutive of* the phenomenon *thereby being* scientifically *studied*, and not as being measurement *of properties* of some phenomenon or object as *common-sensically* conceived. Thus, when a thermometer measures 'degree of heat', *that* is *the* scientific phenomenon.

Dingle, however, hastens to add that while 'We have discovered how to create a world between the elements of which rational relations exist . . . we exploit the *empirical fact* of its *close parallelism* with the *natural world*' (Dingle, 1960, p. 191, my emphasis).

I doubt very much if science would ever have achieved its current status as a most worthwhile and supportable enterprise if this 'parallelism' were *not* manifest.

this. In no book, articles, lecture, or informal discussion does a scientist *not refer* to his perception of a world of common-sensically describable objects. He has a 'lab', i.e. a workroom with walls, a floor, and roof, tables, chairs and apparatus. And all that apparatus can be described in quite common-sense terms, e.g., that big dial over there, those wires, that glass bottle. In his laboratory, at work, he always sees objects in that way *as* his mode of orienting generally to his operating locale. He emphatically does not see only, e.g., protons and electrons. How could he? And not only does it *not matter* that he does not, he *cannot do so*. And his not doing so is part of his getting on with his work properly.[4] Such objects as table, chair, instrument, etc., of course, do not exist in terms of the categories of any scientific theory. Yet they are none the less counted on as features of the world within which those theories are constructed, tested and understood. For the scientist they are 'givens'. Any adequately comprehensive investigation of how common-sense figures in the doing of science, however, must address itself to an examination of such givens.[5]

3. But what of the scientist's manipulations – his detailed handling and observations of his complex instruments? Does he see (and feel) non-common-sense things? No! What he sees and feels are common-sense objects, though what he 'makes of' what he sees is usually far from common sense (but see 2 above). The working scientist sees instruments, i.e. physical objects, with dials, knobs, lines; with fronts, sides and backs. When he pays attention to a pointer, he is observing what any normally sighted human could: it's still, or it's moving and it's now stopped, stopped against scale numbers, the number 2, for example. His 'and therefore . . .' statements which follow could not have followed otherwise, for that's what they invariably follow from. Similarly in observing colour changes, e.g., in gas chromotography (a technique I happened to see being utilized to study 'amino-acids')[6] the scientist observes coloured patches, and his colours are everybody's colours, only he makes something special out of the manner of their appearance on his specially treated sheets of paper.

4. Stebbing (1937) neatly emphasizes and illustrates this point when she argues that a physicist's claim that physical objects are 'really' or fundamentally not-solid depends inescapably and crucially on the common-sense notion of 'solid'. For how else could the conceptual contrast, solid versus not-solid be meaningfully made (Stebbing, 1937, pp. 51–4 of 1958 edn).

5. I am not proposing that science and common sense are identical. The matter is rather that common sense, scientific work and scientific results each manifest stable properties and that the stability of science depends in part on the stability of common-sense procedures (and see 5 on page 25).

6. I am much indebted to Drs John Hughes and Brian Colby for spending hours in their laboratories, showing me how they did their research.

4. Not only does the scientist observe describable events in his laboratory. His response to them itself exhibits quite common-sense features. For example, though he is much concerned with 'accuracy', he does not spend long periods staring at a dial to make sure he's seen its pointer's position 'accurately'. One or two brief stares are enough for his purposes. And it's just the same with making sure the laboratory door is locked at night or that the car's lights have been turned off. Enough is enough for the purpose(s) at hand.[7] More than enough and people begin to wonder about his claims to competence.[8] It is most important here to distinguish very carefully between the scientific *ideal* of accuracy on the one hand, and how this ideal is sanctionably *incorporated* into actual research *performances* as managed accomplishments. It is not regarded as 'reasonable' to insist on ever more accurate meter readings during any given piece of scientific inquiry. The 'reasonableness' of 'enough being enough' is patently obvious to any practising scientist. This being so provides warrant for an inquiry into such 'reasonableness's' foundations, that is, an inquiry into common-sense type practices.[9]

Similarly the scientist does not puzzle about the stability of the world when he's not attending directly to parts of it. Unless something very unexpected happens, the dial observed two days, two hours, two minutes ago is the same dial in all relevant respects (its having aged in the meantime is usually not an issue). Essentially the same consideration holds for everybody. In the perception of tables and chairs, etc., as stable objects, we all see and treat them that way: in fact our so seeing them *is* part of our way of responding to them.

5. The above discussion illustrates and emphasizes how a research scientist works in an environment of perceivedly common-sense objects, and treats them in a manner that itself involves and relies on common-sense ways of procedure. Such an account therefore, not merely supplements that of Nagel. He was largely concerned to depict the differences between science and common sense, whereas I have been concerned with a radically different notion of what the relationship between them in fact is: namely that common-sense modes of perception and operation are an *integral* and *essential feature of* recognized scientific practice.

7. The notion of adequacy for all practical purposes has been extensively discussed by Schutz (see 1962, part 1, *passim*, and 1964, part 1, *passim*).

8. Garfinkel has discussed this specific topic, for example, in connection with the perceivedly proper and adequate performance of a coroner's duties (1967, pp. 9–18). [See Reading 9 – Ed.]

9. The same basic argument holds for the notions of object stability, clarity, schemata of relevance, etc. (see next paragraph in text).

I have, of course, no intention of claiming that science *merely* comprises doing common-sense activities in laboratories, etc. My chief concern in this section has been to briefly mention and discuss features of doing scientific work that the typical philosophy of science account ignores.

References

DINGLE, H. (1960), 'A symposium on the basic problems of measurement', *Scientific American*, vol. 202, no. 6.

GARFINKEL, H. (1967), *Studies in Ethnomethodology*, Prentice-Hall.

KUHN, T. S. (1961), 'The function of measurement in modern physical science', in H. Woolf (ed.), *Quantification: A History of the Meaning of Measurement in the Natural and Social Sciences*, Bobbs-Merrill.

KUHN, T. S. (1962), *The Structure of Scientific Revolutions*, University of Chicago Press.

NAGEL, E. (1961), *The Structure of Science*, Harcourt, Brace & World.

SCHUTZ, A. (1962), *Collected Papers: I. The Problem of Social Reality*, Martinus Nijhoff.

SCHUTZ, A. (1964), *Collected Papers: II. Studies in Social Theory*, Martinus Nijhoff.

STEBBING, L. S. (1937), *Philosophy and the Physicists*, Dover, 1958.

3 Melvin Pollner

Sociological and Common-Sense Models of the Labelling Process

A further development of this paper can be found in Melvin Pollner, 'Mundane and constitutive versions of deviance', in J. Kitsuse and P. Rains (eds.), *The Labeling and Social Differentiation of Deviants*, Basic Books, in press.

Ethnomethodological inquiry is guided by the heuristic 'Treat social facts as accomplishments' (Garfinkel, 1967). Where others might see 'things', 'givens' or 'facts of life', the ethnomethodologist sees (or attempts to see) *process*: the process through which the perceivedly stable features of socially organized environments are continually created and sustained. The ethnomethodologist does not seem to be alone in his endeavors. The formulations of the labeling theorists, for example, are ostensibly congenial to the general ethnomethodological stance. Where others have treated 'deviance' as a property somehow inhering in the acts so designated, the labeling theorist invites the analyst to conceive of deviance as a communal creation. And yet, notwithstanding the seeming affinities, an ethnomethodologist would have reservations about a wholesale endorsement of the labeling perspective. One reason for the reluctance is that some of the leading statements of the labeling position, specifically those found in Howard Becker's *Outsiders* (1963), reveal a deep ambiguity in conceptualizing deviance as a community creation. The ambiguity originates in Becker's simultaneous and entangled use of two distinct models of the relation between actors and 'deviance' to specify the nature of the labeling process.

In this report we shall attempt to show that:

1. There are two models of the relation between community and 'deviance' present in Becker's work. One model is a common-sense model of deviance, the other is a sociological model of deviance.

2. Each model provides for a different understanding of what is meant by the labeling process.

3. Becker confuses the relation between the two models and, consequently, at times advances the common-sense model as part of a sociological perspective on deviance. By contrast, an ethnomethodological inquiry into 'deviance' (and a labelling perspective relieved of ambiguity) would treat the common-sense model as an integral feature of the deviant-making enterprise.

Model I and model II versions of deviance

Becker proposes a sociological view of deviance which stands in contrast to the ways in which deviance has typically been conceived by scientists as well as laymen. The essentials of the distinction are specified in statements such as the following:

What laymen want to know about deviants is: why do they do it? How can we account for their rule-breaking? What is there about them that leads them to do forbidden things? Scientific research has tried to find answers to these questions. In doing so it has accepted the common-sense premise that there is something inherently deviant (qualitatively distinct) about acts that break (or seem to break) social rules. It has also accepted the common-sense assumption that the deviant act occurs because some characteristic of the person who commits it makes it necessary or inevitable that he should. Scientists do not ordinarily question the label 'deviant' when it is applied to particular acts or people but rather take it as given. In so doing, they accept the values of the group making the judgment.

It is easily observable that different groups judge different things to be deviant. This should alert us to the possibility that the person making the judgment of deviance, the process by which that judgment is arrived at, and the situation in which it is made may all be intimately involved in the phenomenon of deviance. To the degree that the common-sense view of deviance and the scientific theories that begin with its premises assume that acts that break rules are inherently deviant and thus take for granted the situations and processes of judgment, they may leave out an important variable. If scientists ignore the variable character of the process of judgment, they may by that omission limit the kinds of theories that can be developed and the kind of understanding that can be achieved (Becker, 1963, pp. 3–4).

. . . social groups create deviance by making the rules whose infraction constitutes deviance, and by applying those rules to particular people and labeling them as outsiders. From this point of view, deviance is not a quality of the act the person commits, but rather a consequence of the application by others of rules and sanctions to an 'offender'. The deviant is one to whom that label has successfully been applied; deviant behavior is behavior that people so label (Becker, 1963, p. 9).

[Deviance] is the product of a process which involves responses of other people to the behavior. The same behavior may be an infraction of the rules at one time and not at another; may be an infraction when committed by one person, but not when committed by another; some rules are broken with impunity, others are not. In short, whether a given act is deviant or not depends in part on the nature of the act (that is, whether or not it violates some rule) and in part on what other people do about it (Becker, 1963, p. 14).

If we take as the object of our attention behavior which comes to be labeled as deviant, we must recognize that we cannot know whether a given act will be categorized as deviant until the response of others has occurred. Deviance is not a quality that lies in behavior itself, but in the interaction between the person who commits an act and those who respond to it (Becker, 1963, p. 14).

If 'deviance' is regarded by the common-sense actor as somehow inhering in the acts so designated, then the proposal that deviance is behavior which persons so label seems to stand the common-sense attitude on its head. That is, from the point of view of the common-sense actor deviance is an 'objective' feature of the environment which invites and in some sense precipitates an appropriate response from the community.[1] Deviance is presumedly 'discovered' not 'manufactured' by the various legal institutions. From the point of view of the common-sense actor, deviance is the pre-existent cause of his response to it. Yet as Becker's remarks suggest, there is a sense in which 'deviance' exists in and by virtue of the response of the relevant community. Viewed sociologically, the deviant character of the act is not intrinsic to the act but depends upon or, more emphatically, is constituted by the subsequent response of the community. If one were concerned to know if a particular act was or was not deviant, then nothing would be gained by examining the act *per se*. Nothing would be gained according to Becker, because the properties with which the act is seemingly endowed are created by the community response to the act.

In contrast to the absolutist proclivities allegedly characteristic of the common-sense actor, the labeling theorist advances a relativistic model. Seen from the 'inside' of an already established symbolic universe, 'deviance' presents itself as a property inhering in the acts so characterized. Yet when viewed from the 'outside', the deviance that such acts are deemed to possess is assured only by virtue of a community's orientation to them as wrong, immoral, evil, etc. From within, deviance is an objective property of an act, or at least constituted by some method other than the immediate response to the act, whereas from without deviance is brought into the world by the communal response.

For the sake of convenience let us call the model of relations presupposed by and implicated in common-sense experience of deviance model I. Model I treats the deviance of an act as existing independently of a community's response. It implicitly posits that certain acts are (or ought to be) responded to in particular ways because they are 'deviant', that is, their 'deviance' is defined by criteria other than the fact that you or I happen to regard or experience the act as deviant. Let us call the model of relations ostensibly advanced in at least some of Becker's statements model II. Model II treats deviance as a property which is created and sustained by a community's response to an act as deviant. It proposes in effect that while the common-

1. For a description of the formal features characteristic of the experience of 'the world of everyday life', see Schutz (1962).

sense actor may regard deviance as a pre-existent cause of his action toward a particular act or person, deviance is being constituted by those very actions.

Model I is an 'insider's' model, a member's model. Model II is an 'outsider's' model,[2] it is a model that the sociologist might use when he turns to the phenomenon of deviance. Unfortunately, there are aspects of Becker's presentation which allow for a possible confusion of the relation between the two models and which ultimately serve to blunt the potentially radical thrust of the distinction. The ambiguity is particularly acute in the observations and reflections which are mobilized to specify what is to be understood by the maxim 'the deviant is one to whom that label has been successfully applied; deviant behavior is behavior that people so label'. In several ways the observations and reflections are derived from a model I understanding of deviance: the resultant conceptualization of the labeling process is but a variant of common-sense recognitions of the sorts of relations which can exist between, say, law enforcement officials and the judiciary on the one hand and 'real' deviance on the other.[3]

Model I and model II understandings of the labeling process

One understanding of the maxim, 'The deviant is one to whom that label has been successfully applied; deviant behavior is behavior that people so label', is derived from the demonstrable inadequacies and variability of the detection and categorization of rule violations. The maxim takes its mandate from the observation that not all those who violate rules are categorized as deviant and not all of those who are categorized as deviant have violated a rule. Presumedly, if the classes of deviance and non-deviance were properly assembled (i.e. in perfect conformity with the criterion of rule violation), if all the faults of police and judicial processing were removed so as to provide for homogeneous categories, then labeling would be superfluous. Rule violation and application of the label 'deviant' would coincide and the deviant would in effect be he who has violated a rule and only incidentally he who has been labeled deviant.

In so far as Becker endorses the notion of 'real deviance' – the evidence is

2. Note that 'outsider' here is not used in Becker's sense [Ed.].
3. For a general treatment of the problems arising from a failure to distinguish clearly between common-sense or members' models and those employed by the sociologist, see Cicourel (1964).

For a seminal and illuminating discussion of model I and model II positions as they apply to the relation of a psychiatric clinic to the 'real demand' for its services and the relation of the police to the 'real amount of crime', see the footnote in Garfinkel (1967, pp. 215–16). With respect to the police, Garfinkel notes that whereas for the police 'real crime' means that it occurs independently of the measures used to detect, describe, report, and suppress it, for the sociologist the 'real amount of crime . . . *consists only and entirely of the likelihood that socially organized measures for the detection and control of deviance can be enforced*' (emphasis in original).

admittedly equivocal – then the labeling maxim is predicated upon and motivated by a modified version of the 'constancy hypothesis' (Gurwitsch, 1966, pp. 4–5). The constancy hypothesis anticipates certain uniform relations between objective stimuli and sensation. Any anomalous relations are accounted for by reference to various supervening processes such as judgement and interpretation (Gurwitsch, 1966, p. 5). The model I version of labeling theory is based on a parallel model of the *social* actor. Specifically, it is based on the assumption that identical objective stimuli, i.e. rule violation or non-rule violation, should yield identical responses from law enforcement and judicial personnel, etc., i.e. categorization as deviant or non-deviant, respectively. Under the auspices of the constancy hypothesis, rule violation is accorded the status of an objective stimulus. Categorizing or not categorizing the act in question marks off the range of possible reactions from the relevant community. Given the model of the actor (or community) and its relation to the world, there is an anticipated (perfect) correlation between the properties of the act and subsequent categorization. Rule violation, the constancy model implicitly predicts, should be categorized 'deviant'; rule compliance should be categorized, minimally, 'non-deviant' or conforming. Given these expectancies specified by the constancy model, discrepancies between the objective properties of a particular act and ultimate categorization are anomalies. Under model I, the labeling process is the theoretical construct through which the anomaly is accounted for. That is, the labeling process serves to account for the disparity between expected and observed categorizations. It represents in effect an appeal to a process which intervenes between detection of the objective property of rule violation and ultimate categorization. Certain rule violators are not categorized as deviant because of the variable exigencies of the process. Thus, for example, a disparity between rule violation and applied label may be accounted for by an appeal to factors which are roughly the analogue of the psychological notion of 'attention'.[4]

A person believed to have committed a given 'deviant' act may at one time be responded to much more leniently than he would be at some other time. The occurrence of 'drives' against various kinds of deviance illustrates this clearly. At various times, enforcement officials may decide to make an all-out attack on some particular kind of deviance, such as gambling, drug addiction, or homosexuality.

4. Merleau-Ponty (1962), makes the following observation regarding the use of the concept of 'attention' in psychological theorizing: 'The object, psychologists would assert, is never ambiguous but becomes so only through our inattention. The bounds of the visual field are not themselves variable, and there is a moment when the approaching object begins absolutely to be seen, but we do not "notice" it. But the notion of attention . . . is no more than an auxiliary hypothesis, evolved to save the prejudice in favour of an objective world' (p. 6).

It is obviously much more dangerous to engage in one of these activities when a drive is on than at any other time (Becker, 1963, p. 12).

The differential concern of legal officials expressed in the notion of 'drives' provides an implicit answer to the question: how is it possible that a person may violate the law and yet not be regarded as deviant while being nevertheless 'deviant'?

The model I formulation of labeling provides a means for resolving the anomaly of the fact that the common-sense actor (or sociologist) can propose that an act really and actually is deviant while other members of the society seemingly do not concur.[5] As we shall see, the model I conception of the role of the labeling process is not so much a unique sociological conception of deviance, as it is a member of the society's way of conceiving of the relation between the activities of the legal system and the violation of the law.

In the model II version of deviance, the labeling process is constitutive not only of particular determinations of deviance, in the sense that certain acts are 'labeled' as deviant while other deviant acts are not so labeled, but of the very possibility of any determination of deviance or rule violation in the first place. Deviance consists of the responses or consequences through which it is realized as an existential possibility. There is no deviance apart from the response; for deviance is in effect the gloss for the processes through which it is realized as such.[6] The 'characters', to borrow Mead's words, of the 'objective' stimuli or rule infraction are assured of in no other way than in and through the definitional response of the individual or relevant community. The properties of the stimuli, when seen from the perspective of model II, are not written into or built into the stimulus. Rather, they are the accomplished creation, so to speak, of the response to them. Thus the labeling process is not merely an intervening process between the 'real' stimulus and its ultimate categorization – as it is regarded under model I. The labeling process, instead, is regarded as constitutive of deviance.

That a particular act is regarded as deviant and that acts are regardable in that way in the first place is assured of only in and through the responses of the significant community and/or individuals. To refer to 'deviance', under model II, is, in effect, to refer in a shorthand way to the process through which deviance is realized as such. Whereas model I renders deviance a static entity in conformity with the implicit recommendation of the natural

5. That is, the 'judgemental activities' collected under the heading of the labeling process serve as a source of solutions to the puzzle posed by the fact that a person identified as deviant and, consequently, a candidate for certain prescribed treatment is not accorded that treatment.
6. The concept of 'gloss' and 'glossing' is taken from Garfinkel and Sacks (1970).

language (i.e. 'deviance' is a noun), model II renders deviance the name of a process of constitution.

Improper and proper relations between models I and II

Model I and model II versions of labeling theory represent distinctive epistemological models. Indiscriminate intercourse between the two spawns an internally contradictory theoretical formulation. One such contradiction manifests itself with dramatic lucidity in Becker's classification or typology of deviant behaviors. The typology is produced by the cross classification of whether or not an act did in fact violate a rule and whether or not the actor is perceived as deviant.

	Obedient behavior	Rule-breaking behavior
Perceived as deviant	falsely accused	pure deviant
Not perceived as deviant	conforming	secret deviant

Figure 1 Types of deviant behavior (Becker, 1963, p. 20)

While the typology may have been advanced to illustrate certain features of model II, it is, in fact, a schematic portrayal of how model I views the relation between community perceptions and deviance. Indeed, given model II presuppositions, the categories 'secret deviant' and the 'falsely accused' are conceptual anomalies (at least in so far as Becker presents the types as 'sociological' observations). If deviant behavior is behavior that persons so label, then secret deviance wherein 'an improper act is committed, yet no one notices it or reacts to it as a violation of the rules' (Becker, 1963, p. 20) is a theoretical *non sequitur*. If the labeling is constitutive of deviance, then the fact that no one reacts to an act as deviant means that it is not deviant.[7] Similarly, the notion of the 'false accusation' is anomalous with respect to model II. If the label is constitutive of deviance then there can be no 'error'.

The typology is not an expression of the sociologist's conceptualization of the phenomenon of deviance. It is a schematic representation of possible relations that a model I reasoner can envision as existing between the response of a community and real deviance (where the latter is treated as a property defined by some method other than the immediate response of the community). For example, the typology is isomorphic with the major fea-

7. This contradiction has been noted by others. See, for example, Gibbs (1966, p. 13).

tures of a traffic court judge's conception of the possibilities which derive
from the interaction between law enforcement officials and violators/non-
violators of the law.[8] What Becker calls 'types of deviant behavior' roughly
characterize the judge's more or less explicit conception of the possible outcomes of judicial and police activities.

Consider, for example, that the judge 'knows' that there is not a one-to-
one correspondence between citations and offenses which warrant a citation.
Offenses, i.e. traffic code violations, are regarded as occurring with increasing frequency and because of the limited size of the available police force,
laxity, etc., some violations go undetected. From the point of view of the
judge, these 'real' but undetected violations constitute a population of
'secret deviants'. They are in effect a collection of acts which, had the police
or the highway patrol been present to observe them, would perhaps have
been citable. Alternatively, the judge 'knows' that the police may for one
reason or another erroneously cite a man for an infraction he has never committed. Such persons would presumedly fall in the category labeled the
'falsely accused'.

There are a number of relatively subtle variants of these categories, but
they are all dependent upon the assumption of objective deviance. That is,
the idiomatic variations assume that the deviance of a particular act is independent of the processes through which it is displayed and detected as
deviant. Police discretion, for example, constitutes an ancillary category of
persons who have committed a deviant act and who are perceived as com-
mitting a deviant act, but because of some situational exigency are not cited.
From the point of view of the judge, these are persons who but for the grace
of the officer would be counted as pure deviants.

The conceivable population assembled by the presumption of police discretion and a host of other categorical possibilities presuppose the independence of the deviant character of the defendant's act from the processes
through which it is labeled by the officer. The judge is aware of the contingencies of the identification process. In a sense, it is conventional labeling
theory or a version of it which provides the mandate for his job. If, for
example, deviance were equated with labeling, then the defendant would,
having been labeled, be deviant. There would in effect be no need for adjudication of the label. It is precisely because the identification of deviance is
presumed to stand in some variable and contingent relation to 'real' deviance that the judgement of the judge is required. The problematic relation of
labeled and real deviance provides also for a defendant's contesting an
officer's accusation in the first place.

8. All of the materials dealing with traffic court were collected through observation
and interviews in a number of municipal courts. See Pollner (1970).

With appropriate terminological modifications, Becker's typology characterizes the possible outcomes of adjudication as they are envisioned by the judge and the legal system in general. Given that a defendant is contesting the officer's accusation, the following relations between the judge's determinations and the presumed actual state of affairs being determined are possible from the point of view of the judge.

	Complied with law	Violated law
Judge finds defendant guilty	falsely convicted	rightfully convicted
Judge finds defendant innocent	rightfully acquited	falsely acquited

Figure 2 Defendant 'actually' or 'really'

From the point of view of the judge, the hatched rectangles define 'justice'. The coincidence of actual and assessed guilt defines a correct decision. The remaining categories are varieties of error and injustice. For the judge, a particular determination may be right or wrong because the determinations of guilt presumptively vary independently of actual guilt. Indeed, the presupposed independence of the defendant's guilt provides for the sensible character of interrogation in order to find out 'what really happened'. Without such an assumption, the sense of the correctness of a determination dissipates – as does the very sense of a determination. If the existential belief in an independent and objective state of guilt or innocence (i.e. did or did not violate a rule) is suspended, then there is no sense in which the judge's determination can correspond or fail to correspond to the actual state of affairs, for there would be no actual state of affairs apart from their determination.

Paradoxically, the model I conception of deviance is a constituent feature of the process through which 'deviance' is realized as such. That is, given that 'deviance' is the gloss for its accomplishment, an integral feature of that accomplishment is the use of the model I version of the relation between judge and the police, on the one hand, and deviant acts on the other. The typology of possible deviant acts and the dimensions along which the typology is assembled (i.e. perception and rule violation) are features of the accounts employed by the judge and/or defendant to explain how there is a less than perfect correspondence between rule violation and categorization. Consider, for example, the following excerpts in which the contingencies of police practice are specifically introduced by the defendant and/or the judge.

In the first excerpt, for example, the defendant uses the fact that not all cars traveling at seventy miles per hour are necessarily cited for speeding as a means for displaying the inconsistency of the police in citing him.

D . . . On the speeding violation, I violated the law . . . there's no argument about that, but 70 miles an hour, on an open freeway . . . there were essentially no other cars . . . I've seen the Highway Patrol cruise, with cars . . . 70 miles an hour, cruise with me, for that matter, at 70 miles an hour, at 3:00, when the freeway was absolutely jam-packed . . .

J Well, but still the law is sixty-five and that's it . . . They cite a lot of people, if it makes you feel any better, at 70 miles an hour.

D I agree . . . I find the Highway Patrol being slightly capricious on this though, your honor. I do agree it's a violation of the law, there's no question about that. I wish they would be a little bit more consistent though. That's all I have to say.

The charge of capriciousness or inconsistency, it should be noted, is predicated on a model I version of the relation between police and rule violations. That is, 'inconsistency' is part of an idiom which presupposes that rule violations are essentially objective stimuli to which the police ought expectably to respond in an objective manner. The feature of overriding import, however, is that this basic model is a constituent feature of the process through which a person or his acts are labeled deviant.

The following excerpt is taken from the judge's opening remarks in one of the largest traffic courts in the United States. The judge is explaining the ways in which cases may be disposed of.

. . . and if I say dismissed, that means not guilty. You are free to go. Now, we are going to dismiss if we are satisfied that the explanation is a good defense and it raises a reasonable doubt, or too, if we are reading the officer's notes, we come to the conclusion that he has made a mistake, in either applying the law or in his judgement and he should not have issued the citation. Now before anybody takes that as a – my remark about the officer's – criticism of these officers, please don't put that emphasis on it. Because that's not my intention at all. Particularly to you young people that are visiting. I'm not criticizing the officers but I have been in this court for two years, and during that time they tell me they've issued two million citations. Now, I review them at the rate of 25,000 a month. That means I've looked at 600,000 samples, and I can't honestly represent to you that officers are infallible, and that they never make mistakes and that they are always right, and that the public is always wrong. Because that is an incorrect statement. You see, officers are very human, and they do make mistakes – they make mistakes just like, oh, doctors and lawyers and accountants, and mechanics, and students and teachers, professional ballplayers, housewives, and judges. I'm told that I make more mistakes than any judge on the bench, and I guess that is right. But I'll see more people today through on to 10 tonight to night court than most judges will see in a year. So I'm bound to make more mistakes. See we recognize the officers' mistakes, and they are dismissed.

As the excerpt indicates, the judge acknowledges the possibility of mistakes both by himself and police officers. The possibility of 'mistakes', of course, requires reference to a state of affairs whose properties are determined by reference to criteria other than the fact of having been given a citation or the judge finding a person to be guilty. It is by reference to those independently established properties that it is possible for an 'error' to occur. In the absence of an independently defined state of deviance, one is deviant, in a Kafkaesque fashion, because one is said to be deviant.

As these illustrations suggest, from within the deviant-making enterprise, model I may be invoked as a method for describing the enterprise. The deviance-making enterprise includes the use of model I as what might be termed an autobiographical conception of itself. Even though deviance is created by what we have glibly referred to as the response of the community, an integral feature of that response is the autobiographical conception of itself as confronting an order of events whose character as deviant is presupposed as independent of the immediate response of the community. Thus, for example, even though the judge is part of an enterprise which constitutes and creates deviance (under model II), a constituent feature of that enterprise is the judge's conception of his activities (and those of the police) as attempting to discover, determine or assess the defendant's guilt or innocence. This autobiographical conception, in turn, grounds the possibility of a common-sense understanding of labeling. It is with respect to the 'real' guilt of the defendant, for example, that the judge entertains the notion that his own assessments as well as those of the police are not infallible and that mistakes are possible. The overriding point, however, is that model I is a constituent feature of the process for which deviance is the gloss. Part of the 'response' through which deviance is constituted includes the community's reflexive conception of itself as responding to essentially objective structures.

The relation between model I and model II can be further specified by considering a typology constructed in strict accord with a model II understanding of the relations between a community and deviance. If a community's response is treated as constitutive of deviance, a typology which expresses those relations would be something like this:

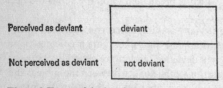

| Perceived as deviant | deviant |
| Not perceived as deviant | not deviant |

Figure 3 Types of deviant behavior

While the typology captures the relativistic thrust of a sociological understanding of the phenomenon of deviance, it seems to preclude a consideration of a variety of commonplace recognitions. After all, for example, as common-sense reasoners we know that some persons who are perceived as deviant are not 'really' deviant – they have been 'falsely accused'. We know further that some persons who have not been perceived as deviant – really are. Indeed, in so far as deviance is radically equated with the response of a particular community, a vast array of common-sense recognitions are denied their possibility. For example:

1. A defendant is deviant (or guilty) simply by virtue of the fact that he is responded to as deviant. He is what he is taken to be.

2. Given that the defendant's status is constituted by or consists of the individual or collective response, the defendant is 'all things to all men'. That is, there are as many statuses as there are determinations of that status, each of which is equally valid and equally correct even though they may directly and unequivocally contradict one another.

3. The equation of 'deviance' with response, moreover, means that given a multiplicity of (contradictory) determinations, there is no appeal nor any concern with an appeal to whether the defendant 'really' is or 'really' is not guilty. The notion of 'real' deviant loses its sense and possibility. In a world where 'deviance' is equated with the processes through which it is realized as deviance, the idea of a status which stands independent of the response is an alien conception. It is also, parenthetically, a world in which there is no possibility of a 'mistake'.

4. The very sense of terms such as 'determination' ('taken to be', 'perceived as', 'judged', etc.) also disintegrates. These are terms derived from the idiom founded upon the duality which is implicitly dissolved in a world where model II is somehow a 'lived' epistemology. The conception of the judge's 'determining' or 'assessing' the guilt of the defendant is derived from a model which presupposes an inquirer confronting an essentially objective world. These terms are but specifications of the possible explicative acts which an inquirer may make with respect to the world and, as such, have currency only within a model which is predicated upon the subject–object duality.

The cherished terms of the deviant-making enterprise such as 'truth', 'bias' and others such as 'perception' and 'judgement' are predicated upon the duality of 'response' and 'real deviance' and, more generally, between subject and object. The disintegration of the duality between the subject and object (or any of the synonyms and variants of that dichotomy) deprives these terms of their sense and possibility. A Pirandellian world where 'it is so if you think so' is a world in which – in so far as its inhabitants are 'aware' of their predicament – the possibility of truth has ceased, for there is no 'reality' apart from the perception of it. Issues of veridicality and verisimilitude can no longer be formulated, for their sense as issues presupposes an autonomous facticity with respect to which perceptions, analyses, responses, etc. may be compared.

A narrow reading of the labeling stance and of the model II version seems to have no conceptual room for the idiom of common-sense possibilities which informs and infuses common-sense talk about deviance. How is the relativism recommended by the sociological attitude to be reconciled with the occasional absolutism of the talk of parties to the deviant-making enterprise?

The reconciliation is achieved through the (analyst's) recognition that while a community creates deviance, it may simultaneously mask its creative work from itself.[9] Thus, for example, while the community creates the possibility of traffic violations in the sense of making the rules which can be violated and developing the agencies for their detection, from within the court the rules may be treated as definitive of 'real' deviance, as establishing that class of acts that are deviant whether or not they are concretely noticed or responded to as such.[10] A consequence of such treatment is that the community can conceive of itself as 'responding' to deviance in a restricted sense: it conceives of its reponse as an effort to correlate its discovery, suppressing, judging activities with the 'real' properties of acts. In so conceiving of its relation to deviance, the community produces for itself all of the common-sense recognitions which turn on the distinction between 'real' deviance and a community's 'assessment' or 'judgement' of deviance. A community member who models himself in such a manner makes available to himself the possibility of 'mistakes' as well as 'truth'. More generally, he becomes a model I reasoner from within a model II process. While creating

9. For a more extensive treatment of the issues raised here, see Berger and Luckmann (1966, pp. 57, 82–3), Garfinkel (1967, p. 182), Merleau-Ponty (1964, p. xiii) and Pollner (1970, pp. 201–41).

10. The vehicle code is but one way of establishing 'real' deviance. Other methods would include the use of common-sense knowledge, functional analysis, revelation, etc. Of course, it is possible for the community to conceive of its rules as an integral feature of its response to deviance. Thus, for example, we have the argument that laws penalizing the sale and use of marijuana are unjust because marijuana is void of demonstrably adverse effects. The significant feature of such arguments for our purposes is that even though the laws themselves are understood by the community as a contingent response, their character as just or otherwise rests upon an appeal to some independent method for assessing whether an act is 'really' wrong, immoral, etc.

See Berger and Luckmann's (1966) discussion of 'objectivation' and 'reification' for a discussion of a community's capacity to comprehend the nature of its productions.

meanings by his actions, he encounters the meanings as the pre-existent cause of his actions.

There are aspects of Becker's formulation of the labeling position, we have proposed, that invite confusion. Specifically, a sociological model and a common-sense model of deviance are entangled with one another. Indeed, at times it appears that a common-sense model is being advanced as a sociological depiction of a community's relation to deviance. Once the relations between the two models are grasped, the use of the common-sense model is visible as an integral feature of the work whereby a community creates deviance.

References

BECKER, H. S. (1963), *Outsiders*, Free Press.

BERGER, P., and LUCKMANN, T. (1966), *The Social Construction of Reality*, Doubleday; Allen Lane The Penguin Press, 1967.

CICOUREL, A. (1964), *Method and Measurement in Sociology*, Free Press.

GARFINKEL, H. (1967), *Studies in Ethnomethodology*, Prentice-Hall.

GARFINKEL, H., and SACKS, H. (1970), 'On formal structures of practical actions', in J. C. McKinney and E. A. Tiryakian (eds.), *Theoretical Sociology: Perspectives and Developments*, Appleton-Century-Crofts.

GIBBS, J. P. (1966), 'Conceptions of deviant behavior: the old and the new', *Pacific Sociological Review*, vol. 9, pp. 9–14.

GURWITSCH, A. (1966), *Studies in Phenomenology and Psychology*, Northwestern University Press.

MERLEAU-PONTY, M. (1962), *The Phenomenology of Perception*, Routledge & Kegan Paul.

MERLEAU-PONTY, M. (1964), *Signs*, trans. R. C. McLeary, Northwestern University Press.

POLLNER, M. (1970), 'On the foundations of mundane reasoning', unpublished Ph.D. dissertation, University of California at Santa Barbara.

SCHUTZ, A. (1962), *Collected Papers; I. The Problem of Social Reality*, Martinus Nijhoff.

4 Dorothy Smith

Theorizing as Ideology

Excerpt from Dorothy Smith, 'The ideological practice of sociology', first published in this volume.

The German Ideology (Marx and Engels, n.d.) describe three tricks which prove 'the hegemony of the spirit in history'. If we do away with their specifically Hegelian reference, we find a recipe for making up an ideological representation of what people think. Here is my version:[1]

Trick 1. Separate what people say they think from the actual circumstances in which it is said, from the actual empirical conditions of their lives and from the actual individuals who said it.

Trick 2. Having detached the ideas, they must now be arranged. Prove then an order among them which accounts for what is observed.

Marx and Engels describe this as making 'mystical connections'. [...]

Trick 3. The ideas are then changed 'into a person', that is they are constituted as distinct entities to which agency (or possibly causal efficacy) may be attributed. And they may be re-attributed to 'reality' by attributing them to actors who now *represent* the ideas.

Contemporary methodological prescriptions to be found in works on theory construction look uncomfortably like this recipe for making ideology. Take for example Zetterburg's recommended procedure.

1. The three tricks appear in Marx and Engels as:
1. One must separate the ideas of those ruling for empirical reasons, under empirical conditions and as empirical individuals, from these actual rulers, and thus recognize the rule of ideas or illusions in history.
2. One must bring an order into this rule of ideas, prove a mystical connection among the successive ruling ideas, which is managed by understanding them as 'acts of self determination on the part of the concept'. (This is possible because by virtue of their empirical basis these ideas are really connected with one another and because, conceived as *mere* ideas, they become self-distinctions, distinctions made by thought.)
3. To remove the mystical appearance of this 'self determining concept' it is changed into a person – 'self consciousness' – or to appear thoroughly materialistic, into a series of persons, who represent the 'concept' in history, into the 'thinkers', the 'philosophers', the ideologists, who again are understood as the manufacturers of history. ... Thus the whole body of materialistic elements has been removed from history and now full rein can be given to the speculative steed (pp. 42–3).

Sociologically definitions are constructed by combining primitives of several actors. Let us assume that our primitives are verbal actions such as 'descriptions', 'evaluations', and 'prescriptions'. As a first operation consider any procedure used to find a 'central tendency'. . . . Central tendencies of the same action types among an aggregate of individuals become their 'social beliefs', 'social valuations', and 'social norms' (Zetterburg, 1965, pp. 54–5).

Zetterburg is telling us how to get from something which actual people actually said to making it over so that it can be treated as an attribute of an 'aggregate'. The process of getting from the original individuals who described, judged and prescribed to the end product of 'social beliefs', 'social valuations', and 'social norms', goes something like this:

1. Individuals are asked questions, presumably in an interview.

2. Their answers are then detached from the original practical determination in the interview situations, and from the part the sociologist played in making them. They become data. Note that the questions are not data (trick 1).

3. The data are coded so as to yield 'descriptions', 'evaluations', and 'prescriptions' (trick 3).

4. There are various intervening procedures which it would be tedious to elaborate on here leading up to the statistical manipulation of the data to find the 'central tendencies' (trick 2).

5. The original individuals are now changed into the sociologist's aggregate. *Their* beliefs, *their* values, *their* norms are now attributed to this 'personage' as '*social* beliefs', '*social* values', and '*social* norms'. It is then perfectly within the bounds of ordinary sociological thinking that social beliefs, norms and values be treated as causing behaviour (though Zetterburg does not recommend this as the next step) (trick 3 and conclude).

Ideology is also a method. Contemporary sociology commands techniques for transforming concepts into currency which were undreamed of in Marx's time. If they are to be reclaimed and made to stand as the preliminary formulation of inquiry, then they must be anchored back into an actual practice of actual living people. The sociologist must begin to discover what people do to bring into being the phenomena which his concepts analyse and assemble. There is clearly an immediate problem with phenomena the only practical substrate of which is the work of sociologists. This arises most obviously in connection with experimental work. But there are similar problems outside the laboratory. It is, for example, ordinary good sociological practice to take a concept such as social class or power and locate it in the real world by creating indicators for it. There are special procedures available for creating special classes of sociological events which stand in the relation of indicators to the concept (there are also instructions for making use of 'naturally' occurring events in a similar way). In this way, so the sociologist learns to believe, he approaches indirectly the reality he can never confront or know directly and which always escapes him. By the criteria used here this is an ideological method. It involves beginning with a concept which is constituted as a traditional piece of sociological currency. The theoretical provenance of the concept which validates its use may be well understood. Its phenomenal provenance remains wholly unexamined. The concept is then embodied in the 'real world' by making happen certain special kinds of events which stand then as its signs. A real world is constituted which points back to and validates the sociological currency.

Trick one of the three tricks enjoins by implication the preservation of the 'subject' or 'agent' in the sociological version and the 'subject' or 'agent' located in a definite historical position. By the preservation of the subject or agent I mean that sociological statements must be grounded in and refer back to descriptions in terms of actual persons in actual contexts of actions and experience. The presence of the subject cannot be so casually dropped as Zetterburg does. Such a step must be justified by an account of how that is done as a feature of social organization. Thus Marx as a preliminary to his theoretical development in *Capital*, begins with a careful analysis of how relations among men come to take on the appearance of relations between things – namely commodities. His analysis of the fetishism of commodities shows precisely how the presence of the subject is separated from the thing so that commodity appears as 'agent'. If men do not appear as agents in their own effects, then that is also something which men have provided for. Thus for example how human action can come to have properties of system must be spelled out. To treat human action in terms of systems necessitates an account of how people may be separated from their actions so that what they do may become the components or parts of a system which assumes the prerogatives of 'agency' *vis-à-vis* the actors. Social systems are ordinarily put together without systematic provision for their ontological status (though the prominence which Parsons gives to the problem of order suggests that that indeed is crucial to the ontological status of his social system). The peculiar abstractness of much organizational theory and its often rather obviously ideological features represent a failure to deal with this problem.

A useful working rule is to insist upon passing through the 'forms of thought' to a description of what people do to make that concept or that statement something *that can be said*. Take for example the kinds of things that are said about technology representing it as a force thrusting us blindly forward into a technologically determinate but humanly indeterminate future. If we follow this rule, technological changes must be transposed out of that generalizing language and into a description of the work of actual men in actual work contexts, with given kinds of equipment paid for in such and such ways. Their work has a product which is appropriated by definite types of socially organized entities which have uses for those products which are not necessarily those of the people who do the work of discovery nor of the people who eventually make use of the product. We should spell out in the same terms how that product is distributed to whom and how and to whom it is further consequential. Such a preliminary description transforms the way in which questions about technological change are asked. It begins to provide the form of an answer in terms of how it actually works as a practical activity and also to how it is *that it may appear to us a force with its own internal dynamic*. It also raises questions about whether a relation such as that posited between technology and social change can be treated as constant throughout history. The underlying determinations of what has been made observable to us as technology on the one hand and social change on the other are seen then as differing greatly in varying institutional contexts. I do not insist of course on the particularities of this account. But I would like to insist upon the practice of formulating a description of how it is done and by whom, as a first and elementary rule of sociological inquiry.

References

MARX, K. (1867), *Capital, A Critical Analysis of Capitalist Production*, Foreign Languages Publishing House, Moscow, 1954.

MARX, K., and ENGELS, F. (n.d.) *The German Ideology*, ed. R. Pascal, International Publishers.

ZETTERBURG, H. L. (1965), *On Theory and Verification in Sociology*, Bedminster Press.

5 W. W. Sharrock

On Owning Knowledge

First published in this volume.

Sociologists routinely treat the activities of society's members as being somehow related to one or another corpus of knowledge: it is supposed that there must be some connection between what members know and what they do. The use of such notions as 'culture', 'perspective', 'ideology' and 'world view' has not only been intended to convey the idea that members' activities are to be construed by reference to some corpus of knowledge but also that the corpus of knowledge itself must be viewed as being in some way associated with the collectivity in which the actors have membership. The problem for sociologists has not, then, been that of finding a relationship between any member's knowledge and his activities but, instead, that of interpreting the relationship between a collectivity's corpus of knowledge and the activities of its members. That relationship has been intensely problematical to sociologists: that there is a relationship seems indubitable but it is more than a little difficult to say what it is. To make an issue of the relation between members' activities and the collectivity's corpus is, however, to distract attention from a prospectively interesting question: how do we come, in the very first place, to conceive of a corpus of knowledge as a *collectivity's* corpus? To suppose that a connection can be made between a collectivity's corpus and its members' activities is to presuppose that there is already such a relationship between the corpus of knowledge and the social structure as will permit the ascription of the corpus to one or another collectivity.

The ascription of the corpus to a collectivity profoundly affects the way in which we conceive the problem of relating members' knowledge to their activities. There are other ways in which we could deal with the entire problem. We could, for example, propose that there is no reason to suppose any special connection between collectivity and corpus and that any set of activities might be understood in relation to any corpus. It would then be the researcher's task to find out which bodies of knowledge were related to which activities. Thus if we were to examine the activities of Americans we could propose that their activities could possibly be understood by reference to any one or more of the following schemes of thought: Chinese geomancy, Azande witchcraft, Russian populism, Cheyenne law, Aboriginal kinship rules. The list of possibilities need not, of course, be terminated here for any identifiable corpus of knowledge could be included in it since any one of them might turn out to be the one that is 'relevant' to the activities of Americans. The researcher's investigations would show us what relationships held between each corpus and the activities of Americans and his findings could lead us to decide which of the various bodies of knowledge on the list would be the one to comprise the 'culture' of America.

If such a proposal were seriously advanced as defining proper investigative procedure, it would no doubt be rejected out of hand by serious sociologists: it seems absurd even to imagine that the corpus of knowledge known to us as Aboriginal kinship rules could turn out to constitute the culture of Americans. If, however, we did not already have an implicit conception of the relation between collectivity and corpus we should have to extend that proposal the most serious consideration: after all, relations between collectivity and corpus would have to be researched and we could not know in advance of our researches which corpus of knowledge would be related in which ways to which activities. Indeed, to apply the kind of procedure suggested above would involve us in achieving a much greater degree of clarity about what it is that makes a corpus of knowledge so 'relevant' to the activities of a collectivity's members that we can count that corpus as the collectivity's culture. We would, under such a procedure, have to decide what made a corpus into a culture and we could then set out to find out whether or not a particular corpus could be legitimately considered as the culture of a specific collectivity. Under present procedures we operate in almost the reverse fashion; having decided that some corpus is properly viewed as a collectivity's culture, we then wonder what it is that relates culture, collectivity and members' activities.

The fact that we can find ourselves in our present situation indicates the common-sense character of sociologists' treatments of the relations between corpus, collectivity and activities: it is common sense in that it trades on knowledge available to us by virtue of our membership in the society. We have an implicit conception of the relationship of corpus and collectivity which renders the kind of investigative procedure proposed above intuitively absurd. It seems obvious, for example that 'physics' is the corpus of knowledge which is relevant to the doings of physicists and that Aboriginal kinship rules relate to the doings of Aborigines. We don't have to do research to find that Aboriginal kinship rules do not comprise the culture of physicists and the very obviousness of that fact suggests that it is a common-sense matter, available to us by virtue of our membership in society. How, then, is our common-sense conception accomplished?

It is clear that the list of bodies of knowledge proposed as candidate cultures for Americans did not consist in the description of each of those bodies of knowledge. The list was not constituted in the following way: that each body of knowledge was constructed from a set of elements. The bodies of knowledge were identified quite adequately by the use of names, as Chinese geomancy and the rest. We must, therefore, recognize that it is a routine and common-sense practice to assign names to bodies of knowledge. The very fact that a corpus of knowledge has a name does not, however, tell us anything about the relation of corpus and collectivity until we begin to examine the *kinds* of names that were used. The names that were employed consisted in two parts, one part of which seemed to indicate the kinds of things that the corpus of knowledge was used to do, to order life by reference to geographical relations, to deal with witches, to regulate civil relations among a society's members, to regulate the relations of kinsmen etc. The other part of the name is, however, of more interest on this occasion in that that part of the name seemed to involve the use of the name of a collectivity: Chinese, Azande, Aborigine, etc. The corpus of knowledge was, then, identified in such a way that it was given the *same* name as a collectivity. Of that fact we need make nothing whatsoever: to give one's son the same name as another person does not necessarily say anything about his or one's own relations with that person. But the giving of the same name *may* indicate that such an operation as 'naming after' has been done, that the naming of one party has been done to provide for the sameness of names. That 'naming after' has been done is a possibility to which members may warrantably orient in cases where the same names occur and it is something which they can on occasion treat as a fact. Thus to find amongst the English that there is an increase in the popularity of a name that has already been given to a member of the royal family is to warrant the conclusion that people are naming their own children after a member of the royal family. Though a corpus of knowledge and a collectivity share a name in common it need not be the case that the name indicates that there is some association between corpus and collectivity but persons may warrantably suppose that there would be, that, for example, Cheyenne law is law that is applied amongst the Cheyenne. They may make this supposition because the giving of the same name as an instance of 'naming after' is not merely to be seen as providing, in the case of personal names, that two persons will have the same name: the naming may be seen to be grounded in the relations among the parties involved. Thus one can be seen to have named one's child after a famous person because one admires, respects, etc. that famous person.

At least we have, then, the possibility that persons find that some corpus of knowledge constitutes the culture of a collectivity by virtue of the fact that corpus and collectivity have the same name. What, in the case of corpus and collectivity, does the giving of the same name recognize?

It would seem, initially, most plausible to suppose that the name is used descriptively: Cheyenne law is so named because it is law applied amongst the Cheyenne, Azande witchcraft so called because such beliefs about witches are held by members of Azande society. Thus we might be led to suppose that the corpus of knowledge so named was known by all and only the members of the collectivity having the same name. A cursory examination of any sociological description will undercut any such presumption: it can easily be found that persons who are not members of a particular collectivity subscribe to and make use of the corpus of knowledge named after that collectivity. We find, for example, in Evans-Pritchard's report on the Azande, the following description of a witch-doctor's operations:

Bögwözu had lately arrived in our neighbourhood and had shown himself to be an able organizer and a resourceful schemer. He at once dominated the local practitioners and browbeat them into accepting his leadership by his far-reaching claims and his imposing figure and personality. He told everyone that his magic was not the old Zande magic of witch-doctors, *böndöku*, but more powerful magic he had learned among the Baka people from a man whose name, Bögwözu, he had taken for his professional cognomen (Evans-Pritchard, 1937, p. 219).

And

I asked Badodo why he remained servile to a man who so freely insulted him. He replied that Bögwözu had acted according to the custom of witch-doctors, though it was true, his own methods were different, for if someone gave him spears, then he would show him all the medicines without further trouble. He would not want spears all the time as this fellow did. Bögwözu was always after their goods, and why? His medicine was the same as theirs, his *mbiro* was the same, his *ranga* was the same, his *togo* was the same. There were, nevertheless, certain small differences between their medicines, and it was on account of these that they made him presents and listened to his talk. His was the medicine of the Baka people. . . . Well, he [Babodo] was anxious to add Baka medicines to his own stock of Zande medicines (Evans-Pritchard, 1937, pp. 223–4).

The naming of a corpus of medical knowledge as Zande medicine is not, then, *merely* descriptive. Though the name signifies that a certain sort of knowledge has currency amongst Zande witch-doctors it does not mean that they are only current among the Zande for there are, according to Evans-Pritchard's informant, similarities between Zande and Baka medicines. We might suppose, if the name were intended only as descriptive, that Evans-Pritchard would revise the name, would now identify the corpus of medical knowledge as, perhaps, Zande-and-Baka medicine or, perhaps, devise some other name which would not make reference to either collectivity. The same ideas are being identified, then, under two different names and the fact of their sameness is formulated here as similarities between Zande and Baka medicines. There are some elements of Baka medicine previously unknown to the Azande that are being learned from Bögwözu. We might suppose that this would entail the renaming of those elements as elements of Azande medicine. However, their acquisition is not described by Evans-Pritchard's informant as the expansion of Azande medicine by way of the transformation of Baka medicine into Azande medicine but, instead, as 'adding Baka medicines to the stock of Zande medicines'. Thus, though these elements of medical knowledge are gaining currency among the Azande, they preserve their name, to be identified as 'Baka medicines'. There are perhaps grounds here for complaints about inconsistent policies in the use of names but such complaints are not very useful and are far less valuable than is the treatment of the practice of naming as a phenomenon. Instead of criticizing Evans-Pritchard and his informant for inconsistency in their use of names, we might ask how such an 'inconsistent' use of names can provide for an apparently coherent and intelligible account of social events; for Evans-Pritchard's account can be read as intelligible and coherent, the way in which he uses names providing for its sense.

The assignment of a name to a corpus sets up the way in which further description is to be done. The name is not, then, *merely* descriptive in that once it has been assigned it becomes a device-for-describing: that is, the name is not to be revised in the light of events but is, rather, to be invoked in the description of whatever events occur. Thus, though the use of names such as 'Zande medicine' and 'Baka medicine' might initially appear as specifying the constituency amongst which a knowledge of those medicines might be found, it does not mean that those names have to be retracted if it is found that knowledge of Baka medicines can be found amongst other persons than members of the Baka: rather, that which those persons know has now to be described by reference to the fact that some elements of knowledge have already been named as 'Baka medicines'. Thus, after they have learned from Bögwözu, the Zande may now be described as 'having a knowledge of Baka medicines'.

Once the corpus of knowledge has been given a name, then, that name is used as a device-for-describing and cannot thus be construed as being literally descriptive of the constituency within which the corpus has currency. Does this mean that there is after all no connection between corpus and collectivity, that the name is common is merely coincidentally held? The idea that the name is intended as literally descriptive is mistaken. The name is never intended to describe the persons amongst whom the corpus has currency but, instead, to specify the relationship which that corpus has to the constituency, a relationship which seems analogous to that of ownership. Thus the naming of a corpus of knowledge as Baka medicine does not imply that that medicine is known only to the Baka but, rather, that such medicine in some sense 'belongs' to them, can be seen to be 'owned' by them. Evans-

Pritchard's informant does not appear to treat the description of some knowledge as 'Baka' as amounting to an assertion that all and only Baka know them any more than Marxists treat the categorization of beliefs as bourgeois as implying that they are ideas peculiar to bourgeois persons: bourgeois ideologies and Baka medicines 'belong' to the bourgeoisie and the Baka respectively no matter which persons subscribe to them.

Let us note that the notion of 'ownership' implies rights in and over things. A simple fact about owned objects is that even when the object is in the possession or use of someone other than its owner, its status as an owned object is not affected: you can live in my house, borrow my car and look after my pets but they remain mine even though you do so. The fact that you are living in my house does not, then, affect the description of the house as *my* house but it most certainly does affect the description of your activities, circumstances and, even, your character. In driving my car around you are engaged in either 'borrowing' or 'theft'; your living in my house may mean that you do not have a place of your own; and your looking after my pets allows you to claim that you are doing me a favour. Once we treat objects as being owned we need not modify ownership descriptions on the grounds that persons other than the owner are now in possession and use of them, though we can describe the activities of those other persons by reference to the owned character of the object and perhaps reconceive their relationship to the owner.

It is these facts about ownership which lead me to suggest that we can usefully apply the idea of ownership to the investigation of the corpus of knowledge and its relationship to the collectivity without having to concern ourselves with determining which persons subscribe to the corpus and whether, in the light of its constituency, we might have to revise the name. Instead, we can start to understand how persons come to describe the world in the ways that they do as a result of the fact that the name of a corpus of knowledge may routinely be seen by members as indicating ownership of the corpus by a particular collectivity.

Michael Moerman (1967)[1] seeking to describe the cultural traits of a Tai people, the Lue, asked members of the Lue to identify such traits for him in order that he might list them. The members obliged, listing such things as hairstyles, ornamentation, utensils and the like. Moerman noted, however, that non-Lue seemed also to wear such hairstyles and ornaments as had been identified for him as 'Lue'. When this fact was pointed out to his Lue informants, these informants did not allow that they had made an error, that the Lue and the neighbouring peoples had the same ways and that there was indeed no Lue culture. Instead they characterized their neighbours as 'cop-

1. See Reading 6 in this volume [Ed.].

iers'. The description of practices as 'Lue' does more, then, than simply identify certain practices: it transforms the relationship between two peoples. The Lue and their neighbours do not simply have practices in common which just happen to be called 'Lue practices'. Rather, the neighbours are seen to have taken their practices from the Lue and, in using them, can be found to be copying. If we were to confine ourselves to treating shared knowledge as, simply, shared knowledge, this would mean that certain kinds of persons and collectivity relations which can now routinely be found in the social structure could not exist. The relationship between two collectivities, did we not ascribe ownership of cultural elements to the one, would be no more than that of resemblance in that they shared the same knowledge or beliefs; but where beliefs can be assigned to an owner, then we are able to conceive of collectivities as standing in an assymetrical relationship. A brief discussion of Latin American politics shows what is involved here. Emmanuel de Kadt, in a discussion of a study of political parties in Latin America, observes that

Alan Angell . . . suggests that the political parties should be seen as conglomerations of the politically ambitious from all classes, rather than as simple instruments of the oligarchy. It is an interesting viewpoint but seems to underestimate the extent to which those lower on the ladder identify with and express the interests of those higher up (de Kadt, 1967, p. 468).

We are here being offered two views of the social structure of political organization. On the one hand, we are offered what might be called 'pluralistic democracy', the view that parties are constructed out of personnel drawn from different social classes and that the parties are not, therefore, aligned with any particular social stratum. The holding of the same beliefs by co-members of a party in such a setting represents the occurrence of a consensus which transcends lines drawn by social class membership. These same facts, that parties are made up of persons drawn from various social classes and that there is some consensus amongst party members independently of their class affiliation, alternatively can be reconstructed and transformed into a picture of political organization in which parties are entirely subordinated to social class, by the simple step of assigning ownership of beliefs and interests to those 'higher up' the status system. The fact that those of higher and lower social status subscribe to the same beliefs is no longer conceived as simple agreement amongst persons of different social status: those who are of lower social status can now be seen as taking their ideas from those of higher status, identifying with them and expressing their views. Without assigning ownership of a corpus to one or another collectivity we should, then, be unable to talk of people 'identifying' with collectivities in which they do not have membership and we would also be unable to populate the social structure with such social types as 'stooges', 'mouth-pieces' and 'tools of the oligarchy' in the ways that we presently do.

The treatment of corpus names as recognizing a relationship of ownership between collectivity and corpus provides us, then, with a method of interpreting the activities of persons in the society, both those who are collectivity members and those who are not. It provides us with a method of assessing the bona fides of actions and thus of managing the distinction between appearances and realities that is fundamental both to the conduct of everyday life and the accomplishment of sociological work. The examination of activities to see if they are premised on a corpus of knowledge owned by a collectivity in which the actor does not have membership equips us to find that his activities are imitations, impersonations, representations and the like, that he is not acting in his own behalf but trying to appear like others or to express their ideas and interests. Thus, under the oligarchic version of Latin American politics, we are equipped to find that lower status politicians are not merely saying what they believe but are, in fact, expressing the beliefs of their social superiors and, in the case of the neighbours of the Lue, we can now find that they are not merely doing what they routinely do but are, in fact, aspiring to be like the Lue.

The treatment of corpus names as expressing an ownership relation also enables us to find in the activities of members some operations of the social structure, gives us ways to make the relationship of one collectivity to another observable. Thus, the identification of the knowledge of the witch-doctor Bögwözu as 'Baka medicine' provides us with a particular way to see his activities: they do not represent an innovation *within* Azande society but, instead, represent the occurrence of culture contact and of cultural borrowing by the Azande from another society. Similarly, the adoption of notions identified as Oriental by members of Western societies provides us with a way of finding that those persons are disaffiliating from Western society and identifying with Oriental societies.

The treatment that has been given in the course of this discussion of the notion of the ownership of knowledge to the corpus of knowledge does not exhaust the problems nor does it even exhaust the metaphor of ownership. There is always the question, what do owners and others do with owned objects? A car owner can drive the car, keep it in a garage, give it away, loan it out, crash it and so forth. Ownership gives the right to do things and to decide what can be done, it also generates obligations and responsibilities. The metaphor might find further useful application to the study of the corpus of knowledge.

References

EVANS-PRITCHARD, E. E. (1937), *Witchcraft, Oracles and Magic among the Azande,* Oxford University Press.

DE KADT, E. (1967), 'Review of Paul Halmos (ed.) "Latin American sociological studies" ', *British Journal of Sociology*, vol. 18.

MOERMAN, M. (1967), 'Being Lue: uses and abuses of ethnic identification', *Proceedings of Spring 1967 Meetings*, American Ethnological Society, pp. 153–69.

6 Michael Moerman

Accomplishing Ethnicity

Michael Moerman, 'Being Lue: uses and abuses of ethnic identification',
in June Helm (ed.), *Essays on the Problem of Tribe*, University of Washington
Press, 1968.

Anthropologists use the word 'tribe' in three distinct, but related ways: to
stipulate an evolutionary stage (e.g., Service, 1962), to distinguish one type
of society from others (as in the literature about India, Africa, and South-
East Asia), and to label any population whose members share a common
culture. This paper is concerned mainly with the third meaning, somewhat
with the second, and only in passing with the first. My interest is not in the
confusions that result from this triple usage. Rather, I will use data about the
Tai-Lue[1] in order to describe anthropology as an enterprise that systematically confuses data with analysis and words with people.

What are the Lue?

Ethnologists of South-East Asia usually use 'tribe' for the members of a set
of societies that are not congregations for a great religion, that have little
supra-village political organization, and that are only superficially involved
in a cash economy. Although negative descriptors are usually no more than
tautologically implied poles for an imaginary continuum (Lehman, 1964,
p. 390), in the context of South-East Asia such negative descriptors of
'tribe' have value. Leach (1954, 1960) and Lehman (1963) have shown that a
South-East Asian society's membership in the set called 'tribal' can be described, defined, and analysed only in terms of that society's contrast to a
civilized society which it may fight, serve, mimic, or even become – but
which it can never ignore. Elsewhere (Moerman, 1965, p. 1216), I have
argued that an individual is a member of some society by virtue of not being a
member of other specific societies. In South-East Asia, a society is a member
of the tribal set by virtue of not being a member of the civilized set. The title
of Burling's book (1965), *Hill Farms and Padi Fields*, is an epigrammatic
formulation of two common rules of South-East Asian ethnology. The first

1. I use *Thai* for the Siamese and *Tai* for the larger language family of which they are
a member. Accessible descriptions of the Tai-Lue can be found in LeBar, Hickey and
Musgrave (1964) and in Moerman (1965). My fieldwork among them was concentrated
in Ban Ping village, Chiengkham district, Chiengrai province, north Thailand but
includes Lue elsewhere in Thailand.

rule is that every South-East Asian society is uniquely and obviously tribal or civilized. The second is that membership in either subset is based upon ecological adaptation. Specifically, civilized peoples are supposed to farm irrigated rice in valleys and river basins, tribesmen to cultivate rice swiddens in the hills. For those who use them, the rules lose no force even when it is pointed out that the Shan live on plateaux, not in valleys, and that many Lao practice shifting, not sedentary, cultivation. When contrasted with their immediate tribal neighbors, the Shan, however paltry their princes, and the Lao, however anarchic their administration, are peoples with a state. Although it is probably this which makes them 'civilized', it is nevertheless clear that the distinction hill versus plains does not bifurcate the real populations of South-East Asia (La Raw, 1967; Lehman, 1967). One reaction to this observation would be, as Lehman (personal communication) suggests, to analyse the rules which underlie the cliché and to thereby also discover the objects (ethnic categories versus groups of people) which those rules concern. The present paper, however, is limited in its central data to the actual clichés of Chiengkham Lue usage and in its initial purpose to pointing out how conventional anthropological 'analysis' is a be-jargoned restatement of those clichés.

South-East Asian peoples are supposed to all fall into one or the other of the two complementary subsets: tribal and civilized. The illiterate Tai who meets a Yao learned in Chinese never doubts which is which. Nor, it seems, does the ethnologist, although he has seen merchants, heard of hunters and fishermen, smells the smoke of Northern Tai burning the hillsides, and knows that Mew silver ornaments are the proceeds of opium that reaches Hong Kong.

Table 1 indicates that the dichotomy between jungle and state (or hill and lowland) peoples is the primary ethnic distinction made by the Lue of Ban Ping village. It seems that the dichotomy is equally basic to other groups in northern South-East Asia. It is folk belief that hill and plains are exhaustive and mutually exclusive categories of peoples, that plainsmen are civilized and tribesmen are not, and that the significant properties of members of each set can be found by negating the properties of the members of the other set. Folk beliefs have honorable status but they are not the same intellectual object as a scientific analysis. The tribal–civilized, or hill–plains dichotomy in South-East Asia is not an analysis or explanation of behavior. It is a native notion, for us anthropologists to analyse and not merely repeat as if it were our own discovery. The dichotomy is not an answer to the complexities of South-East Asian ethnology, but a problematic cultural phenomenon for us to investigate.

As category anomalies, the Lue and other 'tribal Tai' are instructive cases for this investigation. In contrast to hill people, the Lue are civilized, sedent-

Table 1 Lue taxonomy of Chiengkham ethnic groups

```
                                        ┌─ set [animals]
                                        │
                                        └─ kun [people(s)]
                                             ├─ pa· [jungle], dɔj [hill]
                                             │      └─ mew   jaw   hɔ·
                                             │
                                             └─ lap, lum [lowland], me·ŋ [state]
                                                    ├─ [with religion]¹
                                                    │     ├─ phama [Burma]
                                                    │     │     └─ ly· [Lue]   taj, me·ŋ, kalɔ·m,   law    thaj        ka·t      ŋi·w
                                                    │     └─ taj         jo·n [Yuan]   [Lao]  [Siamese]   [Town]   [Shan]
                                                    │
                                                    └─ [no religion]¹
                                                          ├─ cek, nɔ· [Chinese]
                                                          └─ fala·ŋ [Caucasian]
```

1. I am uncertain whether this pair (mi·sá?saná· vs. ɱmi·sá?saná·) belongs in the Lue ethnic label scheme.

ary, irrigating, Buddhist, and patriotic lowlanders. In their immediate societal context, however, the Lue of Chiengkham present themselves as a tribe, in the third sense of that word. They are an ethnic entity which the Yuan villagers about them and the officials above them are compelled to recognize. Although they have lived among the Yuan for 120 years, the women of Ban Ping wear a distinctive Lue sarong and hairstyle. Although they have lived sixty years in the nation of Thailand villagers feel a vague nostalgia for 'the old country', the Sip Song Panna. Although the two dialects are similar, villagers ridicule Yuan and call it ugly. The villagers of Ban Ping maintain details of costume and adornment which permit them to look different from the Lao and Yuan about them. The peculiar tones and vowels of their speech allow them to sound different. They reject close association with the Yuan and, unless it is convenient, refuse to marry or work with them. The problem, then, is how and why the Lue can come across to their neighbors, themselves, and their ethnographer as 'a group the members of which claim unity on the grounds of their conception of a specific common culture' (Nadel, 1942, p. 17). Let me emphasize that I honor the Lue claim only by reporting it and by commenting on the circumstances in which it is made. Personally, I believe neither in the total uniqueness of labeled sets of persons nor in the correspondence between each named set and an homogeneous, distinctive and total 'way of life'. Nevertheless, in some contexts the Lue do seem to subscribe to these rather odd notions, although they are less obsessed by them than professional anthropologists are.

To themselves and their neighbors, the Lue are an ethnic entity despite the evident triviality of their 'distinctive' traits and the total destruction of the political state that once defined them: Chiengrung and the Sip Song Panna.[2] Let us begin our examination of Lue ethnicity with the thirty or so visible traits which the Lue of Ban Ping say distinguish them from their Yuan neighbors (see Table 2). Of these, sixteen are no longer practiced, or are restricted to the old, and eight are shared with the Yuan. Nevertheless, I must tarry with these thirty paltry traits because the Lue do.

The brevity and pettiness of the list are not sufficient reasons for dismissing it. I expect that the product of a similar approach to distinguishing between Americans and Canadians or among Thai, Burmese, and Cambodians might be no more impressive. More generally, trait inventories are clearly irrelevant to 'culture' if one means by that word either something with a structure or a set of native concepts. More importantly, there is no

2. Unlike Berreman (1960, p. 788), I am interested not in how the Lue became 'distinctive', but in why they have remained 'distinctive' despite a high frequency of interaction with other Northern Tai which, just as Berreman would predict (pp. 785f.), has made them objectively resemble their neighbors.

basis for assuming that the profession's judgements of 'minor' (such petty traits) and 'major' (ethnicity) are universally shared by natives.

The superficiality of the traits may perhaps even aid preservation of them and of the ethnicity which they serve to document. The Lue exist only in the context of a larger socio-political system. Unlike such distinctive customs as Iban headhunting or Mormon polygyny, Lue traits do not disturb the neighbors and rulers of the larger society. In addition, since signs of Lueness

Table 2 Inventory of Lue traits

	1 Going and gone	2 Shared with Yuan	3 Currently distinctive
Tattooing	●		
*Male hairstyle	●		
*Female hairstyle	●		Only women over 30
*Male turban	●		
*Female turban	●		Only women over 30
*Male jacket	●		
*Female jacket	●		
*Female sarong		●	
*Decorated trousers	●		
*Home-made work clothes		●	Formerly shared with Yuan
Sword	●		
Silver ornaments	●		Yuan gave them up before Lue did
Silver girdle	●		
*Longhouse	●		
*Sloping walls	●		
*Chopsticks	●		Rarely by men under 50
*Recessed fireplace		●	Now rare
*Blanket			●
*Pillow		●	
*Black mosquito net		●	
*Mattress			●
*Weaving		●	Now very rare among Yuan
*Rice pounder		●	
Dibble		●	
Flail		●	
Village Spirit house		●	
*Cooperative labor groups		●	
*Cycling residence	●		
Folksong (xáplỳ)			●
Lenten games	●		Now restricted to children

have little to do with career advancement or basic economy, the Lue do not yet have to choose between ethnicity and comfortable modernization.

A further characteristic of these traits is their item equivalence to those of the peoples from whom the Lue distinguish themselves. That is, the observer can ask himself questions like, 'If the Lue have this kind of folksong, what kind do the Yuan and the Lao have?' The appropriateness of such isomorphic comparisons suggests both that the Lue and their neighbors are part of a single ethnic system and that the Lue exist as a visible ethnic category only in contrast with and intelligibly to the other Tai groups listed on the last line of Table 1.

Another observation that can be made about most traits on the list, and especially about those which are still practiced, is that, compared to their Yuan equivalents, they conserve cash. The items marked with an asterisk are made within the village, and often within the household. A Lue sarong or mattress or house cannot be bought in town. Their Yuan equivalents, if they are to be good ones, must be bought there. Villagers do not say, 'We are Lue because it's cheaper.' Nevertheless, in discussing some traits, predicting how long they will persist, and in comparing themselves to the Yuan, they recognize that Lue insignia encourage the hard work and frugality that they regard as virtues in which the Yuan and their own young folk fail.

In their view, as in mine, weaving is the most time-consuming and money-saving Lue trait. In Chiengkham, most rural Lue and hardly any Yuan dress in home-woven clothes. The Lue call the Yuan lazy and often prove the observation by referring to their failure to weave. The Yuan call the Lue stingy, which, of course, could be proved just as easily. Because weaving is hard to do and money easier to obtain than it used to be, old villagers fear that the young will give up weaving and with it the distinctive sarongs, mattresses, pillows, and home-woven work clothes. In 1960, and again in 1965, I saw little sign of this prophecy being fulfilled in Ban Ping. In part this was because a trousseau of Lue artifacts and a reputation as a hard worker were important to a young girl's marriageability.

Unlike rabbis among the Jews, there is among the Lue no office concerned with preserving the people's distinctive cultural practices. The Lue suppose that it is the old who do so, and in some ways, especially by story and example, this is true. It should be pointed out, however, that many 'distinctive' Lue traits are associated with the courtship and family-founding institutions which, for reasons other than their cultural conservatism, are of such interest to all Lue. The decorative ornaments, clothing, hair-dress, and sword are usually spoken of by the Lue in the context of courtship. Lue folksongs and musical instruments were also part of courtship, though not exclusively so. Only after their legs were tattooed did boys count as young men; the girls ridiculed those with white legs. Dialect, the most important and distinctive

Lue trait (and one omitted from Table 2) is also associated with courtship. Unlike the Siamese, most Northern Tai have elaborate courtship practices, including allusive dialogues and songs. For the Lue, as for most populations, endogamy affects ethnicity. Lue and Yuan rarely court one another seriously, and a usual reason both give is that the other group cannot speak well when courting.

Consider now the traits which are disappearing or are no longer practiced (column 1 of Table 2), since these provide villagers with data for their explanations of culture change. Some customs (like male top-knots) were given up because the Siamese, who began to administer Chiengkham in 1902, demanded it. The motive usually ascribed to the Siamese officials is that they 'wanted the Lue to be like everybody else'. This motive is quite intelligible to the Lue, since their own most common phrase for culture change is 'copying others' (hén pōn).

It is fair, I think, to translate 'copying others' as 'cultural borrowing' or 'diffusion'. This translation implies a view, which the Lue indeed have and apparently share with many anthropologists, that culture change involves a loss of ethnicity. Perhaps the view arises from the formal properties of most casual schemes of ethnic labels as they are usually used by natives and anthropologists. Each current label is imagined to have always existed, and to cover a total way of life. The sum of labels is supposed to be exhaustive of ways of life. In short, if every human activity can appropriately be given some ethnic label, then substituting one activity for another is tantamount to trading an Indian custom, for example, for an American one.

A common motive which the Lue ascribe for 'copying others', especially more powerful others, is embarrassment at being different from them (áj pōn). The Lue claim that the young are more prone to copy others than the old are, men more than women. They further claim that some areas of life, typically those concerned with marketing and production or which involve contacts with townsmen, change more easily and rapidly than others, which are typically those concerned with family life and language. The more thoughtful villagers analyse culture change in terms of comparative advantage. Specifically, in terms of how rewards – usually leisure, cash, or extra-community power, for the new practice outweigh its costs – usually social – for those who adopt it. In some instances, a parallel analysis is made in terms of constant advantage compared to recently reduced costs, usually because of expanded or redistributed resources.

In general, aside from psychodynamic issues which I did not discuss with them, there is nothing in the anthropological literature on acculturation and culture change which the Lue were unable to volunteer to me in casual conversation. Now, it should come as no news that some of our hard-won anthropological truths are commonplace old wives' tales. The intriguing fact is that these are old *Lue* wives, or more accurately, husbands. That they should share with Americans the folk-beliefs that we anthropologists pretend are scientific discoveries is surely a phenomenon worthy of investigation. There may be something universal to human societies which makes it natural for us to talk about change in terms of diffusion differentiated by sex and generation, progressive homogenization, and calculations of relative economic and social advantage. There is, I think, some reason to believe that the Crô-Magnon talked among themselves about culture change in much the same way as next year's journals will.

Why are the Lue?

Although the 'distinctive customs' of column 2 (Table 2) are not objectively distinctive, villagers labeled, and even described, each of the traits marked in that column as 'Lue'. Sometimes they volunteered, or by observation and questioning I discovered, that the Yuan too, have them.

It is possible, and some villagers claim, that such customs either originated with or are most prevalent among the Lue and that the Yuan merely copied them because, in the conventional village explanation, 'they were embarrassed to be different'. So, for example, one villager volunteered the information that walking backwards when transplanting rice – a practice which I think is shared by all Tai and perhaps by all who transplant – is a Lue custom which the Yuan copied. The example suggests, first, that villagers, like anthropologists, are culture historians, who are interested in the imagined origins of a custom and who take that origin to be a demonstration of the custom's essential ethnicity. Second, although you might want to dismiss it as a deliberate subterfuge on my part, the custom of walking backwards does not appear on Table 2. Trait inventories have a general characteristic of all lists: they offer no closure. A more elaborate listing might contain fifty traits, a more casual one fifteen. The listing is retrospective, not inductive. Having identified some population – in this instance their own – as Lue, informants can then assign the label 'Lue' to anything that population does.

Since professional anthropologists use ethnic labels in much the same way, I may have some difficulty suggesting to readers that this is, in fact, a curious propensity. Consider however, that any person, or group of persons, or set of persons can be assigned any of a large number of identifications. In our own society sex, age, religion, job titles, race, and place of birth or residence are identifications which are quite generally usable. But each of us, both as individuals and as members of sets of persons, is simultaneously identifiable by all of these, and by many more. Since multiple identifications are always present, the 'truth' or 'objective correctness' of an identification is never sufficient to explain its use. It is vacuous to say that the Lue call themselves and their customs 'Lue' because they both *are* Lue. To the serious student of society, the preferring of any identification should be a problematic phenomenon, not a comforting answer. The question is not, 'Who are the Lue?' (cf. Moerman, 1965, 1967) but rather when and how and why the identification 'Lue' is preferred. Truth or falsity is a criterion which should be applied to our analysis; it has no relevance to native category usage.

Once an identification label has been assigned, members can use it for labelling the behavior, possessions, ideas, etc., which are appropriately associated with the labeled category. Through this procedure, villagers can talk about Lue hairdress, anthropologists about peasant values, and journalists about Californian marriages. In America, and apparently in Chiengkham, some identification labels can be used by members to report almost any behavior of persons identified by that label. To anthropologists, and to the Lue, ethnic labels have such general utility. This permits the Lue of Ban Ping to generate a list without limits (i.e. one can probably always add another trait) like that of Table 2. The availability of such a list, like the silliness of the trait 'walking backwards', suggests that the Lue are concerned to *demonstrate* their ethnicity. To put the matter somewhat less motivationally, identification by means of ethnic labels has a higher order of priority for the Lue than it does for Americans, Siamese, and I think, for Yuan. There seems then, to be curious complicity between native and ethnographer. I consider the Lue to be an ethnic entity, a tribe, because they successfully present themselves as one. This is not a matter of my ingenuity as an analyst of native cognitive systems. Rather, like most ethnography, it is a product of the anthropologist's *essential* naïveté.

I am not asserting that the Lue are not in fact a tribe, and that they merely fooled me into thinking them one. Rather, I do assert that Lue ethnicity consists largely of the fact that persons in Chiengkham and neighboring districts often use ethnic labels when they talk about the people and the activities of Ban Ping and certain other villages. Just as a behavior in America is socially the action of, say, a property-owner in that it is by means of that category label that the rules of American society make it appropriate to report the behavior, so, in Chiengkham, the ethnic label 'Lue' has high priority for talking about persons or practices which might, were we not in Chiengkham, be properly associated with other identifications. Further, in order to call themselves by an ethnic label, villagers are semantically required to use or imply a contrastive ethnic label for others. To phrase the issue somewhat more generally and accurately, using one member of a set of identifications provides the context which makes other members of that set appropriate. Using the label 'Negro' provides the context which makes labels like 'White' or 'Mexican' appropriate. The ethnic identification of Table 1 are, in this sense, mutually appropriate. In addition, the socio-political environment of Ban Ping – and natives' awareness of that environment – suggests some reasons why the villagers of Ban Ping might find ethnic labels desirable.

As Table 1 records, hill/jungle and plains/state are exhaustive and mutually exclusive local categories. All Tai are certain that members of the state set are in every way superior. Since all relevant persons regard the Lue as being in that set,[3] ethnic categorization is no disadvantage. Compared to the culturally possible alternative categorization schemes, it is an advantage. In Thailand, the usual distinction among Tai is between officials and peasant, or, with rough equivalence, between townsmen and villagers. In this categorization scheme, villagers are called, both by themselves and by others, *khon bâ·n nɔ̆·k*, which, to quote an unusually sympathetic Thai scholar who avoids the term, means 'backwardness in wealth and knowledge' (Rajadhon 1961, p. 8). To be a *khon bâ·n nɔ̆·k*, a 'hick' or 'peasant', is to participate to an unequal, deprived, and rather contemned degree in the Siamese urban-focused national culture. To the extent that the villagers of Ban Ping can be categorized as Lue, they are members of a distinct tribe. Within the ethnic identification scheme, they refer to the dominant Siamese as *thaj*, an ethnic designation. They call townsmen *taj kă·t* ('market Tai') as if they, too, were but another tribe. Village divergences from town, and from the Yuan who 'copy the *taj kă·t*' thereby become matters of ethnic pride rather than of class embarrassment. As Lue, villagers are not ashamed of using charms and tigers' claws to cure sprains, for it is 'the Lue custom', even though the same practices are found in Central Thai villages. Wide-bottomed trousers for dress wear are not merely old fashioned and rustic, they are 'the Lue custom', even though the Yuan, too, wear them when working in the fields. The propitiation of spirits, rather than an embarrassing sign of religious ignorance, is the Lue way.

Like sociologists, the Lue recognize three socio-economic classes – whether based on wealth or on style of life. In those situations where villagers use class identifications for themselves, they must use a label from the lowest rank in either the wealth-based scheme of Table 3a or the life-style-based scheme of 3b. In the alternative identification scheme afforded by ethnic labels, lowlanders are clearly superior to the sometimes barely human jungle people, those with religion immeasurably better than those without, the *taj* superior to others on level D (Table 1), and the Lue, of course, more moral, honest, hospitable, pacific, hard working, cooperative, clean, and attractive than any other Tai group they, or I, know of.

3. The Chiengkham Lue are unaware that the few Bangkok Thai who have heard of them suppose them to be a hill people. They also seem to be unaware that some Thai newcomers to Chiengkham think that the Lue must once have been a hill people because they walk single-file.

Tai peasants are usually ashamed of their non-urban practices. For Lue, such practices are foci for ethnic pride. As a Lue, the villager sees himself as different from but not inferior to the dominant townsman-official. Ban Ping's customs and knowledge and religion pretend to self-sufficiency. Under the aspect of its Lueness, the village does not see itself as part of a 'little tradition' dependent on the town and nation for ideas and symbols and culture. In other words, in so far as he can regard himself as Lue, the villager need not think himself a peasant.

The Lue of Chiengkham avoid opprobious class identification through asserting the higher priority of a non-stratifiable ethnic identification.[4] Presumably, it requires a few exotic traits, tics, and peculiarities to make their assertion successful. That this use of culture to avoid class is not peculiar to the Lue is suggested by Spicer's account (1940) of the Yaqui of Arizona – a social category which seems to differ from Mexican-American rural proletarians largely in its ability to convince anthropologists and other Anglos of its ethnicity.

Table 3a **Wealth-based class labels**

| I [rich] há·ŋ |
| II [average] bá hâj bà dí· |
| III [poor] tùk |

Table 3b **Life-style-based class labels**

| I [officials] kun kín ŋən də·r, câw naj |
| II [merchant] kun kâ· |
| III [farmer, hick, peasant] kun bâ·n nŏ·k, kun bâ·n, kun het ka·n |

To be a Lue is to have 'Lue' in the set of social identities with which one can be properly labeled. As I suggested for the Lue (Moerman, 1965), and as Goodenough (1965, p. 21) has asserted more generally, 'the qualifications for a social identity are the conditions for being referred to by the linguistic expression that names the identity'. The traits listed in Table 2 can be used as such qualifications. My analysis of their use in Chiengkham, however, is different from the conventional ethnoscientific approach in which a large set of culturally recognized indices is mapped many-to-one on to a smaller set of culturally recognized category labels. Ethnic labeling in Chiengkham (and probably elsewhere) does not have the properties of a conditioned reflex in which cultural traits serve as stimuli which produce an ethnic label as

4. It would not surprise me to learn that other tribesmen in national societies share with the Lue Steward's observation that cultural distinctions are vertical, class distinctions horizontal.

an automatic response. Rather, the set of ethnic labels are *possible* identifications for human objects which can also be properly given labels from other identification sets. From this observation it follows that an ethnic identification is never self-explanatory. From this, in turn, I assume that ethnic labeling is motivated. I further suspect, but cannot demonstrate, that the optative and motivated nature of ethnic labeling is connected to the fact that traits are used retrospectively, not inductively. To put it baldly, once a native decides to give some person an ethnic label, he finds some traits which that person has that can be used to demonstrate that the label has been applied correctly. In addition, it is clear, albeit trivial, that neither the selection of the ethnic identification set nor the properties of the indexical traits can determine the taxonomic level used.

Permit me to review some of the ground we have covered before I probe its solidity. In South-East Asia, the categories 'tribal' and 'civilized' each implies and defines the other. This suggests that it would be foolish to discuss regional history in terms of evolution from tribe to state, since tribes exist only in the context of a state system of social relations which includes them; states exist by coming to terms with tribes (as social types). In a somewhat similar manner, the contemporary tribalism (in the sense of ethnicity) of the Chiengkham Lue depends upon contrast with equivalent ethnic entities. The form of the local set of ethnic identifications, the pettiness and frugality of Lue insignia, and the functions and presumed motives of Lue ethnicity all involve participation in a modern, centralized nation state.

Putting across his ethnic identification involves the villager of Ban Ping in a complex of assumptions which seem to be shared by professional anthropologists whose interest in them is presumably equally pronounced, albeit differently motivated. The villager assumes, as the form of his own Lueness proclaims, that, in some contexts, behavioral insignia, of which dialect is paramount, contrastively identify eternal, mutually exclusive, and exhaustive ethnic entities. Such entities are then, for certain purposes, assumed to correspond to real populations which have internally homogeneous and externally discrete ways of life. Such ways of life, in turn, are in certain contexts, bound to vary from other ways of life (*phàsá· pháj phàsá· man*) which also are eternal and, provided that the group is civilized, equally worthy of respect. That is, the Lue, for some purposes and situations, seem to be cultural relativists who believe in named, somehow timeless, and discrete (and so presumably denumerable) societies, each associated with a culture which is a 'blueprint for living' (Naroll, 1964), at least in the minimal, though really quite strong, sense that assigning an ethnic label to a behavior explains that behavior.

The most weakly grounded argument, I think, concerns the motives for contemporary Lue ethnicity, for this rests upon the accuracy of my observation that ethnic identifications, in particular the label 'Lue', have high priority to the people I studied. I believe that my observation is accurate, I hope that my discussion made it plausible, but I am convinced that the data and methods of participant observation preclude demonstrating the adequacy of this or similar observations.

When are the Lue?

The research interest of our 1959–61 field trip was the study of decisions which had consequences for modernization and for change toward national and lowland types of society. With this in mind, and after a series of compromises, we went to Chiengkham in order to study the Lue. Everyone in Chiengkham town, and everyone in Ban Ping, knew that to be my purpose – largely because we told them so. It is therefore no surprise that events were often reported to us and spoken of in our presence in terms of ethnic, and specifically Lue, categories. I am not merely whistling the tired old tune that 'the Tai' or 'Orientals' or 'peasants' – substitute what word you will – 'tell you what you want to hear'. Rather, I am concerned about something more subtle and more pervasive. My understanding of society as a cognitive system is that people observe what they take to be human occurrences and ascribe them to categories of what they take to be persons. My initial goal as an ethnographer of Lue society is to learn the Lue categories of occurrences and persons and the implicit rules by which they are appropriately associated. It is clear that when an ethnographer asks natives questions which they would not ask each other, he is calling attention to issues which are normally inexplicit and sometimes non-existent. In so far as the significance of an action depends upon the situation in which it occurs, then, to the extent that answering an ethnographer's question is an unusual situation for natives, one cannot reason from a native's answer to his normal categories and ascriptions. But the importance of *the situation*, and particularly of the other persons present in it, goes beyond this to distort the data of even the silent ethnographer. By his very presence as someone interested in culture and cultures, the social scientist establishes the primary relevance to him of ethnic (or kinship, or class, or political) categorization schemes as ways of reporting, recording and analysing human occurrences. He thus pressures those who would talk to him to pay primary attention to these categorizations even when they would not otherwise do so. Consider, for example, the following fieldnote recorded about a month after we arrived in Chiengkham, and before we had moved to Ban Ping. At a funeral, 'I was told [presumably by the Yuan townswoman with whom we were then living] that the deceased was a Shan. Also that most of the guests were Lue or Shan.' I think it safe to suppose that had we not been the specific strangers we were – foreigners interested in learning what the Lue were like – her categorization would not have been ethnic. Instead, she might have thought fit to tell us of kinship relations, relative wealth, official connections, or neighborhood. All of these category sets are, like the ethnic set, used by the people of Chiengkham. I do not believe that the ethnographic stranger can make people use category systems which are unavailable to them. But he can, and does, and in principle can never be sure that he has not altered the local priorities among the native category sets which it is his task to describe.

It is a plausible belief, which I share, that persons who talk or live together must acknowledge rules-in-common which permit them to do so. It is my business as an ethnographer to discover, describe, and analyse those rules whether or not they are explicitly known by the natives who use them. Those rules can be regarded as predicates pertaining to some subjects. Only after we have analysed a large number of rules among a large number of sets of persons will we know what those subjects are. In Ban Ping, for example, I would judge that many of the rules are human universals, but that some pertain to sex-specified subjects, and some others to peasants, to physically isolated communities, to the Tai and to the Lue.

Most of what is called 'cultural anthropology' consists of reporting the folk predicates of folk ethnic identification labels, of assuming that all predicates are properly ascribable to such labels, and of hunting for human populations to which the labels can be pinned. The first section of this paper argued that anthropologists do not distinguish between native clichés about predicates and analyses of them. The second argued that anthropologists, with more naïveté than any native, suppose that all of these imperfectly understood predicates can correctly be ascribed to a single category of subject: the ethnic identification. The last section suggests that the ethnographer's professional obsession with ethnic subjects makes participant observation an inappropriate technique for discovering the native categories that must be reported if we are to be able to analyse the underlying rules which natives use to ascribe events, things, and persons to those categories.

Were it not so generally shared, professionally entrenched, and scientistically justified, the naïveté of anthropology would be amusing. Did I not suspect its naïveté to be irremediable, the present paper might be merely querulous. Anthropologists imagine that it would not be a fish who discovers water, yet believe that the credibility of a cultural analysis varies with the length and intimacy of fieldwork. Anthropologists point out that everyone's viewpoint is rooted in his social position, yet suppose that their own observations are unmotivated and their motives invisible. But the most striking practice is anthropology's apparent inability to distinguish between warm striking human bodies and one kind of identification device which some of those bodies sometimes use. Ethnic identification devices – with their important potential of making each ethnic set of living persons a joint enterprise with countless generations of unexamined history – seem to be universal. Social scientists should therefore describe and analyse the ways in which they are used, and not merely–as natives do–use them as explanations. It would make more sense to first study and analyse social rules, and then worry whether they are descriptive of the Nuer or the Shilluk, the Yuan or the Lue, the Sinhalese or the peasants. It is quite possible that ethnic categories are rarely appropriate subjects for the interesting human predicates.

References

BERREMAN, G. D. (1960), *Hindus of the Himalayas*, University of California Press.

BURLING, R. (1965), *Hill Farms and Padi Fields*, Prentice-Hall.

GOODENOUGH, W. H. (1965), 'Rethinking "status" and "role": towards a general model of the cultural organization of social relationships', in *The Relevance of Models for Social Anthropology*, ASA Monograph no. 1, Tavistock.

LA RAW, M. (1967), 'Towards a basis for understanding the minorities in Burma: the Kachin example', in P. Kundstadter (ed.), *Southeast Asian Tribes, Minorities and Nations*, vol. 2, Princeton University Press.

LEACH, E. R. (1954), *The Political Systems of Highland Burma*, London School of Economics.

LEACH, E. R. (1960), 'The frontiers of "Burma"', *Comparative Studies in Society and History*, vol. 3, pp. 49–68.

LEBAR, F. M., HICKEY, G. C., and MUSGRAVE, J. K. (1964), *Ethnic Groups of Mainland Southeast Asia*, HRAF Press.

LEHMAN, F. K. (1963), 'The structure of Chin society', *University of Illinois Studies in Anthropology*, no. 3.

LEHMAN, F. K. (1964), 'Typology and the classification of sociocultural systems', in R. A. Manners (ed.), *Process and Pattern in Culture: Essays in Honor of Julian H. Steward*, Aldine.

LEHMAN, F. K. (1967), 'Ethnic categories in Burma and the theory of social systems', in P. Kunstadter (ed.), *Southeast Asian Tribes, Minorities and Nations*, vol. 2, Princeton University Press.

MOERMAN, M. (1965), 'Who are the Lue?', *American Anthropologist*, vol. 67, pp. 1215–30.

MOERMAN, M. (1967), 'Reply to Naroll', *American Anthropologist*, vol. 69, pp. 512–13.

NADEL, S. F. (1942), *A Black Byzantium*, Oxford University Press for the International African Institute.

NAROLL, R. (1964), 'On ethnic unit classification', *Current Anthropology*, vol. 5, pp. 283–91, 306–12.

RAJADHON (1961), 'The life of a farmer', in W. J. Gedney (ed.), *Life and Ritual in Old Siam*, HRAF Press.

SERVICE, E. R. (1962), *Primitive Social Organization*, Random House.

SPICER, E. M. (1940), *Pascua: A Yaqui of Arizona*, University of Chicago Press.

STEWARD, J. H. (1955), *Theory of Culture Change*, University of Illinois Press.

7 Egon Bittner

The Concept of Organization

Egon Bittner, 'The concept of organization', *Social Research*, vol. 32, 1965, pp. 239–55.

In recent years a good deal of the very best sociological work has been devoted to the study of organization. Although the term, organization, belongs to the category of expressions about which there is maintained an air of informed vagueness, certain special conventions exist that focus its use, with qualifications, on a delimited set of phenomena. In accordance with these conventions, the term applies correctly to stable associations of persons engaged in concerted activities directed to the attainment of specific objectives. It is thought to be a decisive characteristic of such organizations that they are deliberately instituted relative to these objectives. Because organizations, in this sense, are implementing and implemented programs of action that involve a substantial dose of comprehensive and rational planning, they are identified as instances of formal or rational organization in order to differentiate them from other forms.[1]

It has been one of the most abiding points of interest of modern organizational research to study how well the programmatically intended formal structures of organizations describe what is going on within them, and what unintended, unprogrammed, and thus informal structures tend to accompany them.

How do sociologists go about distinguishing the facts of formal organization from the facts of informal organization? There seem to be two things that matter in the ways this distinction is drawn. There is, in the first place, a certain scholarly tradition in which the distinction is rooted. It dates back to Pareto's definition of rationality, Tönnies' typology, Cooley's concept of primary-group, and – tracing through the seminal achievement of the Haw-

---

1. These characteristics are generally noted when the task is to identify real instances of 'formal organization'. Cf. Blau and Scott (1962), Etzioni (1961) and Parsons (1960, pp. 16–96). Various authors have studied such organizations in ways that seem to disregard the identifying characteristics, or to subordinate them to other interests. To study a phenomenon while suspending the relevance of that feature by which it is recognized is not an unusual procedure, though it produces peculiar problems. G. E. Moore and Edmund Husserl have explored these problems from substantially different perspectives.

thorn studies – the tradition is very much alive today. Being steeped in this line of scholarship allows a sociologist to claim his colleagues' consent to the decisions he makes. In this way the distinction is a fact of life in sociological inquiry, and perceiving it correctly is a trademark of professional competence. Although this is undoubtedly a potent factor in many decisions, it does not furnish a clear-cut rule for the distinction.[2]

The rule, which is the second consideration, can be stated as follows: In certain presumptively identified fields of action, the observed stable patterns of conduct and relations can be accounted for by invoking some *programmatic constructions* that define them prospectively. In so far as the observed stable patterns match the dispositions contained in the program they are instances of formal organizational structure. Whereas, if it can be shown that the program did not provide for the occurrence of some other observed patterns which seem to have grown spontaneously, these latter belong to the domain of the informal structures.

Despite its apparent cogency, the rule is insufficient. The programmatic construction is itself a part of the presumptively identified field of action, and thus the sociologist finds himself in the position of having borrowed a concept from those he seeks to study in order to describe what he observes about them.

In general, there is nothing wrong with borrowing a common-sense concept for the purposes of sociological inquiry. Up to a certain point it is, indeed, unavoidable. The warrant for this procedure is the sociologist's interest in exploring the common-sense perspective. The point at which the use of common-sense concepts becomes a transgression is where such concepts are expected to do the analytical work of theoretical concepts. When the actor is treated as a permanent auxiliary to the enterprise of sociological inquiry at the same time that he is the object of its inquiry, there arise ambiguities that defy clarification. Now, if the idea of formal structure is basically a common-sense notion, what role can it have in sociological inquiry?

The theoretical sense of formal structures of organization

In an influential essay published fifteen years ago, Philip Selznick (1948) explicitly addressed the problem of the theoretical significance of formal constructions by relating them, as facts of life, to functional imperatives of organizations conceived as cooperative-adaptive systems. Arguing along the

2. It should not be thought that such grounds are wholly particular to the procedures of sociological inquiry. The distinguished physical chemist G. N. Lewis pointed out that a traditional conception of causality has led to an arbitrary interpretation of Maxwell's equations with the consequent development of a special electromagnetic theory of light. On purely theoretical grounds an entirely different development was equally justified and did occur later, making possible the development of quantum electromechanics. See Whitrow (1963, pp. 25–35).

lines of structural-functional analysis, he showed convincingly why 'formal administrative design can never adequately or fully reflect the concrete organization to which it refers', but is nevertheless a relevant element in the sociological study of organizations. In his view, the design represents that particular conception of organization which management technicians seek to explicate. Even though there may attach to these explications some descriptive or analytic intent, they are primarily active elements of the concrete phenomenon of organization rather than disinterested statements about it. As such, the presence of rational organizational design in social systems of action is a source of tension and dilemma. These consequences arise out of the 'recalcitrance of the tools of action', relative to the 'freedom of technical or ideal choice' reflected in plans and programs.

It is important to note that in this new and rich context the old conception of formal organization, which is traceable to Max Weber, remained intact. Together with Weber, Selznick assumes that the formal structures represent an ideally possible, but practically unattainable state of affairs. While Weber outlined the contents of the normative idealization in general terms, Selznick pointed out that the normative idealization, to be an effective source of restraint, must be constantly adapted to the impact of functional imperatives of social systems. Thus he furnished the necessary theoretical argument for an entire field of sociological investigations by directing attention to a sphere of adaptive and cooperative manipulations, and to the tensions typically found in it.

Despite the gain, the argument retains a certain theoretical short circuit. While Selznick quite clearly assigns the formal schemes to the domain of sociological data, he does not explore the full range of consequences arising out of this decision. By retaining Weber's conception of them as normative idealizations, Selznick avoids having to consider what the constructions of rational conduct mean to, and how they are used by, persons who have to live with them from day to day. It could be, however, that the rational schemes appear as unrealistic normative idealizations only when one considers them literally, i.e. without considering some tacit background assumptions that bureaucrats take for granted.

In the following we shall endeavor to show that the literal interpretation of formal schemes is not only inappropriate but, strictly speaking, impossible. We shall further show that the tacit assumptions are not simply unspecified, but instead come to the fore only on occasions of actual reference to the formal scheme. Finally, we shall argue that the meaning and import of the formal schemes must remain undetermined unless the circumstances and procedures of its actual use by actors is fully investigated.

Critique of Weber's theory of bureaucracy

We shall introduce our argument by considering Weber's work critically because the short circuit in theorizing occurred first in his work and because most of contemporary research in formal organization claims to stand in some sort of relationship to the definitions formulated by him. We shall be discussing the theory of bureaucracy as the most general case of many possible, more specific, rational schemes. But what we say about the general form is applicable to such specific instances as manuals of operations, tables of organization or programs of procedure.

Weber used the concept of organization to refer to a network of authority distribution.[3] As is well known, he asserted that such a network may be said to exist when and in so far as there prevails a high degree of correspondence between the substance of commands and conditions favoring compliance with them. Confining our interest to bureaucracy, we note that the condition favoring compliance with its authority structure lies in its acceptance as being efficient (Gerth and Mills, 1948, pp. 214–16). From this premise, pure bureaucracy obtains when the principle of technical efficiency is given overriding priority above all other considerations. The ideal type of bureaucracy is, consequently, the product of ostensibly free conceptual play with this principle.

To say, however, that the resulting scheme is a meaningful conceptualization indicates that the ideal of efficiency is exercised over a domain of objects and events that are known to exist and that are known to possess independent qualities of their own. The efficiency principle merely selects, identifies, and orders those existing elements of a scene of action that are perceived as related to it. The relevance of the known qualities of things becomes very apparent when one considers that it must be at least possible for them to be related in ways that the idealization stipulates. What sorts of things are taken for granted may vary, but it is not possible to have any rational construction of reality that does not rest on some such tacit assumptions.[4]

3. Unfortunately there exists some confusion on this point. Weber himself uses the term organization as we have stated; cf. Weber (1954, Kapitel IX, Abschnitt I, #3). The German term 'Organisation' is translated by Shils and Rheinstein as 'organization' in Rheinstein (1954, ch. 12, sect. 3). On the other hand, Henderson and Parsons translate Weber's German term 'Betrieb' as 'organization'. The reason for this choice is that Weber's definition of 'Betrieb' coincides with Alfred Marshall's definition of 'organization' in economic theory. More important than the question of 'authenticity' is, however, the fact that Weber's statement on 'Betrieb' is almost never cited in modern organizational studies while his work on authority is widely used.

4. It has been proposed that this restriction extends to all types of rational constructions. For a critique of Russell's mathematical logic along these lines see Charlsworth (1959, ch. 2).

It could be said that this is not an unusual state of affairs. In scientific inquiry it is always the case that in order to assert anything one must leave some things unsaid. Such unsaid things stand under the protection of the *ceteris paribus* clause. The use of this clause is, however, restricted and its contents are always open to scrutiny.[5]

When one lifts the mantle of protection from the unstated presupposition surrounding the terms of Weber's theory of bureaucracy one is confronted with facts of a particular sort. These facts are not sociological data, or even theoretically defensible hypotheses. Instead, one is confronted with a rich and ambiguous body of background information that normally competent members of society take for granted as commonly known. In its normal functioning this information furnishes the tacit foundation for all that is explicitly known, and provides the matrix for all deliberate considerations without being itself deliberately considered. While its content can be raised to the level of analysis, this typically does not occur. Rather, the information enters into that commonplace and practical orientation to reality which members of society regard as 'natural' when attending to their daily affairs. Since the explicit terms of the theory are embedded in this common-sense orientation, they cannot be understood without tacit reference to it. If, however, the theorist must be persuaded about the meaning of the terms in some prior and unexplicated way, there then exists collusion between him and those about whom he theorizes. We call this unexplicated understanding collusive because it is a hidden resource, the use of which cannot be controlled adequately.

Some examples will help to clarify this point. Consider the term 'employee'. There is little doubt that Weber presupposed, rather than neglected, a whole realm of background information in using it. Certainly employees must be human beings of either the male or female sex, normally competent adults rather than children, and in many ways familiar types of persons whose responsiveness, interests, inclinations, capacities and foibles are in a basic sense known as a matter of course. All this information is obvious, of course, but does not by any means coincide with the scientifically demonstrable or even scientifically tenable. Rather, the full meaning of the term 'employee', as it is used in the theory of bureaucracy, refers to that understanding of it which fully franchised persons in society expect from one another when they converse on matters of practical import. That is, in so far as the term refers meaningfully to some determinate object, it does so only in the context of actors making common sense of it in consequential situations.

Let us consider the ideal of efficiency itself. While Weber is quite clear in

5. Concerning the role of the *ceteris paribus* clause in economic analysis see Kaufman (1958, ch. 16).

stating that the sole justification of bureaucracy is its efficiency, he provides us with no clear-cut guide on how this standard of judgement is to be used. Indeed, the inventory of features of bureaucracy contains not one single item that is not arguable relative to its efficiency function. Long-range goals cannot be used definitively for calculating it because the impact of contingent factors multiplies with time and makes it increasingly difficult to assign a determinate value to the efficiency of a stably controlled segment of action. On the other hand, the use of short-term goals in judging efficiency may be in conflict with the ideal of economy itself. Not only do short-term goals change with time and compete with one another in indeterminate ways, but short-term results are of notoriously deceptive value because they can be easily manipulated to show whatever one wishes them to show (cf. Haire, 1962, especially pp. 8–10). Clearly, what Weber had in mind when speaking about efficiency was not a formally independent criterion of judgement but an ideal that is fully attuned to practical interests as these emerge and are pursued in the context of every-day life. The standard itself and the correct way to use it are, therefore, a part of the selfsame order of action that they purport to control. The power and right to judge some procedure as more or less efficient require the same kind of sensitivity, responsiveness and competence that using the procedure presupposes in the first place. Only those who have serious business in doing what must be done are also franchised to judge it.

Weber, of course, intended to achieve an idealized reconstruction of organization from the perspective of the actor. He fell short of attaining this objective precisely to the extent that he failed to explore the underlying common-sense presuppositions of his theory. He failed to grasp that the meaning and warrant of the inventory of the properties of bureaucracy are inextricably embedded in what Alfred Schutz called the attitudes of every-day life and in socially sanctioned common-sense typifications (Schutz, 1953).

Thus, if the theory of bureaucracy is a theory at all, it is a refined and purified version of the actors' theorizing. To the extent that it is a refinement and purification of it, it is, by the same token, a corrupt and incomplete version of it; for it is certainly not warranted to reduce the terms of common-sense discourse to a lexicon of culturally coded significances to satisfy the requirements of theoretical postulation. This is the theoretical shortcut we mentioned at the beginning of our remarks.

The study of the concept of organization as a common-sense construct

Plucked from its native ground, i.e. the world of common sense, the concept of rational organization, and the schematic determinations that are subsumed under it, are devoid of information on how its terms relate to facts.

Without knowing the structure of this relationship of reference, the meaning of the concept and its terms cannot be determined.

In this situation an investigator may use one of three research procedures. He can, for one thing, proceed to investigate formal organization while assuming that the unexplicated common-sense meanings of the terms are adequate definitions for the purposes of his investigation. In this case, he must use that which he proposes to study as a resource for studying it.

He can, in the second instance, attach to the terms a more or less arbitrary meaning by defining them operationally. In this case, the relationship of reference between the term and the facts to which it refers will be defined by the operations of inquiry. Interest in the actor's perspective is either deliberately abandoned, or some fictitious version of it is adopted.

The investigator can, in the last instance, decide that the meaning of the concept, and of all the terms and determinations that are subsumed under it, must be discovered by studying their use in real scenes of action by persons whose competence to use them is socially sanctioned.

It is only the last case which yields entirely to the rule specifying the relevance of the perspective of the actor in sociological inquiry. This is so because in order to understand the meaning of the actor's thought and action, which Weber sought, one must study *how* the terms of his discourse are assigned to real objects and events by normally competent persons in ordinary situations.

In so far as the procedures and considerations actors invoke in relating terms of rational common-sense construction to things in the world exhibit some stable properties, they may be called a method. It is, of course, not proper to assume that this method is identical with, or even similar to, the method of scientific inquiry. Garfinkel proposed that in order to differentiate the study of this method from the study of the methods of scientific inquiry it be called ethnomethodology.

In the following we shall propose in brief outline a program of inquiry which takes as its object of interest the study of the methodical use of the rational constructions subsumed under the concept of organization. We shall also present examples of this program. The concept itself and its methodical use are, of course, defined as belonging entirely to the domain of facts.

We must emphasize that our interest is in outlining a program of inquiry, not in producing a theory of organization. It has to be this way because the inquiry cannot get under way without first employing the very sensibilities that it seeks to study, i.e. the common-sense outlook. At the outset the phenomenon of organization comes to our attention in just the way it comes to the attention of any normal member of our linguistic community. Even as we turn to the investigation of the common-sense presuppositions in which it is embedded, and from which it derives its socially sanctioned sense, other common-sense presuppositions will continue to insinuate themselves into our thinking and observation. The important point in the proposed study is that we must be prepared to treat every substantive determination we shall formulate as a case for exploring the background information on which it in turn rests.

By way of defining our task we propose that *the study of the methodical use of the concept of organization seeks to describe the mechanisms of sustained and sanctioned relevance of the rational constructions to a variety of objects, events and occasions relative to which they are invoked.*

In order to free ourselves progressively from the encumbrance of presumptive understanding we shall take two preliminary measures. First, the author of the rational scheme, typically the managerial technician who deals with organization in the 'technical sense', will not be treated as having some sort of privileged position for understanding its meaning. By denying him the status of the authoritative interpreter we do not propose to tamper with the results of his work in the least. From our point of view he is merely the toolsmith. It seems reasonable that if one were to investigate the meaning and typical use of some tool, one would not want to be confined to what the toolmaker has in mind.

Second, we will not look to the obvious or conspicuous meaning of the expressions used in the scheme to direct us to objects and events which they identify. Rather, we will look for the way the scheme is brought to bear on whatever happens within the scope of its jurisdiction. The consequence of this step is that the question of what the scheme selects and neglects is approached by asking how certain objects and events meet, or are made to meet, the specifications contained in the scheme.

After denying the technician and his scheme the authority to organize the field of observation for the sociologist, the question of how they, nevertheless, organize it in some other sense is open for investigation.

If one suspends the presumptive notion that a rational organizational scheme is a normative idealization with a simple import, i.e. demanding literally what it says it demands; and if one views a rational organizational scheme without information about what it is ostensibly meant to be, then it emerges as a *generalized formula to which all sorts of problems can be brought for solution.* In this sense there is no telling what determinations a formal organizational scheme contains prior to the time that questions are actually and seriously addressed to it.

More important than the open capacity and applicability of the formula is, however, the fact that *problems referred to the scheme for solution acquire through this reference a distinctive meaning that they should not otherwise have.* Thus the formal organizational designs are schemes of interpretation that competent and entitled users can invoke in yet unknown ways whenever it suits their purposes. The varieties of ways in which the scheme can be invoked for information, direction, justification, and so on, without incurring the risk of sanction, constitute the scheme's methodical use. In the following we propose to discuss some examples of possible variations in the methodical use of organizational rationalities.

Examples of variation in the methodical use of the concept of organization
The gambit of compliance[6]

As we have noted earlier, the concept of rational organization is often regarded by sociologists and management technicians as a normative idealization. Even though one finds only '*is*' and '*is not*' in the substantive determination, there attaches the sense of '*ought*' to the entire scheme.

Conceived as a rule of conduct, the concept of organization is defined as having some determining power over action that takes place under the scope of its jurisdiction. This power to produce an intended result is uncertain and depends for its effectiveness on complex structural conditions. Hence, research informed by the conception of organization as a rule of conduct will seek to procure estimates of its effectiveness, and will relate the findings to factors that favor or mitigate against compliance. All such research is necessarily based on the assumption that the relationship of correspondence between the rule and the behaviors that are related to it is clear. A cursory consideration of the significance of rules as social facts reveals, however, that their meaning is not exhausted by their prospective sense. Aside from determining the *occurrence* of certain responses under suitable conditions, rules are also invoked to clarify the *meaning* of actions retrospectively. For example, one knows what a driver of an automobile signaling intent to make a left turn is doing in the middle of an intersection because one knows the rule governing such procedures. Indeed, it is a readily demonstrable fact that a good deal of the sense we make of the things happening in our presence depends on our ability to *assign them* to the phenomenal sphere of influence of some rule. Not only do we do this but we count on this happening. That this is so is richly documented in the work of Goffman who has shown how persons conduct themselves in such a way as to enable observers to relate performances to some normative expectation.

When we consider the set of highly schematic rules subsumed under the concept of rational organization, we can readily see an open realm of free play for relating an infinite variety of performances to rules as responses to these rules. In this field of games of representation and interpretation, the

6. We would like to point out that this example corresponds to what Selznick (1948, p. 32) suggests when he urges the study of the 'manipulation of the formal processes and structures in terms of informal goals'.

rule may have the significance of informing the competent person about the proper occasion and form for doing things that could probably never be divined from considering the rule in its verbal form. Extending to the rule the respect of compliance, while finding in the rule the means for doing whatever need be done, is the gambit that characterizes organizational acumen.

We propose that we must proceed from the theoretical clarification of the essential limitation of formal rules achieved by Selznick to the investigation of the limits of maneuverability within them, to the study of the skill and craftsmanship involved in their use, and to a reconsideration of the meaning of strict obedience in the context of varied and ambiguous representations of it. This recommendation is, however, not in the interest of accumulating more materials documenting the discrepancy between the lexical meaning of the rule and events occurring under its jurisdiction, but in order to attain a grasp of the meaning of the rules as common-sense constructs from the perspective of those persons who promulgate and live with them.

The concept of formal organization as a model of stylistic unity

It is often noted that the formal organization meets exigencies arising out of the complexity and large scope of an enterprise. The rationally conceived form orders affiliations between persons and performances that are too remote for contingent arrangement, by linking them into coherent maps or schedules. The integration transcends what might result from negotiated agreements between contiguous elements, and lends to elements that are not within the sphere of one another's manipulative influence the character of a concerted action. As a consequence of this, however, each link derives its meaning not so much from the specific rule that determines it, but from the entire order of which the rule itself is a part. Each link is intrinsically a member of a chain or fabric of links which conducts a reproducible theme. In this context, many specific instances or elements can be compared with each other as variations of a single pattern. For example, a simple polarization of authority pervades the whole order of an organization and can be found as a redundant thematic focus in many segments of it. A rational principle of justice may prevail in the entire structure while governing differentially correct associations between particular performances and rewards. The varieties of demeanors that are appropriate to a particular status within the system may be perceived as variations of a more general pattern.

We are suggesting the possibility of a principle of discipline that derives from the formal style of the rational scheme and which works against centrifugal tendencies and heterogeneity. The resulting coherence will be in evidence as outwardly proper conduct and appearance. One would then ask how the sensibility of esthetic appreciation is summoned for direction, information and control in various concrete situations. The dominant consideration underlying this construction would not be found in the field of means-end relations but in an all-pervading sense of piety (i.e. in accordance with Burke's definition of the term, a sure-footed conviction of 'what properly goes with what') (Burke, 1954, pp. 74 ff.).

The question whether the syntactic composition of the formal scheme is the leading metaphor for the interpretation of the composition of actual performances and relations is obviously difficult to investigate. A tentative approach may be in the investigation of ties and performances that appeal to bureaucrats as incongruous or in bad taste, and the study of those observed proprieties and tolerated licenses that are restricted to 'on the job' circumstances. In further development the problem could lead to experimental studies. For example, the features of the stylistically normal could be studied by having subjects perform tasks that are not related or even contrary to their routine activities. The subjects would be induced to perform these tasks under the gaze of their work associates, and would be penalized for attracting attention and rewarded for remaining unnoticed.

The concept of organization as corroborative reference

There is another problem which is related to the problem of stylistic unity. A large-scale and complex organization is often composed of fragmented tasks and relations that are not capable of acquiring a phenomenal identity of their own or, at least, it is thought to be extremely difficult to value them for their intrinsic merits. Whether it is enough to relate these tasks to work obligation, and whether work requires any corroboration of worth beyond pointing to its market price is an open question. If it does, however, the formal scheme could be invoked to attest to it.

When from the perspective of a fragmentary involvement the actual contingent outcome of one's work cannot be appraised, or appears senseless, then it can be understood and judged in terms of its overall functional significance by invoking the formal scheme. For example, mismanagement and waste could be defined as merely accidental or perhaps even justified, relative to the total economy of the enterprise. This consideration of the formal scheme not only persuades the participants of some correct or corrected value of their duties, but can also be used as a potent resource for enforcing prohibitions when interest dictates that such prohibitions should be justified.

In this construction, the formal scheme is used as a resource for bringing anything that happens within an organization under the criterion of success or failure when real results are not visible, or must be discredited. This is not a simple matter, of course, because the scheme does not promote a single ideal of economy but specifies a field of economy in which various aspects of an operation may compete for priority. For example, in an industrial enterprise certain ways of doing things may have one value relative to interest in

production and an altogether different value relative to interest in maintenance. The problem that requires investigation is how various evaluations can
be used as credits, and what sorts of credits have the consequence of assimi-
lating some partial performance closer to the larger enterprise. The investigation of this problem would reveal the negotiable relationship between
policy and politics.

Conclusion

We have cited the gambit of compliance, stylistic unity, and corroborative
reference merely as examples of the possible methodical use of the concept of
organization by competent users. The examples are based on reflections
about ethnographic materials depicting life in large-scale and formally pro-
grammed organizations.[7] We have indicated earlier that such formulations
must be regarded as preliminary at best. Whether what we have tentatively
called the reference through the sensibility of esthetic appreciation exists
effectively or not, is a matter to be decided by empirical research. Without
doubt, these suggestions will have to be revised and amplified, but they must
suffice to illustrate the ethnomethodological study of rational organization.

In conclusion, we should like to mention that there remains for this inquiry one more problem that we have mentioned in passing but have not discussed adequately. We have noted that the methodical use of the concept of
organization must be studied by observing *competent* users. We mean, of
course, socially recognized competence. Consequently it is not within the
prerogative of the researcher to define competence. Instead, while he looks
for the right way to use the rationalities subsumed under the concept of
organization, he must also be looking for the rules governing the right to use
the concept.

References

BARNARD, C. R. (1938), *The Functions of the Executive*, Harvard University Press.
BLAU, P. M., and SCOTT, W. R. (1962), *Formal Organizations*, Chandler Publications.
BURKE, K. (1954), *Permanence and Change*, 2nd rev. edn, Hermes Publications.
CHARLSWORTH, M. J. (1959), *Philosophy and Linguistic Analysis*, Duquesne
   University Press.
DALTON, M. (1959), *Men who Manage*, Wiley.
ETZIONI, A. (1961), *Complex Organizations*, Free Press.
GERTH, H. H., and MILLS, C. W. (eds.) (1948), *From Max Weber: Essays in
   Sociology*, Routledge & Kegan Paul.
HAIRE, M. (1962), 'What is organization in organization?', in M. Haire (ed.),
   Organization Theory in Industrial Practice, Wiley.
KAUFMAN, F. (1958), *Methodology of the Social Sciences*, Humanities Press.

7. Some prominent examples of works containing excellent ethnographic descriptions of conduct in formal organizations are Barnard (1938), Dalton (1959), Roethlisberger and Dickson (1939) and Selznick (1949).

PARSONS, T. (1960), *Structure and Process in Modern Societies*, Free Press.

RHEINSTEIN, M. (ed.) (1954), *Max Weber on Law in Economy and Society*, Harvard University Press.

ROETHLISBERGER, F. J., and DICKSON, W. J. (1939), *Management and the Worker*, Harvard University Press.

SCHUTZ, A. (1953), 'Common sense and scientific interpretation of action', *Philosophy and Phenomenological Research*, vol. 14, pp. 1–38.

SELZNICK, P. (1948), 'Foundations of the theory of organization', *American Sociological Review*, vol. 13, pp. 25–35.

SELZNICK, P. (1949), *T V A and the Grass Roots*, University of California Press.

WEBER, M. (1954), 'Herrschaft durch "Organisation"', *Wirtschaft und Gesellschaft*, 4th edn, Mohr.

WHITROW, G. J. (1963), *The Natural Philosophy of Time*, Harper & Row.

Part Three
Practical Reasoning in Organizational Settings

A number of Readings in this section deal predominantly with organizational record-keeping. Organizational records traditionally have been accorded the status of 'information' with respect to the domain for which the organization has a mandate, and as such have become data for sociological characterizations of those domains. Cicourel's observations on the production of police records suggest that official records and statistics create information with respect to their domains (e.g. crime, delinquency) over the course of responding to organizationally enforced notions and rules regarding e.g. accountably relevant features of the domain, standards of 'good work', economy of resources, career contingencies and other practical constraints. Again, then, the shift of attention is towards investigating the *production practices*, the 'doings' which constitute social order, and away from the products (e.g. records) conceived of as independent of these practices.

In short, these Readings illuminate organizational workings within the framework documented by Bittner. Garfinkel discusses what suicides amount to, for those charged with the determination; Sudnow looks at one class of events in hospital life as sanctionably attended to by hospital staff; Zimmerman discusses what may be 'properly' doubted and what stands as self-evident fact for the workers in a social assistance bureau. There is no attempt to legislate the use of terms divorced from the practical reasoning engaged in by members competent in the ways of their settinged activities.

The thrust of these studies is in the direction of establishing that the organized ways of counting, keeping clinic case histories, accounting for inmates' recalcitrance, etc. are materials for discovery, description and analysis. The intended pay-off is that we shall come to understand the orderliness of everyday life as an accomplishment to which we are all party, and that we shall uncover the formal properties of that accomplishment.

8 Aaron V. Cicourel

Police Practices and Official Records

Excerpt from Aaron V. Cicourel, *The Social Organization of Juvenile Justice*, Wiley, 1968, pp. 112–23.

I have argued that police and probation officials 'make the system work' despite many problems associated with classifying juveniles, events labeled 'offenses', 'family settings', and the like. How the day-to-day activities of the police, probation, and other officials associated with the court or detention facilities produce information that becomes part of an official file on the juvenile (as distinct from the ways in which the file may be interpreted after its assembly) is not understandable without reference to the improvised but 'normal' rules and theories utilized by officials. The rules and theories, however, have their roots in common sense or folk typifications making up law-enforcement officials' stock of knowledge. Without some understanding of everyday categories – the 'strange', 'unusual', 'wrong', and what is 'routine', 'normal', 'harmless', 'right' – we cannot understand how improvisation necessarily enters into the picture in making the formal legal and clinical categories invoked by law-enforcement officials work.

The everyday language of reports and contacts between policemen, juveniles, probation officers, and parents (as articulated with or as abstract referents of nonverbal communication) provides the information. The crucial task is to specify how the content of messages contained in interviews and official reports provide the law-enforcement official and the juvenile, parent, or school official with the basis for deciding 'what happened' and the next course of action. A detailed analysis of the language of conversations and the language of official reports has the methodological significance of not relying upon illustrative quotations examined only by implication and indirectly; the researcher must make explicit remarks as to the meaning of the communication exchanges. Thus, a particular case must reveal something of the structure of all social action, reflect the ways in which the actor's theories are combined with organizational rules and practices for 'making sense' of 'what happened' and 'preparing' the scene for further inference and action. Therefore, references to communication content are not intended as anecdotes left for the reader to interpret.

The police must locate events and objects they investigate in some legal context, or characterize the situation in such a way that their presence or interference can be warranted now and later on if further justification is required. The police must map the event and social objects into socially and legally relevant categories as a condition for inference and action. The officer's tacit knowledge combines with information he has received, and his own observations of the action scene, to provide him with a preliminary mapping, but he invariably asks fairly standardized questions about 'what happened' and who were the principal actors involved. The initial search procedures combine with prior assumptions and information to give the scene structure, but body motion, facial expressions, voice intonation, and the like, can make problematic the routine use of social and legal categories, and alter or 'push' the interpretation of events and objects into categories calling for more or less 'serious' action. 'Normal' appearances are crucial here for routine action. Two general classes of encounters are common in juvenile cases: (1) patrol being called to the scene or they may be passing a situation that is viewed as suspicious, and (2) juvenile officers making telephone or personal inquiries in the field or at the station. In the first class of encounters, appearances are critical for invoking a presumption of guilt and deciding 'what happened'. Practical solutions are immediate, for readily available categories usually exist for subsuming the events described by the participants. For example, a street fight, a variety store clerk with a male or female juvenile accused of stealing candy or cosmetics, juveniles with 'questionable' grounds for not being in school, and a juvenile unable to identify his ownership of a car or establish an appropriate link with the owner are all viewed as routine objects and events easily categorized. The 'game' is understandable because it is possible to map some general features of the objects and events involved, with categories and general practices 'known' to fall within the policeman's proper domain of activities. When the patrol officer finds that the situation does not readily fit available categories for deciding 'what happened', he may take down more than the routine kind of face sheet data and description and bring everyone involved down to the station for further interrogation or for detention, until a juvenile officer or detective (depending on the policy of the organization) can pursue the matter further. The imputed suspicions of the patrolman may be communicated in the official report as something like 'they couldn't give a straight story as to what they were up to around the garage so I brought them in'. Or the report may say 'The same suspects have been known to break into houses in the X area so the undersigned decided it was best to have the juvenile bureau talk to them.' The initial remarks, however, may be loaded or indirect, depending upon how much information the officer had prior to arrival or what was immediately observable as he pulled up, and, of course, the particular style the officer employs for such occasions: 'What's up?' 'What's going on around here?' 'OK, what are you guys up to?' 'OK, who did it?' 'Which one of you started it?' 'OK, now, who are you? What are you doing here?' 'In trouble again, huh?' 'OK, let's have it.' 'OK, what else did you take?' If the patrolman is involved with a more complicated problem involving witnesses and several possible offenders, the initial question may be followed by more systematic attempts to establish the sequence and timing of 'what happened'. The critical feature of the initial remarks, coupled with any prior information related or observed, is that some attempt at mapping the objects and events into a readily understandable police situation is signaled by the language used and the categories therein. Thus the body motion, facial expressions, voice intonation, a known past record by the juveniles involved provide the officer with an initial basis for inferences, judgements, routinized evaluations as revealed in the language categories he employs. My field experiences, however, differ little from those reported elsewhere and I would not be adding much to repeat similar descriptions.

The case of interrogations by juvenile officers in the field or at the station is another matter for several reasons.

1. The juvenile officer is skilled in his ability to interview suspects and has had considerable experience with virtually every 'type' known to the police. There is little that is likely to surprise him and he will seldom lack appropriate categories with which to classify, evaluate, or summarize any concrete case.

2. The juvenile officer can pursue the case and contact different witnesses or others relevant to the case such as school officials, parents, neighbors, and victims. He can draw upon whatever information the police have on the suspect and supplement it by other contacts. Thus the 'picture' can be fairly complete prior to the interrogation. The language of the interview is often more managed than those encounters experienced by patrolmen in the field.

3. The juvenile officer has had experience with a variety of offenders and possible dispositions, troublesome parents, probation, and a particular style of interviewing he follows, depending upon the initial assumptions he makes about the case at hand. The interrogation, therefore, is often based upon some fairly definite interpretations of 'what happened' and a kind of plan of action for reaching a particular disposition. The alternatives that might emerge here are contingent upon the suspect's demeanor, the details he reveals about participation in activities under investigation, his past record, the kind of imputations the officer makes about his home situation, and the control the officer assumes can be exercised by the parents and police over his future conduct.

4. Because the juvenile officer has more information available and accessible, and because of his knowledge of probation-court procedures, he is able to

manipulate the interview more than the patrolman. The juvenile officer, therefore, becomes a critical gatekeeper in the administration of juvenile justice because the same information can lead him to make quite different recommendations. Thus he is in a position to bargain with the juvenile and negotiate terms under which some disposition will be accomplished. The bargaining and negotiations reveal how members 'close' activities, resolve contingencies, and arrive at seemingly 'clear' accounts as to 'what happened'.

The juvenile officer interview is oriented by a variety of hunches, theories, rules of thumb, general procedures, and on the spot strategies for dealing with different juvenile suspects. The officer's past experience and the information available prior to the interview, lead him to make quick evaluations of his client as soon as there is a confrontation. The interrogation, therefore, is highly structured in the sense that the information revealed by the juvenile is evaluated quickly in terms of a set of categories which the officer invokes by means of questions posed for the suspect. The interrogation is designed to confirm the officer's suspicions or firm beliefs about 'what happened' and how the particular suspect is implicated. The language used links the juvenile to particular activities, relations with peers, family, school officials, and the like, locates the suspect in a network of social relationships, and imputes routine motives and grounds to his action. For example:

POLICE OFFICER Hi, you Jack Jones?
JUVENILE Yaa, that's me.
OFFICER Fine, sit down, Jack, I wanta ask ya a few questions about that dance out at the — Club last Saturday night. You were there, weren't you?
JUVENILE Yaa, I guess I was there. Why?
OFFICER I wanta ask ya a few questions, that's all.

The officer may not reveal that the juvenile is the prime suspect in an incident involving an assault with a deadly weapon, that is, not until he can establish certain factors as to the youth's presence, for instance, his knowledge of what happened, his friends, his whereabouts at the time of the incident, his general manner of talking, the confidence he reveals about his affairs and their description. But the officer does seek to establish some immediate conditions for preparing the youth for a particular line of questioning. The initial gambit seeks to establish a nonthreatening setting if the officer assumes the juvenile's presence cannot be clearly established by witnesses. If this information is available to him (i.e. there are witnesses of the youth at the dance), then the opening line may include a 'pleasant' or 'neutral' tone of voice and seemingly a routine line of questioning without any apparent implications about the guilt or innocence of the youth. The meaning of the message and the particular line of questioning are constrained by the social context. Now it is possible that the officer has no prior information, the suspect is a kind of shot in the dark, and he intends to bluff his way while 'playing it by ear'. The officer may plunge into the following: 'Why do you cheat, lie, and act this way?' The decision to 'bluff' a 'hard line' may be motivated by the fact that a serious offense was committed and there are few leads to follow. The many possibilities, however, are endless, but they are not all 'independent' cases; some can be analysed for routinized patterns. The officer engages in a preliminary mapping of events and objects into social categories to establish the relevance of prior knowledge, present assumptions, and what is 'happening'. The language employed, therefore, may or may not reflect the initial strategy of the policeman's intentions, but locates officer and juvenile in a preliminary network of relationships. The officer seeks to keep the suspect in a state of 'informational imbalance'. The sense of bargaining or fatality that is communicated can vary with the particular officer's style of interviewing, his estimation of who is guilty or implicated, the juvenile's demeanor, the juvenile's past record, and how much information the officer possesses that can be used to convey particular power conditions he has available. Now each of these conditions is not available to the officer as an explicit and obvious possibility he will or can utilize to 'nail down' the case, but the conditions are revealed to the researcher in two ways. First, the interview itself, as it unfolds, reveals something of the officer's strategy. Second, in discussing cases with officers, general conditions of interrogation are described over and over again in distinct cases and cut across officers.

Some idea of police interrogation strategies can be obtained from reading the official policy of large metropolitan juvenile bureaux such as the following from a large city in southern California:

Interrogation. Juveniles are to be interrogated, keeping in mind the same procedures and techniques used with adults, with one exception: the interrogation of a female under the age of eighteen years regarding sex matters shall be conducted by a policewoman, except if none is available and the situation demands immediate investigation.

Many times a juvenile is anxious to tell the entire story about his suspected crimes immediately upon arrest. After a period of waiting in a police station without being interrogated, he may gain composure or he may think about the reaction of his parents when they learn of his arrest. This waiting period may afford him a good opportunity to think of an excuse or a story to cover his arrest. Many admissions have no doubt been lost by the fact that officers failed to interrogate juvenile suspects properly upon initial contact.

Juveniles are more inclined to 'cop-out' than an adult, and a good interrogation will result often in the admission of other crimes and the identification of accomplices.

Notice how the above general statement of policy and strategy stresses the importance of interrogation under conditions where the juvenile may not be 'composed'. The 'suspect' appears to be viewed as 'guilty', even though the language does not make the apparent presumption clear. The statement makes explicit reference to the possibility of obtaining information about 'other crimes and the identification of accomplices.' What remains unclear, of course, is how one 'interrogate(s) juvenile(s) properly'.

A caution is necessary at this point. I am not saying that it is typical for officers to follow the same line of questioning or strategy, given the different conditions of demeanor, past record, information available, and discretionary power to the follow the same strategy. Various routinized procedures exist for the ways in which the juvenile is prepared for adjudication of his criminality or competence or illness *vis-à-vis* the event or events in question. The 'preparation' leading to inferences and further action extends to the juvenile's future in that an estimation of projected future behavior can influence the present course of action. The initial categories used to describe the juvenile depend upon the information available to structure the 'set' or 'stance' assumed by the officer when he enters the action scene with the juvenile. The language employed in the course of the interview reveals the interplay between the conditions mentioned and provides the researcher with a basis for deciding 'what happened' based upon a commitment to the manner in which the participants made sense of 'what happened'. The fact that the officer is not bound by explicit rules governing adversary settings with adults, such as right to council (particularly its effective use), and the fact that the juvenile is often aware that he is dealing with a unilateral arrangement, whereby he is at a disadvantage that can become considerably worse if he does not demean himself in a way that the officer considers 'appropriate', invariably lead the officer to make fairly explicit statements about his evaluation of the juvenile, his disposition feelings, and what the juvenile can expect in future encounters. The generalization I propose is that irrespective of different types of officer as social types, of different interviewing strategies, of different conditions of information about the juvenile (seriousness of offense, past record, demeanor, etc.), the 'preparation' of the juvenile's case, leading to decisions, follows consistent patterns of encoding information into language categories assumed to have 'obvious' meaning.

Juvenile problems and their social settings

I should like to outline typical juvenile problems in order to orient the reader further about everyday police activities, but the price is that of reifying the empirically observable features of actual juveniles as they appear to the researcher in different encounters with the police. Any set of types must be an exaggerated depiction of those juveniles actually seen by the police, but I justify the use of such a set here because it will sensitize the reader to the implicit one the police utilize in making their decisions about the social object in question, 'what happened', and taking further action. The seriousness of the offense from the point of view of the police and their interpretation of the penal code, does not reveal how much time the police spend with different classes of juveniles. The following typology suggests the order of decreasing time spent with different classes of juvenile cases.

1 Dependency cases

These cases seldom involve acts, regarded as criminal or delinquent, committed by juveniles. Information is supplied to the police by school or welfare authorities, neighbors, and even the juveniles themselves, to the effect that children are being neglected, the home is 'unfit', the parents 'beat' the children excessively, and the like. In such cases the police intervene into the everyday lives of the family and have considerable discretion over search and seizure procedures in deciding that immediate action is justified. Differences between the probation department, the welfare department and the police are not uncommon here, since the police seem to react more strongly than the former agencies in seeking to separate the children from parents and bringing charges against the parents. The probation officials may view the home as 'adequate' for the 'type of people' involved, while the welfare representative may feel the police are not informed sufficiently about the 'real' problems of the case.

2 Family and juvenile problems

The police are frequently called in by the parents to intervene in problems where juvenile responses at home are viewed as excessive, abusive, or unwarranted; the youth doesn't 'mind' or do 'what he is told' and is abusive to the parents, siblings, friends, neighbors, or the like. Many cases of incorrigibility and runaways are included here. In some middle-class homes, this might include parental requests that the police interfere with the juvenile's 'going around with the wrong crowd,' or going out with members of the opposite sex viewed as 'bad' types or 'embarrassing', for example, middle-income families concerned with their girls dating lower-income or ethnic males. A frequent problem involves juveniles who wish to marry against their parents' wishes and continually run away. In these cases, police intervention is welcomed by the family, and controlling of the activities of juveniles viewed as 'bad', 'disrespectful', 'wild', or 'immature' becomes the issue.

3 'Minor' misdemeanors or 'normal' juvenile 'delinquency'

In every city in the United States the weekend invariably includes any number of dances, parties, and gatherings at popular juvenile 'hangouts' such as drive-in restaurants, ice-cream parlors, drug stores, and hot-dog stands. Most of these activities are known to the police, and calls to 'break up' a crowd, 'check out' a party, and so forth, are routine activities. The lateness of the gatherings is an immediate basis for interference by the police, and there is a tacit assumption that drinking, sexual activity, curfew, fighting, and the like, accompany such gatherings. From a routine investigation of a drunken party, the police may uncover clues or suspects involved in something more serious; such inquiries are not viewed as trivial. Juveniles considered 'bad', or 'punks', for reasons like prior petty theft, grand theft auto, burglaries, and malicious mischief may be recommended for serious disposition because of activities (otherwise viewed as trivial) in drunk parties, fighting, and so on.

4 'Normal' misdemeanors

This category represents activities for which persons in the community expect to hear juveniles are in trouble. A striking feature of juveniles picked up for such activities as petty theft, malicious mischief, joyriding, shooting in the city limits, battery, etc., is that the police report (but not always the 'rap sheet' summarizing offenses) may mention many additional cases the juvenile admits to when questioned by the officer. Many juvenile officers routinely ask: 'Now tell me about how many other times you did the same thing.' Many parents register surprise when the officer tells them their child has been involved in many past incidents, thus challenging the parents' claim to an official 'first offense.' The confrontation, where the juvenile admits before the parent the information revealed to police during private interrogation, provides the officer with leverage for making threats about what will happen in the future and allows him to give the juvenile 'another chance' even though a more severe disposition may be warranted. The important feature of this category is that, the juveniles in question are not merely engaged in occasional delinquent activity, but systematic criminal activities for which they are seldom apprehended. But inasmuch as it is difficult to link these reported acts with prior complaints from victims, the confessed acts do not become part of the official material from which official statistics are constructed. Such information provides the officer with routine grounds for recommending a court hearing and applying informal pressure on the probation officer even though the official record does not contain all of the details about past activities. The cards ('rap sheets') of all juveniles often include such statements as 'this boy like to rub cheeks with other boys', 'this boy is a liar', 'this boy is a mama's boy', or 'this boy can't be trusted'. Notice that many of the juveniles in this category may systematically engage in activities that the police and, presumably, a juvenile court consider to be misdemeanors, and juveniles confess to such activities freely (according to various interrogation procedures).

5 'Serious' offenses and general felonies

It is important to distinguish between those juveniles who routinely may be involved in one or more of the categories described above and those who are viewed as a kind of 'hard core' type of criminal for whom the label 'delinquent' is merely a euphemism for 'gangster' or common thief. The former juveniles may routinely fall into categories 2 or 3 above, but on some particular occasion become involved in an offense considered serious. Depending upon the family situation, demeanor of the juvenile, and his official past record, such cases may not lead to a Youth Authority commitment but, at most, removal from the community to a boys' ranch or a private school if the family can afford it. The 'hard core' cases, however, will be sent to the Youth Authority, and may be parolees from state institutions. The police are convinced 'hard core' cases are involved routinely in systematic criminality. This latter group of juveniles (a minority of the total 'delinquency' population) will include the stereotypical ethnic group cases, school dropouts, those who come from 'bad' homes, and candidates for adult criminality. To the police, this group of juveniles *are* criminal types.

The above five general types are not intended as equivalence classes to enable the researcher to subsume actual cases, nor are they in one-to-one correspondence with types employed by police and probation officers. The probation officer's clinical orientation tends to take the edge off the criminal categories the police use with 'hard core' types. The five categories represent my efforts to identify agencies' organized attempts to generate data placed in official files, and from which stem official or community notions of delinquency. Thus, even though category 5 occupies the least part of the police officer's time, it tends to provide generic notions of delinquency, in both community and social science conceptions, viewed as typical.

The generation of delinquent categories

Constructing rates of delinquency from police records provides *one* method for showing how law-enforcement activities generate data said to reflect 'delinquent behavior'. The socially organized ways in which juvenile activities are translated into types of 'delinquents' by observing behavior during initial encounters with the police and, by subsequent interrogations and official reports, provide a *second* method for showing how notions of delinquency are generated. What the two methods have in common is that the same juvenile activities lead to different pictures of something called delinquency.

The two methods for generating delinquency provide a basis for understanding how process and structure are inferred by sociologists and enable the researcher to compare the formal or ideal conceptions of community-defined problems as handled by the legal system, and the practiced and enforced activities making up the routine character of everyday problems. The first method does not reveal the bargaining or negotiated character of all legal procedures. Through day-to-day encounters with the police, juvenile cases are filtered so that some cases assume typical 'delinquent' features, that is, coming from broken homes, exhibiting 'bad attitudes' toward authority, poor school performance, ethnic group membership, low-income families, and the like. The official records mask the filtering, particularly when the first method is used. When we merely abstract information from official records so that structural comparisons are possible (e.g. broken home, low income, ethnicity, negative social character), the contingencies of unfolding interaction, the typifications (theories of 'good' and 'bad' juveniles, families, etc.), are excluded from our understanding of how legal or other rules were invoked to justify a particular interpretation and course of action. We are forced to interpret the categories established in accordance with *ad hoc* or improvised theoretical or substantive rules. There is no articulation between procedural rules and observable referents, joined by a theory of action. The 'logic-in-use' of the organizational actors (for example, policemen, probation officers) is obscured because the organizational records contain information reconstructed for various practical reasons. Knowledge of how reports are assembled is needed to transform the formal report descriptions into processual statements about the public and private ideologies of law-enforcement agencies.

If the routine procedures and ideologies of police and probation officials filter juveniles into various categories and courses of action, then the researcher's construction of tables based upon structural information must reflect the typifications employed by officials. The structural or so-called objective data extracted from official records are labels stripped of their contextual significance. The meanings, which the researcher assigns to 'broken home', 'bad attitude towards authority', 'gang influence' and 'bad neighborhood', are divorced from the social context in which the labeling and actor's routine activities occur. These labels provide meanings to the police and probation officers for making both evaluations and disposition decisions. Offense categories, therefore, cannot be divorced from the typifications employed by the police and probation officials.

The initial police encounter produces typical 'face-sheet' data about the juvenile and a few cryptic notes. The formal report is often literal in the language employed (for example, 'he then urinated against the side of the building', 'as they drove past the girl, X put his bare bottom out the car window', 'X said that Z told him to leave his house, but he refused, whereupon Z went up the stairs and X and Y followed him to his bedroom where Z bent over and came up with the rifle'), but the report can also be general (for example, 'it is obvious to the undersigned that X is not about to listen to his mother and is headed for a lot of trouble with this department').

The descriptions I shall give in this and in subsequent chapters presuppose my acceptability to the police as trustworthy and able to simulate being a 'policeman'. The same assumption would have to be true of probation descriptions. Therefore, my accounts represent a view of how delinquent types are produced by assuming 'inside' knowledge, the routine social meanings employed by law-enforcement personnel in face-to-face encounters, and the more managed language of the official report. The tape-recorded accounts of interaction sequences are not sufficient for the observer to derive his interpretation of the encounters merely by reference to actors' categories. The physical appearance of the juveniles, their facial expressions, affectual communication, and body motion are all integral features of the action scene. The officer's sense of the enterprise he is engaged in, namely, assisting juveniles who need 'help', juveniles who are no different than adult criminals, juveniles who need a 'good whipping' by their parents, juveniles who need to have the 'shit kicked out of them', juveniles who could use different parents, and so forth, suggests the researcher must untangle the use of language categories reflecting everyday organizational theories and practices, together with the features of legality and justice or procedural due process.

Legal requirements often lead to a kind of window dressing necessary to making the sometimes nasty business of police work compatible with demands for legal safeguards. The police assume their violation of a person's civil rights will not occur 'in the long run' if the accused is 'really innocent'. The assumption of guilt or innocence on intuitive, common-sense grounds, based on considerable experience in typing different persons suspected or labeled offenders, is the core of law enforcement. Legal rules and conceptions of justice or fairness, before arraignment, are not relevant when the police are engaged in pursuing an adversary who is already viewed as guilty or suspect, and for whom no advantages are viewed as warranted. The adversary legal system with procedural due process, is viewed as a hindrance by the police because of a belief in their own integrity and their devotion to the control of persons variously 'known' as 'bad', 'criminal', or 'punks'. Practical theorizing, based on extensive day-to-day contacts with various types of juveniles and adults in the community, provides the police with the *only* basis with which they feel comfortable and knowledgeable for tacking legal rules onto their routine activities.

9 Harold Garfinkel

Suicide, for all Practical Purposes

Excerpt from Harold Garfinkel, *Studies in Ethnomethodology*, Prentice-Hall, 1967, pp. 11–18.

The Los Angeles Suicide Prevention Center (SPC) and the Los Angeles Medical Examiner-Coroner's Office joined forces in 1957 to furnish Coroner's Death Certificates the warrant of scientific authority 'within the limits of practical certainties imposed by the state of the art'. Selected cases of 'sudden, unnatural death' that were equivocal between 'suicide' and other modes of death were referred by the Medical Examiner-Coroner to the SPC with the request that an inquiry, called a 'psychological autopsy',[1] be done.

The practices and concerns by SPC staff to accomplish their inquiries in common-sense situations of choice repeated the features of practical inquiries that were encountered in other situations: studies of jury deliberations in negligence cases; clinic staff in selecting patients for out-patient psychiatric treatment; graduate students in sociology coding the contents of clinic folders into a coding sheet by following detailed coding instructions; and countless professional procedures in the conduct of anthropological, linguistic, social psychiatric, and sociological inquiry. The following features in the work at SPC were recognized by staff with frank acknowledgement as prevailing conditions of their work and as matters to consider when assessing the efficacy, efficiency, or intelligibility of their work – and added SPC testimony to that of jurors, survey researchers, and the rest:

1. An abiding concern on the part of all parties for the temporal concerting of activities.

2. A concern for the practical question *par excellence*: 'What to do next?'

3. A concern on the inquirer's part to give evidence of his grasp of 'What Anyone Knows' about how the settings work in which he had to accomplish his inquiries, and his concern to do so in the actual occasions in which the decisions were to be made by his exhibitable conduct in choosing.

1. The following references contain reports on the 'psychological autopsy' procedure developed at the Los Angeles Suicide Prevention Center: Curphey (1961, 1967), Litman *et al.* (1963), Shneidman (1963) and Shneidman and Farberow (1961).

4. Matters which at the level of talk might be spoken of as 'production programs', 'laws of conduct', 'rules of rational decision-making', 'causes', 'conditions', 'hypothesis testing', 'models', 'rules of inductive and deductive inference' in the actual situation were taken for granted and were depended upon to consist of recipes, proverbs, slogans, and partially formulated plans of action.

5. Inquirers were required to know and be skilled in dealing with situations 'of the sort' for which 'rules of rational decision-making' and the rest were intended in order to 'see' or by what they did to insure the objective, effective, consistent, completely, empirically adequate, i.e. rational character of recipes, prophecies, proverbs, partial descriptions in an actual occasion of the use of rules.

6. For the practical decider the 'actual occasion' as a phenomenon in its own right exercised overwhelming priority of relevance to which 'decision rules' or theories of decision-making were without exception subordinated in order to assess their rational features rather than vice versa.

7. Finally, and perhaps most characteristically, all of the foregoing features, together with an inquirer's 'system' of alternatives, his 'decision' methods, his information, his choices, and the rationality of his accounts and actions were constituent parts of the same practical circumstances in which inquirers did the work of inquiry – a feature that inquirers if they were to claim and recognize the practicality of their efforts knew of, required, counted on, took for granted, used, and glossed.

The work by SPC members of conducting their inquiries was part and parcel of the day's work. Recognized by staff members as constituent features of the day's work, their inquiries were thereby intimately connected to the terms of employment, to various internal and external chains of reportage, supervision, and review, and to similar organizationally supplied 'priorities of relevances' for assessments of what 'realistically', 'practically', or 'reasonably' needed to be done and could be done, how quickly, with what resources, seeing whom, talking about what, for how long, and so on. Such considerations furnished 'We did what we could, and for all reasonable interests here is what we came out with' its features of organizationally appropriate sense, fact, impersonality, anonymity of authorship, purpose, reproducibility – i.e. of a *properly* and *visibly* rational account of the inquiry.

Members were required in their occupational capacities to formulate accounts of how a death *really*-for-all-practical-purposes-happened. 'Really' made unavoidable reference to daily, ordinary, occupational workings. Members alone were entitled to invoke such workings as appropriate grounds for recommending the reasonable character of the result *without necessity for furnishing specifics.* On occasions of challenge, ordinary occupational workings would be cited explicitly, in 'relevant part'. Otherwise those features were disengaged from the product. In their place an account of how the inquiry was done made out the how-it-was-actually-done as appropriate to usual demands, usual attainments, usual practices, *and* to usual talk by SPC personnel talking as *bona fide* professional practitioners about usual demands, usual attainments, and usual practices.

One of several titles (relating to mode of death) had to be assigned to each case. The collection consisted of legally possible combinations of four elementary possibilities – natural death, accident, suicide, and homicide.[2] *All* titles were so administered as to not only withstand the varieties of equivocation, ambiguity, and improvisation that arose in every actual occasion of their use, but these titles were so administered as to *invite* that ambiguity, equivocality, and improvisation. It was part of the work not *only* that equivocality is a trouble – is *perhaps* a trouble – but also the practitioners were directed to those circumstances in order to *invite* the ambiguity or the equivocality, to invite the improvisation, or to invite the temporizing, and the rest. It is not that the investigator, having a list of titles, performed an inquiry that proceeded step-wise to establish the grounds for electing among them. The formula was not, ' Here is what we did, and among the titles as goals of our research *this* title finally interprets in a best fashion what we found out.' Instead titles were continually postdicted and foretold. An inquiry was apt to be heavily guided by the inquirer's use of imagined settings in which the title will have been 'used' by one or another interested party, including the deceased, and this was done by the inquirers in order to decide, using whatever 'datum' might have been searched out, that *that* 'datum' could be used to mask if masking needed to be done, or to equivocate, or gloss, or lead, or exemplify if they were needed. The prevailing feature of an inquiry was that nothing about it remained assured aside from the organized occasions of its uses. Thus a routine inquiry was one that the investigator used particular contingencies to accomplish, and depended upon particular contingencies to recognize and to recommend the practical adequacy of his work. When assessed by a member, i.e. viewed with respect to actual practices for making it happen, a routine inquiry is not one that is accomplished by rule, or according to rules. It seemed much more to consist of an inquiry that is openly recognized to have fallen short, but in the same ways it falls short its adequacy is acknowledged and for which no one is offering or calling particularly for explanations.

2. The possible combinations include the following: natural; accident; suicide; homicide; possible accident; possible suicide; possible natural; (between) accident or suicide, undetermined; (between) natural or suicide, undetermined; (between) natural or accident, undetermined; and (among) natural or accident or suicide, undetermined.

What members are *doing* in their inquiries is always somebody else's business in the sense that particular, organizationally located, locatable persons acquire an interest in light of the S P C member's account of whatever it is that will have been reported to have 'really happened'. Such considerations contributed heavily to the perceived feature of investigations that they were directed in their course by an account for which the claim will have been advanced that for all practical purposes it is correct. Thus over the path of his inquiry the investigator's task consisted of an account of how a particular person died in society that is adequately told, sufficiently detailed, clear, etc., for all practical purposes.

'What really happened,' over the course of arriving at it, as well as after the 'what really happened' has been inserted into the file and the title has been decided, may be chronically reviewed as well as chronically foretold in light of what might have been done, or what will have been done with those decisions. It is hardly news that on the way to a decision what a decision will have come to was reviewed and foretold in light of the anticipated consequences of a decision. *After* a recommendation had been made and the coroner had signed the death certificate the result can yet be, as they say, 'revised'. It can still be made a decision which needs to be reviewed 'once more'.

Inquirers wanted very much to be able to assure that they could come out at the end with an account of how the person died that would permit the coroner and his staff to withstand claims arguing that that account was incomplete or that the death happened differently than – or in contrast to or in contradiction of – what the members to the arrangement 'claimed'. The reference is neither only nor entirely to the complaints of the survivors. Those issues are dealt with as a succession of episodes, most being settled fairly quickly. The great contingencies consisted of enduring processes that lay in the fact that the coroner's office is a political office. The coroner's office activities produce continuing records of his office's activities. These records are subject to review as the products of the scientific work of the coroner, his staff, and his consultant. Office activities are methods for accomplishing reports that are scientific-for-all-practical-purposes. This involved 'writing' as a warranting procedure in that a report, by reason of being written, is put into a file. That the investigator 'does' a report is thereby made a matter for public record for the use of only partially identifiable other persons. Their interests in why or how or what the inquirer did would have in some relevant part to do with his skill and entitlement as a professional. But investigators know too that other interests will inform the 'review', for the inquirer's work will be scrutinized to see its scientific-adequacy-for-all-practical-purposes as professionals' socially managed claims. Not only for investigators, but on all sides there is the relevance of 'What was really found out for-all-practical purposes?' which consists unavoidably of how much can you find out, how much can you disclose, how much can you gloss, how much can you conceal, how much can you hold as none of the business of some important persons, *investigators* included. All of them acquired an interest by reason of the fact that investigators, as a matter of occupational duty, were coming up with written reports of how, for-all-practical-purposes persons-really-died-and-are-really-dead-*in*-the-society.

Decisions had an unavoidable consequentiality. By this is meant that investigators needed to say *in so many words*, 'What really happened?' The important words were the titles that were assigned to a text to recover that text as the title's 'explication'. But what an assigned title consists of as an 'explicated' title is at any particular time for no one to say with any finality even when it is proposed 'in so many words'. In fact, *that* it is proposed 'in so many words', *that* for example, a written text was inserted 'into the file of the case', furnishes entitling grounds that can be invoked in order to make something of the 'so many words' that will have been used as an account of the death. Viewed with respect to patterns of use, titles and their accompanying texts have an open set of consequences. Upon any occasion of the use of texts it can remain to be seen what can be done with them, or what they will have come to, or what remains done 'for the time being' pending the ways in which the environment of that decision may organize itself to 'reopen the case', or 'issue a complaint', or 'find an issue' and so on. Such ways for SPCers are, as patterns, certain; but as particular processes for making them happen are in every actual occasion indefinite.

SPC inquiries begin with a death that the coroner finds equivocal as to *mode* of death. That death they use as a precedent with which various ways of living in society that could have terminated with that death are searched out and read 'in the remains'; in the scraps of this and that like the body and its trappings, medicine bottles, notes, bits and pieces of clothing, and other memorabilia – stuff that can be photographed, collected, and packaged. Other 'remains' are collected too: rumors, passing remarks, and stories – materials in the 'repertoires' of whosoever might be consulted via the common work of conversations. These *whatsoever* bits and pieces that a story or a rule or a proverb might make intelligible are used to formulate a recognizably coherent, standard, typical, cogent, uniform, planful, i.e. a professionally defensible, and thereby, for members, a *recognizably* rational account of how the society worked to produce those remains. This point will be easier to make if the reader will consult any standard textbook in forensic pathology. In it he will find the inevitable photograph of a victim with a slashed throat. Were the coroner to use that 'sight' to recommend the equivocality of the mode of death he might say something like this. 'In the case where a body looks like the one in that picture, you are looking at a suicidal death because the wound shows the "hesitation cuts" that accompany the great wound. One can imagine these cuts are the remains of a procedure whereby the victim first made several preliminary trials of a hesitating sort and then performed the lethal slash. Other courses of action are imaginable, too, and so cuts that look like hesitation cuts can be produced by other mechanisms. One needs to start with the actual display and imagine how different courses of actions could have been organized such that *that* picture would be compatible with it. One might think of the photographed display as a phase-of-the-action. In any actual display is there a course of action with which that phase is uniquely compatible? *That* is the coroner's question.'

The coroner (and SPCers) ask this with respect to each *particular* case, and thereby their work of achieving practical decidability seems almost unavoidably to display the following prevailing and important characteristic. SPCers must accomplish that decidability with respect to the 'this's': they have to start with *this* much; *this* sight; *this* note; *this* collection of whatever is at hand. And *whatever* is there is good enough in the sense that *whatever* is there not only *will* do, but *does*. One makes whatever is there *do*. I do not mean by 'making do' that an SPC investigator is too easily content, or that he does not look for more when he should. Instead, I mean: the *whatever* it is that he has to deal with, *that* is what will have been used to have found out, to have made decidable, the way in which the society operated to have produced *that* picture, to have come to *that* scene as its end result. In this way the remains on the slab serve not only as a precedent but as a goal of SPC inquiries. *Whatsoever* SPC members are faced with must serve as the precedent with which to read the remains so as to see how the society could have operated to have produced what it is that the inquirer has 'in the end', 'in the final analysis', and 'in *any* case'. What the inquiry can come to is what the death came to.

References

CURPHEY, T. J. (1961), 'The role of the social scientist in medico-legal certification of death from suicide', in N. L. Farberow and E. S. Shneidman (eds.), *The Cry for Help*, McGraw-Hill.

CURPHEY, T. J. (1967), 'The forensic pathologist and the multi-disciplinary approach to death', in E. S. Shneidman (ed.), *Essays in Self-Destruction*, International Science Press.

LITMAN, R. E., *et al.* (1963), 'Investigations of equivocal suicides', *Journal of the American Medical Association*, vol. 184, pp. 924–9.

SHNEIDMAN, E. S. (1963), 'Orientations toward death: a vital aspect of the study of lives', in R. W. White (ed.), *The Study of Lives*, Atherton Press.

SHNEIDMAN, E. S., and FARBEROW, N. L. (1961), 'Sample investigations of equivocal suicidal deaths', in N. L. Farberow and E. S. Shneidman (eds.), *The Cry for Help*, McGraw-Hill.

10 David Sudnow

Counting Deaths

Excerpt from David Sudnow, *Passing On: The Social Organization of Dying*,
Prentice-Hall, 1967, pp. 36–42.

On high-death wards, staff members frequently ask, upon coming to work,
'How many today?' Deaths are counted, not with any special interest, but
along with such matters as the number of new admissions, the number of
occupied beds, the number of discharges, and other demographic facts.
During 'report', that ritual wherein the new shift of nurses receives its brief-
ing from the outgoing shift – a changing of the guards – the number of deaths
on the previous shift, along with other demographic occurrences, is a matter
routinely reported. The opening of the report session, with a staff nurse reviewing nursing care matters with a group of incoming nurses, typically includes the following kinds of prefatory tallies: 'We have a full house, Mrs W
was discharged this a.m., a patient is expected in tonight who'll go to Room
7, Mrs P died this morning'; or 'No deaths, three empty beds, quiet night
ahead.' Then the details of patients' progress and treatment schedules are
reviewed. Nurses on these wards leave work at the close of their shift expect-
ing that some of the patients they have cared for during the day will have died
during their absence, and frequently they make inquiries upon arriving at
work to confirm their expectations. Some nurses characteristically look into
doorways of those rooms wherein dying patients had been known to be the
day before, to see if they are still alive and present. The following recorded
sequents of conversation between nurses at shift change indicate the manner
in which such inventories are made and convey a sense of the general import
of noting the occurrence of a death:

A Hi Sue, bet you're ready to go home.
B You ain't just kiddin' – it's been a busy one!
A What's new?
B Nothin' much. Oh yes, Mrs Wilkins, poor soul, died this morning, just after I got here.
A I didn't think she'd make it that long. Do we have a full house?
B Just about. Number two's empty, and seven I think.

A Mrs Jones die?
B I think so, let me see. (Looks at charts.) Guess so. (Turns to other nurse.) Did Mrs Jones die today?

C She was dead before I got into work this morning, must have died during the night.
A Poor dear. I hardly knew her but she looked a nice old lady.

A You look tired.
B I am. Lucky you, it's all yours.
A I hope it's a quiet night. I'm not too enthusiastic.
B They all died during the day today, lucky us, so you'll probably have it nice and easy.
A So I saw. Looks like three, four, and five are empty.
B Can you believe it, we had five deaths in the last twelve hours.
A How lovely.
B Well, see you tomorrow night. Have fun.

The announcement of a death from one shift member to another can and does occur in the course of an ordinary greeting conversation, and on these wards, where deaths are not so much announced as they are mentioned, their mention does not noticeably inhibit ordinary conversation. When a death occurs in an unexpected place within the hospital, or when deaths occur in rather unusual circumstances, news spreads quickly and the conversation about death is much more dramatically attenuated. On one occasion, a diabetic woman died in childbirth, a relatively infrequent happening, and by the time a nurse arrived on the O B ward for the evening shift she had already heard of the morning's death. She was greeted by a daytime nurse as she approached the station with, 'Have you heard?' and answered, 'Yes, Mrs B stopped me in the hall downstairs and told me', whereupon a conversation was entered about 'what happened' with a level of interest, detailed reporting of 'what she said', 'why did they do that?' 'then what did he do?' etc., far exceeding that which normally attends the discussion of deaths on the medical and surgical wards. On the latter settings, the greeting 'have you heard?' would not be taken to refer to a death, unless some rather special circumstance surrounded it, nor would it be used as a way of conveying news of an 'ordinary' one.

New student nurses and, apparently, young medical students make it a habit of counting such events as deaths, and locate their own growing experience and sophistication by reference to 'how many times' such and such has been encountered, witnessed, done, etc. Throughout the medical world, numerical representations of phenomena are accorded central status as marks of experience. The frequency of encounters with an event, disease type, constellation of symptoms, and the like, is taken to attest significantly to the practitioner's competence and authority and to the warrantability of his suggestions. It is hence useful to consider, if only briefly, some of the ways in which such 'counting' occurs and is properly presented.

One apparent mark of sophistication among one's peers is reached at that point when some occurrences are no longer counted, i.e. when 'I've lost count' is properly given as an answer. It is instructive to describe the way this point is achieved. A student nurse informant reported that young students count, and report their counts in informal conversation, nearly everything from the number of injections they have given and enemas administered to the number of operations they have witnessed, autopsies attended, deaths of their patients, other patients' 'dead bodies seen', etc. Some events, like giving injections and administering enemas, quickly lose their countability; in fact the count seems to end once the first occasion is superceded by a second. Other events are counted for a more extensive period of time, and only partially so, it seems, because they accumulate more slowly. While it is apparently relevant to report, 'I have given my first injection today', once that point is reached, the 'second injection' is considered to be of no special interest, for example, it is not sensibly used in conversation for demonstrating 'more' experience than is attested by citing the first injection. Experience in giving injections or administering enemas, while perhaps producing skill in doing so, is not conversationally additive as a competence attesting matter, so that having given one is just as good as having given a hundred.[1] The girl who would report that she had administered her 'second' or 'third' injection would be regarded by her peers, my informant reports, as one who was too taken by the trivial tasks of nursing.

In referring to the fact that specific counts of frequent occurrences have 'long since been lost', we often find persons pointing to that feature by announcing some number, or using some quasinumerical way of talking which conveys 'having lost count' in a somewhat more powerful way. Examples are 'I've given so many injections in my day . . .,' 'In the thousands of operations I have seen . . . ,' 'I have seen dozens of. . . .' These kinds of 'numerical' ways of describing some state of experience are to be clearly distinguished from those which involve specific reference to an actual number, e.g. 'I have seen twelve of . . .', 'In the seven cases of. . . .' Deaths are specifically counted in this latter sense, so it appears, to about half a dozen. The highest specific (i.e. nonsummary account like 'dozens', 'hundreds', etc.) count I was able to elicit when asking the question of nurses, 'How many have you seen?' was eight. Never did a student report a figure of more than eight, that number being the approximate maximum point at which 'losing count' occurs, or must be reported as having occurred. To report a number greater than a handful is, seemingly, to appear overly concerned

1. It is a matter of general sociological interest that a significant transformation occurs when an event comes to be seen as having ordinal properties, i.e. where it is not merely an occurrence but one which is seen as an event in a series. A major shift in ways of looking at the institution of marriage, for example, can be said to attend talk of a 'first marriage'.

about death, in either a worried, upset, fearful, or over-fascinated way. With respect to deaths, at least, the student can safely say, 'I've seen so many I've lost count', and not be sanctioned for pretentiously suggesting 'having been around a lot' should the actual number she has witnessed turn out to be just slightly over a handful.

Within any specific setting in the hospital and for different groups in the age-graded and occupational system, there is a culturally defined collection of properly counted items. For the novice, certain grossly delimited categories of events are counted, for example, deaths witnessed, operations seen, etc. For nearly everyone but the novice, counts cease to be made in these classes, experience in dealing with them being conveyed by pointing to the fact that specific counts have 'long since been lost'.[2] What occurs as one becomes more established in some work setting is that the classes of initially countable events become partitioned into subclasses, the elements of which are themselves counted although those of the class as a whole no longer are. It is relevant and proper – proper in the sense of being sanctionably usable in conversation and not a mark of over-concern, naïveté, etc. – to count the 'number of children you have seen die', but not the 'number of deaths you have witnessed' if that latter number exceeds an handful. Likewise, the student nurse who 'rotates' through the operating room counts the number of operations she witnesses up to a few, and then, the student informant reported, it is regarded as strange for her to continue to count and report counts of events in the class 'operations in general'. Further counts would then be made and remembered and reported upon within subcategories, like the number of appendectomies, open heart surgeries, gall bladders, and the like.

It can be noted that the differentiation of classes into highly subdivided classes, and the counting of events within these increasingly differentiated subclasses, provides a way for demonstrating 'experience', 'familiarity', and historical involvement in some scene which, unlike the novice's way, via the use of tallies of gross and frequent occurrences, relies on the relative 'rareness' of events. Frequently occurring events are counted only for a short time, among newcomers. Old timers seem to maintain numerical tallies of infrequent events, or at least view certain classes of occurrences as prospectively and retrospectively countable, and typically report those tallies by

2. It is to be pointed out that the use of this way of talking can be presumptuous for one who, in fact, has not been around very long. 'Having lost count', while in any given case perhaps accurately descriptive, is not thereby usable. It is not so much the usage's correctness which warrants it, but what that usage says about its user's claims to certain membership statuses; entitlement to it may be based on other facts: for example, the user's status in the group in which it is used. Among others of his own station an intern will talk of 'having lost count' but should an elderly physician be present, an inappropriate disregard for his place as a novitiate in the world of medicine might be conveyed.

specifying time intervals, for example, 'I haven't seen a woman die in childbirth in five years.' The relevant way to report experience with events becomes by reference to their relative as against absolute frequency; the length of expired time between occurrences becomes a sign of experience. By pointing to a relatively rare event (and rare events can be said to be discovered through the process of subdividing general classes into delimited ones) a person proposes his experience by way of the fact that he has been involved in events in which only one who has 'been around' would be.

While an extensive discussion of the variant forms, purposes, and conditions of 'counting' is beyond the scope of the present discussion, it is relevant to note that as one moves from one scene to another within the hospital, the way deaths are counted shifts. Each scene, as an environment of events, has a culture that prescribes typical frequencies of typical events and domains of infrequent occurrences, the latter of which apparently retain their countable character for long periods of time, even by long-term employees. On the medical and surgical wards all deaths are routinely counted on a daily basis as part of the general demographic inventory which is taken, on a variety of occasions, throughout the work week. While administrative personnel maintain long-term counts of deaths (along with many other events), ward personnel do not add up the daily death counts in any systematic way. In a very busy week a nurse will occasionally and unsolicitedly point to the fact that there have been 'lots of deaths' during the week. But no nurse of any tenure on the medical wards can begin to recall the total number of deaths she has witnessed. The day is the relevant unit of temporal specification, and counting 'deaths in general' is merely part of counting a host of daily, recurrent happenings. With respect to these wards, one has to ask about some rather special variety of death to elicit specific numerically portrayed descriptions. All the nurses on the medical and surgical wards can with little hesitation report the number of suicidal patients whose deaths they were involved in or which have occurred on their wards during their periods of employment. In conversation with a medical service nurse it can be learned that she remembers that she has seen 'two patients die from barium enema exams'. (Very infrequently barium enemas produce death when there is a rupture in the intestinal tract and the barium solution escapes into the abdominal cavity; this sort of occurrence, one which can be construed as an error, often becomes a major topic of staff conversation.) Nearly everywhere in the hospital, including the pediatrics ward, personnel can report the number of very young children whose deaths they have witnessed or were in any way involved in. One nurse on that service reported that a particular death was her 'thirteenth'. If one asks OB nurses, however, to recall how many deaths of newborns they have witnessed, they all (with the exception of the very recent newcomer) report they 'have no idea'. In certain wards, like the OB ward, adult deaths take on a quite different character. A nurse who was commenting on 'delivery room nursing' reported that it was the most 'rewarding kind of nursing' with the exception that sometimes it can be very 'unpleasant'. When questioned about its unpleasantness, she alluded to the fact that when a mother dies in childbirth it can be very upsetting, enough, apparently, to make the ward not altogether a pleasant working place. This nurse was the head of the delivery room nursing division; on further questioning she reported that 'seven years ago was the last time one (death) occurred'. That single death retained its character as a relevant fact about the OB setting. A senior operating room nurse, of some thirty years' experience on the division, related, on the occasion of a death that occurred on the operating table, that this was the sixth she had seen in her time, that she remembered each vividly, and could describe the circumstances surrounding every one.

The hospital can be viewed as an environment of occurrences and the place of a death as one hospital occurrence takes on its character as more or less prominent, more or less worth remembering, more or less characteristic of the work of a hospital, etc., depending upon the scenic background of typical occurrences. Particularly noteworthy deaths, those about which lively talk spontaneously occurs, are those which take place in settings where deaths are uncommon, those which occur in atypical fashions, those which result from accidents or diagnostic and treatment errors, and those which result in the very young patient. Any given death, however, is always a potential candidate for later retrospective comment when, for some reason, an instant death suggests a principle of categorization and provides for the relevance of searching over 'past ones'. So, for example, when a patient died and his wife fainted on the hall corridor when told of his death, a nurse mentioned that that was the third time she had seen a 'relative actually faint' at the news of a death. When a patient died during the course of a routine morning round a doctor recounted that he had 'had that happen to him', once before in medical school. Any given death is typically discussed by reference to its similarity with others in the past. The more infrequent the occurrence of death on a given ward, the more likely one can elicit talk about death that is specific by virtue of the classification which the ward's specialization naturally provides for, for example, on the pediatrics ward the discussion of death is immediately directed to the special troubles staff confront in dealing with children's death. The more frequent the occurrence of death on a ward, the more talk of death is specially focused by performing classificatory operations which are not given in the very nature of the ward itself. As hospital events, deaths are attended via their membership in whatever class an instant one lies, and such classification is either given in the fact of a specialized ward, or the result of some classificatory operation designed to delineate the properties of deaths which the character of the ward itself does not immediately suggest. Such concerns as 'how horrible death is', 'how long he linger-ed', and such general philosophic considerations do not naturally generate talk and interest in death in daily hospital life, but are only addressed under prodding from an outside party, and then only with difficulty. As organiza-tionally relevant, the commonly discussed aspects of death have to do with ward social structure, i.e. what given death-related occurrences imply about or entail for the activities of ward life and its personnel.

11 Harold Garfinkel

'Good' Organizational Reasons for 'Bad' Clinic Records

Harold Garfinkel (in collaboration with Egon Bittner), ' "Good" organizational reasons for "bad" clinic records', in Harold Garfinkel, *Studies in Ethnomethodology*, Prentice-Hall, 1967, pp. 186–207.

The problem

Several years ago we examined selection activities of the Out-patient Psychiatric Clinic at the UCLA Medical Center, asking 'By what criteria were applicants selected for treatment?' Kramer's method (Kramer *et al.*, 1956) for analysing movements of hospital populations was used to conceive the question in terms of the progressive attrition of an initial demand cohort as it proceeded through the successive steps of intake, psychiatric evaluation, and treatment. Clinic records were our sources of information. The most important of these were intake application forms and case folder contents. To supplement this information we designed a 'clinic career form' which we inserted into case folders in order to obtain a continuing record of transactions between patients and clinic personnel from the time of the patient's initial appearance until he terminated contact with the clinic. Clinic folders contain records that are generated by the activities of clinic personnel, and so almost all folder contents, as sources of data for our study, were the results of self-reporting procedures.

In promised applicability and results, the cohort method was clear-cut and rich. There were no questions of access to the files. Hence, when we prepared the grant application we thought that closely supervised personnel could get the information from clinic folders that we needed. A pilot attempt to learn what information we could and could not get caused us to upgrade needed training and skill to the level of graduate assistants in sociology. We permitted coders to use inferences and encouraged diligent searching. Even so there were few items in our schedule for which we obtained answers. Some kinds of information that we had hoped to get from clinic files, that we got, with what estimated credibility is illustrated in Table 1. For example, patient's sex was obtained in practically all cases; patient's age in 91 per cent of cases; marital status and local residence in about 75 per cent; race, occupation, religion, and education in about a third of the cases; and occupational history, ethnic background, annual income, household living arrangements, and place of birth in less than a third. Of forty-seven items that dealt with the

Table 1 **Availability of desired information and how it was obtained in the 661 cases**

Item of information	*Per cent of 661 cases for which*			
	There was no information	*Information was obtained by uncertain inference*	*Information was obtained by certain inference*	*Information was obtained by inspection*
(a) *Patient's 'face sheet' characteristics*				
Sex	0·2	–	0·3	99·5
Age	5·5	2·9	0·4	91·2
Marital status	11·8	5·4	3·9	78·9
Social area	21·4	0·4	3·6	74·6
Race	59·5	0·2	0·6	39·7
Occupation	55·6	0·4	5·0	39·0
Religion	51·7	9·5	2·3	36·5
Education	60·7	1·4	2·6	35·3

Eliminated because of no information
Occupational history
Duration of marriage
Married first time or remarried
Ethnic background
Income
Household arrangements
Principal contributor to patient's support
Place of birth
Length of residence in California.

Item of information	There was no information	Information was obtained by uncertain inference	Information was obtained by certain inference	Information was obtained by inspection
(b) *First contact*				
How contact was made	7·2	0·4	2·3	90·1
If patient was accompanied, by whom	–	2·0	2·0	96·0
Type of referral	3·5	0·4	7·8	88·3
Outside persons involved in the referral	2·5	0·2	3·0	94·3
Clinic person involved in first contact	3·6	–	–	96·4
Number of clinic persons contacted	4·8	–	2·0	93·2
Disposition after first contact	5·0	0·3	11·9	82·8

Table 1 – *continued*

Item of information	Per cent of 661 cases for which			
	There was no information	Information was obtained by uncertain inference	Information was obtained by certain inference	Information was obtained by inspection
(c) *Intake interview and psychological tests*				
Patient's appearance at intake interview	0·4	0·5	2·1	97·0
Clinic person involved in intake interview	0·3	–	–	99·7
Outcome of psychological testing	0·2	0·3	1·5	98·0
If no psychological tests, reason	16·3	2·5	17·5	63·7
(d) *Intake conference and treatment*				
Scheduled or improvised intake conference	44·6	10·9	34·9	9·6
Staff member in charge of intake conference	50·3	–	–	49·7
Conference decision	8·0	9·7	10·3	72·0
If patient was assigned to therapist, name of therapist	8·3	–	–	91·7
Name of first therapist	3·8	–	–	96·2
If patient was on waiting list, outcome	–	0·3	9·6	90·1
If patient was not accepted, reason	19·7	1·2	7·7	71·4
If patient was not accepted, how notified	31·5	2·7	6·8	59·0

Eliminated because of no information
Composition of intake conference
Number of prior admissions
Collateral cases
Scheduling of psychological testing
Scheduling of intake interviews

Table 1 – *continued*

Item of information	There was no information	*Information was obtained by uncertain inference*	*Information was obtained by certain inference*	*Information was obtained by inspection*
		Per cent of 661 cases for which		

Number of appointments for intake interview
Notification of impending termination after intake interview
Psychological tests administered
Type of recommended treatment
Number of scheduled treatment sessions
Number of missed appointments
Number of interviews with spouses, parents, relatives, friends, etc.
Treatment supervisor
Planned visit regime
Actual frequency of visits
Reasons for termination after treatment

(e) *Psychiatric characteristics*

Item	no info	uncertain	certain	inspection
Nature of patient's complaints	7·0	0·2	1·9	90·9
Psychiatric diagnosis	17·2	–	–	82·8
Prior psychiatric experience	19·0	1·7	46·5	32·8
Motivation for therapy	32·0	11·3	28·3	28·4
'Psychological mindedness'	40·2	14·0	23·9	21·9

(f) *Clinic career*

Item	no info	uncertain	certain	inspection
Point of termination	–	0·9	6·2	92·9
Circumstances of termination	2·6	1·1	5·6	90·7
Where was patient referred	3·5	0·3	7·6	88·6
Type of clinic career	0·2	0·8	5·1	93·9
Number of days in contact with clinic	1·5	3·0	3·5	92·0
Number of days outside of intreatment status	2·0	3·8	3·9	90·3
Number of days in treatment	8·8	0·4	0·4	90·4

history of contacts between applicants and clinic personnel we had returns on eighteen items for 90 per cent of our cases; for twenty other items we got information from between 30 per cent to none of the cases.

When, after the first year's experience, we reviewed our troubles in collecting information from the files, we came to think that these troubles were the result of our seeking information that we or anyone else, whether they were insiders or outsiders to the clinic, could probably not have, because any self-reporting system had to be reconciled with the routine ways in which the clinic operated. We came to tie the unavailable information to the theme of 'good' organizational reasons for 'bad' records. It is this theme to which our remarks are addressed.

'Normal, natural troubles'

The troubles that an investigator can encounter in using clinic records can be roughly divided into two types. We may call the first type general methodological troubles, and the second 'normal, natural troubles'. We shall make very brief remarks about the first type; the burden of our interest is with the second.

General methodological troubles furnish the topic of most published discussions about the use of clinic records for research purposes. Interest in these troubles is directed by the task of offering the investigator practical advice on how to make a silk purse out of a sow's ear. Instead of 'silk purse' we should say a container of sorts that might, with the investigator's sufferance, be permitted to hold a usable percentage of the sorry and tattered bits that are removed from the files and put into it. Such discussions attempt to furnish the investigator with rules to observe in bringing the contents of case folders to the status of warranted answers to his questions. What is generally involved here is the rephrasing of actual folder contents so as to produce something like an actuarial document that hopefully possesses the desired properties of completeness, clarity, credibility, and the like. The transformed content of the record lends itself more readily than the original to various kinds of social scientific analyses on the assumption, of course, that there exists a defensible correspondence between the transformed account and the way the information was meant in its original form.[1]

Any investigator who has attempted a study with the use of clinic records, almost wherever such records are found, has his litany of troubles to recite. Moreover, hospital and clinic administrators frequently are as knowledgeable and concerned about these 'shortcomings' as are the investigators themselves. The sheer frequency of 'bad records' and the uniform ways in which they are 'bad' was enough in itself to pique our curiosity. So we were

1. For an account of social scientific uses of clinical records consult Kuno (1962).

led to ask whether there were some things that could be said by way of describing the great uniformity of 'bad records' as a sociological phenomenon in its own right.

We came to think of the troubles with records as 'normal, natural' troubles. We do *not* mean this ironically. We are *not* saying, 'What more can you expect?!' Rather, the term 'normal, natural' is used in a conventional sociological sense to mean 'in accord with prevailing rules of practice'. 'Normal, natural troubles' are troubles that occur because clinic persons, as self-reporters, actively seek to act in compliance with rules of the clinic's operating procedures that for them and from their point of view are more or less taken for granted as right ways of doing things. 'Normal, natural' troubles are troubles that occur because clinic persons have established ways of reporting their activities; because clinic persons as self-reporters comply with these established ways; and because the reporting system and reporter's self-reporting activities are integral features of the clinic's usual ways of getting each day's work done – ways that for clinic persons are right ways.

The troubles we speak of are those that any investigator – outsider or insider – will encounter if he consults the files in order to answer questions that depart in theoretical or practical import from organizationally relevant purposes and routines under the auspices of which the contents of the files are routinely assembled in the first place. Let the investigator attempt a remedy for shortcomings and he will quickly encounter interesting properties of these troubles. They are persistent, they are reproduced from one clinic's files to the next, they are standard and occur with great uniformity as one compares reporting systems of different clinics, they are obstinate in resisting change, and above all, they have the flavor of inevitability. This inevitability is revealed by the fact that a serious attempt on the part of the investigator to remedy the state of affairs, convincingly demonstrates how intricately and sensitively reporting procedures are tied to other routinized and valued practices of the clinic. Reporting procedures, their results, and the uses of these results are integral features of the same social orders they describe. Attempts to pluck even single strands can set the whole instrument resonating.

When clinic records are looked at in this way the least interesting thing one can say about them is that they are 'carelessly' kept. The crux of the phenomenon lies elsewhere, namely in the ties between records and the social system that services and is serviced by these records. There is an organizational rationale to the investigator's difficulties. It is the purpose of this paper to formulate this rationale explicitly. Toward that end we shall discuss several organizational sources of the difficulties involved in effecting an improvement in clinic records.

Some sources of 'normal, natural troubles'

One part of the problem, a part to which most efforts of remedy have been directed, is contributed by the marginal utility of added information. The problem for an enterprise that must operate within a fixed budget involves the comparative costs of obtaining alternative information. Because there are comparative costs of different ways of keeping records, it is necessary to choose among alternative ways of allocating scarce resources of money, time, personnel, training, and skills in view of the value that might be attached to the ends that are served. The problem is in strictest terms an economic one. For example, information about age and sex can be had almost at the cost of glancing at the respondent; information about occupation puts a small tax on the time and skill of the interviewer; occupational history is a high-cost piece of information. The economic problem is summarized in the question that is almost invariably addressed to any recommended change of reporting procedure: 'How much of the nurse's (or the resident's or the social worker's, etc.) time will it take?'

If the troubles in effecting an improvement amounted entirely to how much information the clinic could afford on a strict time-cost basis, the remedy would consist of obtaining enough money to hire and train a large staff of record keepers. But it is enough to imagine this remedy to see that there are other troubles in effecting 'improvements' that are independent of the number of record keepers.

Consider a part of the trouble, for example, that is contributed by the marginal utility of information when the information is collected by clinic members according to the procedures of an archive – i.e. where uniform information is collected for future but unknown purposes. An administrator may be entirely prepared to require of persons in his establishment that whatever is gathered be gathered consistently. But he must be prepared as well to maintain their motivation to collect the information in a regular fashion knowing that the personnel themselves also know that the information must be gathered for unknown purposes that only the future can reveal. Over the course of gathering the information such purposes may vary, in their appearances to personnel, from benign to irrelevant to ominous, and for reasons that have little to do with the archives.

Further, partisans in the clinic for one reporting program or another are inclined to argue the 'core' character of the information they want gathered. Administrators and investigators alike know this 'core' to be a troublesome myth. Consider, for example, that a sociologist might urge the regular collection of such minimum 'face sheet' information as age, sex, race, marital status, family composition, education, usual occupation, and annual income. The question he must argue against competitors to archive rights is not '*Is* the information worth the cost?' but '*Will it have been* worth the cost?' One need not be a trained investigator to understand that by addressing almost any definitive question to the archives one can reveal the shortcomings of the collection enterprise. Whether or not it turns out that what has been gathered will not do after all, and will have to be gathered all over again, will depend upon what constraints the investigator is willing to accept that are imposed by the necessity of his having to frame questions for which the archives will permit answers. For such reasons, an administrator with an eye to the budgeted costs of his reporting procedures is apt to prefer to minimize the burden of present costs and to favor short-term peak load operations when the investigator has decided his needs in a formulated project.

There are the further difficulties of ensuring the motivation to collect 'core' information that occur when 'good reporting performance' is assessed according to research interest. Such standards frequently contradict the service interests of professional persons within the organization. Moreover, founded priorities of occupational responsibility may motivate vehement and realistic complaints as well as – and with greater likelihood – informal and hidden recording practices that permit the recorder to maintain the priority of his other occupational obligations while keeping the front office appropriately misinformed.

This point touches on a related source of troubles in effecting improvement, troubles having to do with ensuring compliance of self-reporting personnel to record keeping as a respectable thing for them to be doing from their point of view. The division of work that exists in every clinic does not consist only of differentiated technical skills. It consists as well of differential moral value attached to the possession and exercise of technical skills. To appreciate the variety and seriousness of troubles contributed by this organizational feature one need only consider the contrasting ways in which records are relevant to the satisfactory accomplishment of administrative responsibilities as compared with professional medical responsibilities and to the wary truce that exists among the several occupational camps as far as mutual demands for proper record-keeping are concerned.

Clinic personnel's feelings of greater or lesser dignity of paper work as compared with the exercise of other skills in their occupational life, are accompanied by their abiding concerns for the strategic consequences of avoiding specifics in the record, given the unpredictable character of the occasions under which the record may be used as part of the ongoing system of supervision and review. Records may be used in the service of interests that those higher up in the medical-administrative hierarchy are probably not able, but in any case are neither required nor inclined beforehand, to specify or give warning about. Inevitably, therefore, informal practices exist which are known about by everyone, that as a matter of course contradict officially depicted and openly acknowledged practices. Characteristically, the specifics of who, what, when, and where are well guarded team secrets of cliques and cabals in clinics, as they are in all bureaucratically organized settings. From the point of view of each occupational team, there are the specifics that facilitate the team's accomplishment of its occupational daily round which is none of the business of some other occupational team in the clinic. This is not news of course, except that any investigator has to confront it as a fact of his investigative life when, for example, in order to decide the import of what is in the record, he has to consult materials that are not in the record but are nevertheless known and count to someone.

Another source of troubles: clinic personnel know the realities of life in the clinic in their capacity as socially informed members, whose claims to 'have the actual account of it' derive in good part from their involvements and positions in the social system, involvements and positions which carry, *as a matter of moral obligation*, the requirement that incumbents make good sense of their work circumstances. As a consequence of that moral obligation there is the long standing and familiar insistence on the part of self-reporters: 'As long as you're going to bother us with your research why don't you get the story right?' This occurs particularly where standard reporting forms are used. If the researcher insists that the reporter furnish the information in the way the form provides, he runs the risk of imposing upon the actual events for study a structure that is derived from the features of the reporting rather than from the events themselves.

A closely related source of trouble stems from the fact that self-reporting forms – whatever they may consist of – provide not only categories with which clinic personnel describe clinic events, but simultaneously and inevitably, such forms constitute rules of reporting conduct. The self-reporting forms consist of rules that for personnel define correct self-reporting conduct as a work obligation. It is not startling that the investigator can obtain a description of clinic events precisely to the extent that the reporting form is enforced as a rule of reporting conduct upon reporting personnel. But then it should also come with no surprise that the information the investigator can have, as well as the information he cannot have, is subject to the same conditions that investigators are aware of in other areas of rule governed conduct: namely, that well-known differences and well-known sources of differences occur between rules and practices, differences that are notoriously recalcitrant to remedy.

Such differences are not understandable let alone remediable by attempting to allocate blame between reporters and investigators. Consider, for example, the case where a staff member may seek to report in compliance with what the investigator's forms provide, and, precisely because he attempts to take the reporting form seriously, finds it difficult to reconcile what he knows about what the form is asking with what the form provides as a rule for deciding the relevance of what he knows. For example, consider a question which provides the staff member with fixed alternative answers, for example, 'Yes' or 'No', yet from what he knows of the case he is convinced that a 'Yes' or 'No' answer will distort the question or defeat the inquirer's aim in asking it. Taking the study seriously the reporter might ask himself if a marginal note will do it? But then is he asking for trouble if he writes it? Perhaps he should wait until he encounters the investigator and then remind him of this case? But why only *this* case? He knows, along with other reporters like him, of many cases and of many places throughout the reporting form, so that his complaint is entirely a realistic one that were he to engage in marginal jottings, he might have innumerable remarks to make for many items in many cases.

The investigator, for his part, wants nothing more of the self-reporter than that he treat the reporting form as the occasion to report what the self-reporter knows *as he knows it*. Thus we find that the self-reporter may distort the reality of the case precisely because he wants to be helpful and thereby complies with the reporting form. He may know he is distorting and resent it or otherwise suffer it. One can easily imagine that his resentment and suffering are matched on the investigator's side.

Further, while the terminology in self-reporting forms is fixed, the actual events that these terms refer to, as well as the ways in which actual events may be brought under the jurisdiction of the form's terminology as descriptions, are highly variable. The relevance of the reporting form's terminology to the events it describes is subject to the stability of the on-going clinic operations and depends upon the self-reporter's grasp and use of the regular features of the clinic's operation as a scheme of linguistic interpretation. Upon any change of clinic policy, organization, personnel, or procedure the terms on the reporting forms may change in their meaning without a single mimeographed sentence being altered. It is disconcerting to find how even small procedural changes may make large sections of a reporting form hopelessly ambiguous.

Difficulties that are introduced either because the clinic members are reporting on their own activities or because the self-reporting activities are carried on with the use of prepared forms, may be extended and illuminated by considering that candor in reporting carries well known risks to careers and to the organization. Speaking euphemistically, between clinic persons and their clients, and between the clinic and its environing groups, the exchange of information is something less than a free market.

A critical source of trouble: actuarial versus contractual uses of folder contents

The foregoing troubles were introduced by recommending, as a context for their interpretation, that reporting procedures and results, as well as their uses by clinic persons, are integral features of the same orders of clinic activities they describe; that methods and results of clinic record-keeping consist of and are closely regulated by the same features they provide accounts of.

But though the above troubles *can* be interpreted with this context, nothing *about the troubles* requires it. The troubles we have discussed, one might argue, merely document some insufficiency in the rational control of clinic practices. We have enumerated, as troubles with reporting procedures, matters that strong management could undertake to remedy, and in this way the conditions that contribute to bad records could be eliminated, or their impact on record-keeping could be reduced.

But to think of such troubles as a managerial problem of bringing record-keeping performances under greater or more consistent control, overlooks a critical and perhaps unalterable feature of medical records as an element of institutionalized practices. We propose that the enumerated troubles – and obviously our enumeration is by no means complete – either explicate or themselves consist of properties of the case folder as a reconstructable record of transactions between patients and clinic personnel. This critical feature of clinic records brings the enumerated troubles under the jurisdiction of their status as 'structurally normal troubles' by relating reporting systems to the conditions of the clinic's viability as a corporately organized service enterprise. We shall now endeavor to show that clinic records, such as they are, are not something clinic personnel get away with, but that instead, the records *consist of procedures and consequences of clinical activities as a medico-legal enterprise.*

In reviewing the contents of case folders it seemed to us that a case folder could be read in one or the other of two contrasting and irreconcilable ways. On the one hand it could be read as an *actuarial*[2] *record.* On the other hand it could be read as the *record of a therapeutic contract* between the clinic as a medico-legal enterprise and the patient. Because our understanding of the term 'contract' departs somewhat from colloquial usage, but not from the understanding which Durkheim taught, a brief explanation is in order.

Ordinarily 'contract' refers to a document containing an explicit schedule of obligations, the binding character of which is recognized by identifiable parties to the agreement. In contrast, and because we are talking specifically about clinics, we use the term 'contract' to refer to the *definition* of normal

2. David Harrah's model of an information-matching game is taken to define the meaning of 'actuarial' procedure. See Harrah (1961). More extensive discussion that is compatible with Harrah's formulation is found in Meehl (1954, 1958).

transactions between clientele and remedial agencies in terms of which agencies' services are franchised and available to clients. One of the crucial features of remedial activities is that its recipients are socially defined by themselves and the agencies as incompetent to negotiate for themselves the terms of their treatment.

Thus it is the socially acknowledged normal course of affairs that a patient 'puts himself in the hands of a doctor' and is expected to suspend the usual competence of his own judgement about his well being, what he needs, or what is best for him. The same applies to the criminal, *mutatis mutandis*, who is the sole person barred from contributing his opinion to the formulation of a just sentence. Despite these limitations of competence, neither patients nor criminals lose their right to the 'treatment they deserve'. This is so because treatment consists of occasions for performances that in the eyes of participants accord with a larger scheme of obligations. The larger scheme of obligations relates the authorization in terms of which a remedial agency is deputized to act to the technical doctrines and practical professional ethics which govern the operations of the agency. By assuming jurisdiction in specific cases, medical and legal agencies commit themselves to honoring legitimate public claims for 'good healing' and 'good law'. An indispensable though not exclusive method whereby clinics demonstrate that they have honored claims for adequate medical care consists of procedures for formulating relevant accounts of their transactions with patients.

Further remarks are needed about our use of the concept of contract. Even colloquial usage recognizes that what a contract specifies is not simply given in the document that attests to the contract's existence. Nor are terms, designations, and expressions contained in a document invoked in any 'automatic' way to regulate the relationship. Instead, the ways they relate to performances are matters for competent readership to interpret. As is well known, culturally speaking, jurists are competent readers of most contracts; it is for *them* to say what the terms really mean. Indeed, the form in which legal contracts are put intends such readership.

Sociologically, however, legal contracts are only one variant of the class of contracts. The larger conception of contract, namely, its power to define normal relations, also requires that questions of competent readership be considered. Thus we were obliged to consider how the designations, terms, and expressions contained in the clinic folders were read to make them testify as answers to questions pertaining to medico-legal responsibility. In our view *the contents of clinic folders are assembled with regard for the possibility that the relationship may have to be portrayed as having been in accord with expectations of sanctionable performances by clinicians and patients.*

By calling a medical record a 'contract' we are not claiming that the record contains only statements of what should have happened as opposed to what did happen. Nor are we proposing that a contractual reading of the medical record is even the most frequent reading, let alone the only reading that occurs. Clinic records are consulted upon many different occasions and for many different interests. But for all the different uses to which records may be put and for all the different uses that they serve, considerations of medico-legal responsibility exercise an overriding priority of relevance as prevailing structural[3] interests whenever procedures for the maintenance of records and their eligible contents must be decided.

Although folder materials may be put to many uses different from those that serve the interests of contract, *all* alternatives are subordinated to the contract use as a matter of enforced structural priority. Because of this priority, alternative uses are consistently producing erratic and unreliable results. But also because of this priority every last suggestion of information in a medical record can come under the scope of a contractual interpretation. Indeed, the contract use both addresses and establishes *whatsoever* the folder might contain as the elements of a 'whole record' and does so in the manner that we shall now describe.

When any case folder was read as an actuarial record its contents fell so short of adequacy as to leave us puzzled as to why 'poor records' as poor as these should nevertheless be so assiduously kept. On the other hand, when folder documents were regarded as unformulated terms of a potential thera-peutic contract, i.e. as documents assembled in the folder in open anticipa-tion of some occasion when the terms of a therapeutic contract might have to be formulated from them, the assiduousness with which folders were kept, even though their contents were extremely uneven in quantity and quality, began to 'make sense'.

We start with the fact that when one examines any case folder for what it actually contains, a prominent and consistent feature is the occasional and elliptical character of its remarks and information. In their occasionality, folder documents are very much like utterances in a conversation with an unknown audience which, because it already knows what might be talked about, is capable of reading hints. As expressions, the remarks that make up these documents have overwhelmingly the characteristic that their sense cannot be decided by a reader without his necessarily knowing or assuming something about a typical biography and typical purposes of the user of the expressions, about typical circumstances under which such remarks are written, about a typical previous course of transactions between the writers and the patient, or about a typical relationship of actual or potential inter-action between *the writers and the reader*. Thus the *folder contents, much less*

3. By calling interests 'structural' we wish to convey that the interest is not governed by personal considerations in advancing a cause but is related to demands of organized practice which the member treats as his real circumstances.

than revealing an order of interaction, presuppose an understanding of that order for a correct reading. The understanding of that order is not one, however, that strives for theoretical clarity, but is one that is appropriate to a reader's pragmatic interest in the order.

Further, there exists an entitled use of records. The entitlement is accorded, without question, to the person who reads them from the perspective of active medico-legal involvement in the case at hand and shades off from there. The entitlement refers to the fact that the full relevance of his position and involvement comes into play in justifying the expectancy that he has proper business with these expressions, that he will understand them, and will put them to good use. The specific understanding and use will be occasional to the situation in which he finds himself. The entitled reader knows that just as his understanding and use is occasional to the situation in which he finds himself, so the expressions that he encounters are understood to have been occasional to the situations of their authors. The possibility of understanding is based on a shared, practical, and entitled understanding of common tasks between writer and reader.

Occasional expressions are to be contrasted with 'objective' expressions, i.e. expressions whose references are decided by consulting a set of coding rules that are assumed, by both user and reader, to hold irrespective of any characteristics of either one, other than their more or less similar grasp of these rules.

The documents in the case folder had the further feature that what they could be read to be *really* talking about did not remain and was not required to remain identical in meaning over the various occasions of their use. Both actually and by intent, their meanings are variable with respect to circumstances. To appreciate what the documents were talking about, specific reference to the circumstances of their use was required: emphatically *not* the circumstances that accompanied the original writing, *but the present circumstances of the reader* in deciding their appropriate *present* use. Obviously, the document readers to whom we refer are clinic persons.

A prototype of an actuarial record would be a record of installment payments. The record of installment payments describes the present state of the relationship and how it came about. A standardized terminology and a standardized set of grammatical rules govern not only possible contents, but govern as well the way a 'record' of past transactions is to be assembled. Something like a standard reading is possible that enjoys considerable reliability among readers of the record. The interested reader does not have an edge over the merely instructed reader. That a reader is entitled to claim to have read the record correctly, i.e. a reader's claim to competent readership, is decidable by him and others while disregarding particular characteristics of the reader, *his* transactions with the record, or *his* interests in reading it.

To recite investigators' troubles in the use of clinic folders is to remark on the fact that a negligible fraction of the contents of clinic folders can be read in an actuarial way without incongruity. An investigator who attempts to impose an actuarial reading upon folder contents will fill his notebook with recitation of 'shortcomings' in the data, with complaints of 'carelessness', and the like.

However, the folder's contents *can* be read, without incongruity, by a clinic member if, in the way that an historian or a lawyer might use the same documents, he develops a *documented representation*[4] of what the clinic-patient transactions consisted of as an orderly and understandable matter. The various items of the clinic folders are tokens – like pieces that will permit the assembly of an indefinitely large number of mosaics – gathered together not to describe a relationship between clinical personnel and the patient, but to permit a clinic member to formulate a relationship between patient and clinic as a normal course of clinic affairs when and if the question of normalizing should arise as a matter of some clinic member's practical concern. In this sense, we say that a folder's contents serve the uses of contract rather than description, for a contract does not and is not used to describe a relationship. Rather it is used to normalize a relationship, by which is meant that the *quid pro quo* of exchanges is so ordered in an account of the relationship as to satisfy the terms of a prior and legitimate agreement, explicit or implicit.

Folder contents are assembled against the contingent need, by some clinic member, to construct a potential or a past course of transactions between the clinic and the patient as a 'case', and thereby as an instance of a therapeutic contract, frequently in the interests of justifying an actual or potential course of actions between clinic persons and patients. Hence, whatever their diversity, a folder's contents can be read without incongruity by a clinic member if, in much the same way as a lawyer 'makes the brief', the clinic member 'makes a case' from the fragmented remains *in the course* of having to read into documents their relevance for each other as an account of legitimate clinic activity.

From this perspective a folder's contents consist of a single free field of elements with the use of which field the contractual aspect of the relationship may be formulated upon whatsoever occasion such a formulation is required. Which documents will be used, how they will be used, and what meanings their contents will assume, wait upon the particular occasions, purposes, interests, and questions that a particular member may use in addressing them.

In contrast to actuarial records, folder documents are very little constrained in their present meanings, by the procedures whereby they come to be

4. For further descriptions of documentary representation see Mannheim (1962).

assembled in the folder. Indeed, document meanings are disengaged from the actual procedures whereby documents were assembled, and in this respect the ways and results of competent readership of folder documents contrast, once more, with the ways and results of competent actuarial readership. When and if a clinic member has 'good reason' to consult folder contents, his purposes at the time define some set of the folder's contents as constituent elements of the formulated account. If, in the course of consulting the folder, his purposes should change, nothing is suffered since the constituent set of documents is not completed until the reader decides that he has enough. The grounds for stopping are not formulated beforehand as conditions that an answer to his questions has to satisfy. The possible use of folder documents might be said to follow the user's developing interests in using them; not the other way around. It is quite impossible for a user to say when he starts to work out a contract what documents he wants, let alone what ones he would insist on. His interests require a method of recording and retrieval that makes full provision for the developing character of his knowledge of the practical circumstances for the management of which the folder's contents must stand service. Above all, it is desired that folder contents be permitted to acquire whatsoever meaning readership can invest them with when various documents are 'combinatorially' played against and in search of alternative interpretations in accordance with the reader's developing interests on the actual occasion of reading them. Thus the actual event, when it is encountered under the auspices of the possible use to be made of it, furnishes, on that occasion, the definition of the document's significance. Thereby, the list of folder documents is open ended and can be indefinitely long. Questions of overlap and duplication are irrelevant. Not only do they not arise but questions of overlap cannot be assessed until the user knows, with whatever clarity or vagueness, what he wants to be looking for and, perhaps, why. In any case questions of overlap and omission cannot be decided until he has actually examined whatever he actually encounters.

Further contrasting features of 'duplication' and 'omission' in the two reporting systems require comment. In an actuarial record, information may be repeated for the sake of expediency. But the statement of a present state of a bank account does not add any information to what can be readily gathered from the account's earlier state and the subsequent deposits and withdrawals. If the two do not match, this points irrefutably to some omission. The record is governed by a principle of relevance with the use of which the reader can assess its completeness and adequacy at a glance.

A clinical record does not have this character. A subsequent entry may be played off against a former one in such a way that what was known then, now changes complexion. The contents of a folder may jostle each other in bidding to play a part in a pending argument. It is an open question whether things said twice are repetitions, or whether the latter has the significance, say, of confirming the former. The same is true of omissions. Indeed, both come to view only in the context of some selected scheme of interpretation.

Most important, the competent reader is aware that it is not only that which the folder contains that stands in a relationship of mutually qualifying and determining reference, but parts that are not in it belong to this too. These ineffable parts come to view in the light of known episodes, but then, in turn, the known episodes themselves are also, reciprocally, interpreted in the light of what one must reasonably assume to have gone on while the case progressed without having been made a matter of record.

The scheme for interpreting folder documents may be drawn from anywhere at all. It may change with the reading of any particular item, change with the investigator's purposes in making a case of the documents he encounters, change 'in light of circumstances', change as the exigencies require. What the relationship of any document's sense is to the 'ordering schema' remains entirely a prerogative of the reader to find out, decide, or argue as he sees fit in each particular case, after the case, in light of his purposes, in light of his changing purposes, in light of what he begins to find, and so forth. The documents' meanings are altered as a function of trying to assemble them into the record of a case. Instead of laying out beforehand what a document might be all about, one waits to see what one encounters in the folders and from that, one 'makes out', one literally finds, what the document was all about. Then, whether or not there is continuity, consistency, coherence between the sense of one document and another is for the reader to see. In no case are constraints placed upon the reader to justify beforehand or to say beforehand what in the folder counts for what, or what he is going to count or not count for what.[5]

5. It is possible to deliberately design a system for reporting, search, and retrieval with such properties. For example, scholars may deliberately employ such a system precisely because their enterprise is such that they may not be willing to permit their knowledge of the situations that their reporting system is intended to permit an analysis of to be confined in its development by a method that places known limits to what is imaginable about the various readings and ideas they have encountered in their work. To their interests such an *ad hoc* system of classification and retrieval has the virtue of maximizing opportunities for imaginative play. Not knowing as of any Here and Now what might develop later, yet wanting later developments to be used to reconstrue the past, an *ad hoc* strategy for collection and retrieval promises to permit the scholar to bring his corpus of documents to bear upon the management of exigencies that arise as a function of his actual engagement with a developing situation.

What the scholar might do on his own as an aid to thought is done by clinicians in each other's company, under the auspices of a corporately organized system of supervision and review, with their results offered not as possible interpretations but as accounts of what actually happened. Their uses of folders are entirely similar to the many methods of psychotherapy, just as both are legitimate ways of delivering clinical

In order to read the folder's contents without incongruity, a clinic member must expect of himself, expect of other clinic members, and expect that as he expects of other clinic members they expect him to know and to use a knowledge (1) of particular persons to whom the record refers, (2) of persons who contributed to the record, (3) of the clinic's actual organization and operating procedures at the time the folder's documents are being consulted, (4) of a mutual history with other persons – patients and clinic members – and (5) of clinic procedures, including procedures for reading a record, as these procedures involved the patient and the clinic members. In the service of present interests he uses such knowledge to assemble from the folder's items a documented representation of the relationship.[6]

The clinic that we studied is associated with a university medical center. By reason of the clinic's commitment to research as a legitimate goal of the enterprise an actuarial record has high priority of value in the clinic's usual affairs. But the contract character of the contents of case folders has a competing priority of value which is associated with practical and prevailing necessities of maintaining viable relationships with the university, with other medical specialties, with the state government, with the courts and with the various publics at large by making out its activities to be those of a legitimate psychiatric remedial agency in the first place.

Between the two commitments there is no question on the part of the many parties concerned, patients and researchers included, as to which of the two takes precedence. In all matters, starting with considerations of comparative economics and extending through the tasks of publicizing and justifying the enterprise, the conditions for maintaining contract folders must be satisfied. Other interests are necessarily lesser interests and must be accommodated to these.

To all of this it is possible to answer that we are making too much of the entire matter; that after all the clinic's records are kept so as to serve the interests of medical and psychiatric services rather than to serve the interests of research. We would answer with full agreement. This is what we have been saying though we have been saying it with the intent of tying the state of the

---

services. And, if one asks – be he insider or outsider – for the rational grounds of the procedure, in both cases too these grounds are furnished by the personnel's invocation of the clinic's ways as socially sanctioned medico-legal ways of doing psychiatric business.

6. It is important to emphasize that we are not talking of 'making some scientific best of whatever there is'. Organizationally speaking, any collection of folder contents whatsoever can, will, even must be used to fashion a documented representation. Thus an effort to impose a formal rationale on the collection and composition of information has the character of a vacuous exercise because the expressions which the so ordered documents will contain will have to be 'decoded' to discover their real meaning in the light of the interest and interpretation which prevails at the time of their use.

records to the organizational significance of the priority that medical and psychiatric services enjoy over research concerns. Where research activities occur in psychiatric clinics one will invariably find special mechanisms whereby its research activities are structurally separated from and subordinated to the activities whereby the character and the viability of the clinic as a service enterprise are guaranteed. This is not to suggest that research is not pursued seriously and resolutely by clinicians.

References

HARRAH, D. (1961), 'A logic of questions and answers', *Philosophy of Science*, vol. 28, pp. 40–46.

KRAMER, M. *et al*. (1956), 'Application of life table methodology to the study of mental hospital populations', *Psychiatric Research Reports*, June, pp. 49–76.

KUNO, BELLER E. (1962), *Clinical Process*, Free Press.

MANNHEIM, K. (1962), 'On the interpretation of "Weltanschauung"', in P. Kecskemeti (ed.), *Essays on the Sociology of Knowledge*, Oxford University Press.

MEEHL, P. E. (1954), *Clinical versus Statistical Prediction*, University of Minnesota Press.

MEEHL, P. E. (1958), 'When shall we use our heads instead of the formula?', *Minnesota Studies in the Philosophy of Science*, vol. 2.

12 Don H. Zimmerman

Fact as a Practical Accomplishment

Abridged from Don H. Zimmerman, 'Record-keeping and the intake process in a public welfare agency', in Stanton Wheeler (ed.), *On Record: Files and Dossiers in American Life*, Russell Sage Foundation, 1969, pp. 319–54.

The concern of this chapter is illustrated by an incident a caseworker in a public assistance agency reported to her co-workers. An applicant had told her that she could not find the citizenship papers that were to be used to verify her age – a critical issue in determining her eligibility for a certain category of assistance. The applicant went on to say that at one time she had copied her birth-date on a piece of paper, which she then handed to the worker. The caseworkers greeted the story with laughter.

As this incident suggests, not just any piece of paper will do for establishing the objective and factual grounds for administrative action. What is it that confers upon a particular piece of paper its authority for the determination of matters of fact? How do such records achieve the authority of objective and impersonal accounts of persons' lives? What features give them currency, i.e. permit their utilization in varied contexts distinct from the special purposes for which they were originated?

The Lakeside Office, as it will be called here, is one of several district offices of a Bureau of Public Assistance located in a metropolitan county of a large western state.[1] The setting is characterized, first, by the routine collection, production, and use of records; and second, by the way in which the factuality, objectivity, and impersonality of the information contained in those records is an everyday, practical concern, and an everyday, practical accomplishment.

1. The major focus of the author's field work was the Intake Division of the Lakeside Office. The Intake Division has the responsibility of certifying the eligibility of applicants for assistance. The Approved Division manages such cases subsequent to certification. The Intake Division was organized into eight intake units, each consisting of a supervisor, five caseworkers, and a unit clerk. Six months were spent in the Lakeside Office during which time the author divided his effort equally between three units. Detailed observations were made of the work routine of three supervisors, three clerks, and fourteen workers. More casual observation and interaction took place with the remaining five supervisors and a portion of the remaining workers. Field methods included direct observation, informal interviewing, and the analysis of records. Tape recordings of actual work interactions between personnel were made whenever possible. For a more detailed account of the design and methodology of the study see Zimmerman (1966).

The use and production of records is a particularly prominent part of the intake process through which applicant eligibility for assistance is determined. Thus, attention to the investigation of eligibility at Lakeside is an appropriate strategy for addressing the issues raised above.[2]

The intake caseworker's task

In broad outline, the intake caseworker's task is to assemble and assess information pertaining to the set of eligibility factors specified for the particular program of assistance in question. The intake interview is usually the worker's first contact with a new applicant. Subsequently, she will call upon the applicant in her home and in some cases see the applicant again in the office. In the initial interview, and over the course of the investigation, the applicant's 'story' unfolds. The story presents, from the applicant's point of view, the relevant facts about herself and her circumstances which have led to her obvious and pressing need for assistance (given the facts as she has depicted them).

To be counted as doing an acceptable job by her supervisor, the worker must treat the applicant's story as no more than a loosely organized and unprocessed collection of *claims* lacking evidential value as such for the issue of eligibility. In short, the applicant's report of her standing *vis-à-vis* the factors of eligibility cannot, for the most part, be taken at face value. Nor, for that matter, can the worker's unsupported opinions serve as grounds for decision.

To approve an application for assistance, evidence must be marshaled showing that eligibility and need criteria have been satisfied. Documents such as birth certificates, bank statements, medical records, and similar 'official reports' bearing upon age, financial resources, state of health, and other factors furnish such evidence.

The investigative stance[3]

A prominent feature of the investigative process is what may be called the 'investigative stance'. From the point of view of experienced personnel, the 'stance' consists of a thoroughgoing skepticism directed to the applicant's claim to be eligible for assistance. As a mode of conducting an investigation, it is encountered in the setting by the observer (and by new personnel) as characterizations of 'good work', and as advice extended by supervisors and 'old hands' to novices. In relation to the intake worker's task of making the investigation of eligibility an accountably rational enterprise, 'being skeptical' is a way of displaying commitment to establishing the 'facts of the matter' (as against the applicant's mere *claims*) as well as being a method for

2. The perspective of this study follows Garfinkel's formulation of the indexicality and reflexivity of accounts. See Garfinkel (1967, especially ch. 1).
3. Discussed in Zimmerman (1969).

locating the courses of documentation which will determine the relevant facts.

'Doing' skepticism, or assuming the investigative stance is often taught to novices by insisting that they undertake some routine inquiry or initiate some procedure to verify some matter of which they are already persuaded. In one case, a new worker was adamant about giving an emergency grocery order (EGO) to one of her AFDC[4] applicants, even though much investigation remained. She was convinced that the applicant was in immediate need. Her supervisor acquiesced on the condition that she deliver it personally and 'look the situation over'. Of course, the supervisor yielded nothing. What she required was the usual procedure of making a home call before the issuance of aid.

The worker took the EGO to the applicant, and found, somewhat to her chagrin, that the house (as she later reported) was 'full of men' and that one of them was called 'daddy' by the woman's child (although 'daddy' was supposedly not on the scene). She did not give the applicant the EGO.

The point is this: the intake function as an *investigative* process comes to be appreciated through the discovery that the routine procedures insisted upon by supervisors can and do produce information which may run counter to the applicant's account of her situation and the worker's initial assessment of the case. Perhaps more important is the appreciation that the conduct of a recognizably adequate investigation involves displaying the *active* assumption of the investigative stance. A case is assembled over a series of interactions involving workers and their supervisors as well as workers and applicants. Supervisors were observed to be closely attentive to the ways in which their workers talked about their cases, and quick to point out where and how a worker failed to transform a feature of the applicant's story into a questionable matter resolvable through some course of documentation. For example, talk of the applicant's dire need over and against her eligibility was, for supervisors, a sure sign of a faulty grasp of the actual task of the intake division. This lack of appreciation of the 'real' character of the task signaled the need for close supervision, particularly in the context of caseload and processing time limitations, as discussed below.

Work relevancies

The task of investigating a case is understood against the background of work relevancies enforced in the setting. In general terms, these relevancies are (1) the reduction of a worker's caseload; and (2) an emphasis on dispos-

4. Aid to Families with Dependent Children, a federally mandated program of assistance for children deprived of support through death, desertion, or incapacitation of a parent. References to programs of assistance in this paper are to those programs as they existed in 1964-5.

ing of the case within a thirty-day period so that it does not become 'delinquent'. The consequences of such constraints appear to require an organization of work which will permit the worker to exercise a timely demand both on ancillary functions of the Bureau itself and on the applicant to expedite the collection of the requisite documents (see Zimmerman, 1969). The achievement of such work organization does not appear to consist merely in the disciplined control over a set of routines (although this is deemed important) but initially upon the achievement of an understanding by the novice of the technical, investigative character of the task, and how it may be competently conducted.

A crucial consideration in the investigative process is the role of the applicant. She is the primary source of the information needed to initiate the documentation that will warrant a decision in the case. Often the generation of some requisite documentation depends upon her taking certain actions, for example keeping appointments at medical examinations arranged for her, contacting the absent father (if she knows his whereabouts) and asking him to come in for an interview, pressuring a doctor to submit a medical report, making application for unemployment insurance, securing addresses and names of persons and places to be contacted, and so on. This reliance on the applicant is formulated by personnel as 'applicant responsibility'. For example, a worker was asked: 'What about the case where you have a complex situation? The applicant has moved around a lot, he hasn't led his life so as to leave convenient traces.'

The reply was:

Then we have to say the burden of proof is up to him. In other words, this is the agency feeling. You are applying for public assistance and it seems to me that if you are applying for a job with the government where you had to have a security clearance, you will have to have those addresses and if you really want it, the job, you are going to come up with them one way or another.

The caseworker's problem is to grasp what will need to be verified through the assembly of particular documents, to ask the applicant for such documents, and if she does not possess them, to initiate the procedures required to secure them.

In terms of the preceding, the investigative stance may be taken to refer to the variety of practices personnel employ to locate and display the potential discrepancy between the applicant's subjective and 'interested' claims and the factual and objective (i.e. rational) account that close observance of agency procedure is deemed to produce. Producing an account which is recognized as adequate in these terms involves procuring and interpreting documents within the constraints of the work relevancies discussed above.

Documents as objective and factual accounts

It will be useful to recall here the assumption that the applicant has a vital interest in the outcome of her claim. The 'facts', therefore, must be established by appeal to authoritative sources of information that can be viewed as independent of the influence or control of the applicant. What is required is some means for 'objectively' deciding, for all practical organizational purposes, the factual character of the applicant's story. This problem may be illustrated by the examination of an OAA[5] case in which there was an issue of legal possession of funds.

The applicant was found to possess a joint bank account with her daughter, a relatively common occurrence in the OAA category. If the amount in the joint account (in conjunction with the value of other personal property possessed by the applicant) exceeds the maximum allowable amount, the applicant is ineligible.

The applicant, however, claimed that half of the amount was her daughter's property, a fact which, if established, would reduce her total personal property holdings below the maximum, and hence render her eligible, other factors constant. The issue, of course, was *how* this division of property was to be established.

In terms of the banking regulations governing joint tenancy, the tenants have equal legal access to the *full* amount in the account. Hence, in the absence of further documentation which would indicate the ownership of the funds deposited in the account (for example, bank records of withdrawals from each individual's account matching deposits in the joint account), the issue of division of property was resolved by appeal to banking regulations. The statements of the parties concerned are not sufficient. The records of the bank, understood *against the background of banking conventions*, supersede the statements of the interested parties.

The authority of documents

A discussion of the ways in which bureaucratic records come to arbitrate and finally establish matters of fact is best launched by considering two related features of the use of documents in the setting. It may be observed, first of all, that in many situations, personnel simply treat a variety of documents as reports of 'plain fact' for all practical organizational purposes.[6] In other

5. Old Age Assistance, a federally mandated program of assistance to persons over the age of sixty-five whose income or resources fell below a specified minimum.

6. The major types of documents employed in the eligibility investigation were: (1) primary organizational records, for example marriage certificates, bank records, etc.; (2) the applicant's own records, i.e. records for which the applicant is accountable to some organization or, more generally, to some body of law, for example, tax returns,

words, on many occasions the information found in official records is accepted without question. For example, the records generated by the reception process at Lakeside are ordinarily 'plain facts' for intake workers. But, in other circumstances, personnel engage in the construction of accounts of *how* a document is to be honored as reporting 'plain fact', i.e. they present grounds for accepting the testimony of the document over and against the testimony of the applicant. The latter work usually occurs in the context of worker-supervisor interaction over the details of a case, and over the course of instructing novice workers.

'*Plain fact*'. The 'plain fact' character of documents-in-use in the setting is observable in the following ways. As suggested above, personnel regularly employ documents to decide issues of eligibility without comment, without question, and without challenge from superiors. The *de facto* authority thus achieved for documents by such routine decision making contrasts markedly with the thorough-going skepticism concerning the applicant's claim characteristic of the investigative stance. To oversimplify to some extent, the essentially problematic character of the applicant's claims is addressed and resolved by reliance on the essentially *un*problematic character of official documents. That is, the applicant's claims, as a general class, are *from the outset* open to doubt, just as the official document, as a general class, is *from the outset* seen as reliable. That personnel find an applicant's claims to be correct, or discover a record to be in error in a particular case, does not appear to alter their view of the essential character of either class.

It has already been indicated that the applicant, as a general rule, is not seen to be 'trustworthy'. On the other hand, the faith placed in official documents may be further exemplified by the following. The author posed the *global* doubt that records could be trusted as a matter of course, that indeed, they might be systematically falsified. The two workers queried in this fashion treated the suggestion as incredible. For them, the possibilities opened up by such a doubt, including the possibility of a conspiracy between the applicant and the document-producing organization, were not matters for idle speculation. The possibility of error was admitted, but only as a departure from ordinarily accurate reportage.[7]

The preceding seems to suggest that personnel automatically accept the

---

business records, etc.; (3) documents produced by transactions, for example transactions between *individuals* acting in specifiable 'formal' role relationships, for example doctor–patient or landlord–renter (but not affidavits executed by 'interested' third parties); and (4) the County's determination of the applicant's situation, i.e. the outcome of some procedure applied by the County or the Bureau to determine some issue such as an applicant's capacity or willingness to work.

7. The application of this procedure to only two workers provides meagre evidence, to be sure, but its results fit closely with observations on the features of accounts of the authority of official records to be considered below.

testimony of official documents in most cases. However, over a range of cases *and* workers, challenges to the authority of particular documents as decisive arbiters of eligibility do arise. For example, supervisors (and others in authority) view the display of the investigative stance by workers as a critical element of their competence as employees. Hence, as supervisors see it, there is a distribution of competence in the setting related in large part to the distribution of experience. It is *not* the case that inexperienced workers are seen to reject the authority of documents in principle; rather, they are seen to *miss the point* of documentary verification. That is, they are not properly skeptical of the applicant's claims; they do not display skill in relating the particulars of the applicant's story to the kinds of information made available by documents; they do not assign first priority to the collection of pertinent documents and perhaps most troublesome of all to their superiors, they tend to side with the applicant and attempt to 'explain away' discrepancies between her story and the evidence of the record.[8]

Under such circumstances, supervisors usually provide *accounts* which display the ways in which the documentary evidence is visibly more reliable, more objective, more trustworthy than the applicant's word, and in the final analysis is required by the nature of the organization's mission. The general features of such accounts will be outlined shortly.

Challenges arise in other ways. Documents are often found to be ambiguous or difficult to interpret; sometimes they produce marked incongruities for workers if they are taken as definitive of some matter, for example, age. Again, these challenges are not global, but are occasioned by problems encountered in particular cases, and resolved in terms leaving the essential character of records (and applicants) unchanged as organizationally actionable matters.

Accounting for 'plain facts'. Accounts of the 'plain fact' character of documents are done by members of the organization for members of the organization; they are integral features of the situations they make observable and hence organize. By means of these accounts, the documents passing through the hands of agency personnel are seen as documents of the orderly processes of society, and as produced by them. (The Lakeside office is itself one such orderly process.)

Whether or not such accounts are accurate descriptions of document-producing enterprises is an issue here only in so far as it is an issue in the setting. How that issue is solved when it arises is how the 'plain fact' character of documents is preserved in the face of a variety of contingencies and occasioned doubts encountered in the course of using documents to advance the

8. See Zimmerman (1969) for a discussion of these 'troubles'.

work of the organization, i.e. the work of accountably rational investigation and decision-making.

First, accounts displaying the 'plain fact' character of documents show them to depict such activities as buying and selling property, consulting doctors, getting married and divorced, paying taxes and so on. Witnesses to these accounts are invited to see that such activities are everyday, matter-of-course pursuits, i.e. 'natural' occurrences in the society. Further, the outcome of these pursuits, as accomplished-events-in-society, are to be seen as *produced* or *constituted* on the occasion in which the record is generated (for example, the transfer of a title deed). The account *ties* the activity to a record-keeping enterprise.

Making observable the 'necessary' link between an activity and the occasion in which it becomes a matter of record also makes visible the *transactional* character of the document-producing context. Apart from the person undertaking some ordinary activity, there are others involved whose task it is to monitor, facilitate, and record the course and outcome of that activity. In turn, the transaction between such persons is made accountable in terms of the *motivationally transparent* character of their respective roles. That is, the person whose affairs a document reports is a person who, via the account, is seen to be pursuing some commonplace project (for example, buying property) for understandable reasons appropriate to that project, and others are viewed as going about *their* commonplace projects, (for example, selling property, recording titles, assessing taxes, etc.) for reasons appropriate to their occupational obligations. And that occupational obligations are viewed to be binding provides the way of seeing the transaction as under the control of some set of (usually unspecified) procedures.

In short, the authority of various documents is made accountable in terms of the routine, organized ways in which these unremarkable projects are geared to one another under the auspices of typified, generally known interests or motives, and with adumbrated reference to the more or less standardized procedures that presumably control the gearing.

The features discussed above are not offered as exhaustive. Nor can they be viewed as a set of criteria usable by the observer to decide the status of documents independently of their occurrence as features of an account delivered on some occasion of work in the setting. The adequacy of an account is not guaranteed by merely possessing these features. It remains to be seen, in particular cases, how these general features are achieved in the work actually done to make them observable and enforceable over the contingencies of interaction in the setting.

Investigating a case

The occasion for the AFDC-U[9] application to be examined here was the default in payment due the applicant, Mr A., for masonry work he performed as an 'independent contractor'. The work was contracted by the owner of a manufacturing firm for improvements on his private residence. The applicant had been given a check for $300, which proved to be worthless. Mr A. was persuaded to resume his work on the promise of an additional $350, which was never forthcoming, leaving him without funds and in debt. At the time of the application, Mr A. presented a notice from the Labor Law Commission setting a date for a hearing over the dispute.

Verification. A major task for G. B., the worker on the case, was verifying a list submitted by the applicant of the places at which he had sought employment. One requirement of the AFDC-U program is that the unemployed parent actively seek work and give evidence of having done so. This requirement is enforced by the use of a record form on which is entered the name and address of the employers contacted, date and name of the person approached. The entries on the form are checked by phone to establish their 'factual' character. It is important to note that the results of such a procedure, recorded in the case narrative, have the status of a document.

G. B.'s first call produced the promise of a return call, since the person likely to have interviewed the applicant was not in, as was the case for his second call. G. B. was concerned to make what he called a 'breakthrough' on the calls:

It will be easier to go through because we will have some more factual information to go by. You see theoretically, if worse should come to worse, if he were a complete fraud and just listed these places and Mr D (the debtor) is just a friend who will go along with his story – but the one bit of factual information is that letter I got this morning from the Labor Law Commission so if I were looking at it strictly from a fraud point of view, the only document I have concerning this whole dispute is that letter and the phone call and theoretically, that phone call could be arranged. He might have given me the number of a friend *but knowing the operation and having gone through a receptionist – through a general bureaucracy the way it is here – I can intuitively grasp that this is not a phony setup.*

These remarks merit comment. First, G. B. has raised the possibility, that the applicant's representations (and the evidence he has offered in their support) are fraudulent. Second, the character of the factual information G. B. is concerned to collect consists of information outside a 'reasonable' possi-

9. Aid to Families with Dependent Children-Unemployed, a special program designed to provide assistance in those family cases where the reason for the child's 'deprivation' is the unemployment of the principal breadwinner, typically the father.

bility of collusion or manipulation. The one 'bit of factual information' he possessed would seem to qualify as such for him. In discussing the matter of his contact with the debtor, Mr D., he speculates that it could have been 'arranged'. But he discounts this as a likelihood because, in calling Mr D. 'at work', his call went through a switchboard – a 'general bureaucracy the way it is here'.

One may well ask the value of the latter fact. On the basis of earlier discussion, one aspect of the evidential force of documents produced by official agencies is formulated in terms of what it would entail to entertain the notion of a 'conspiracy' with the applicant entered into by that agency. G. B. is evidently willing to consider that possibility with respect to a friend of the applicant, but not with respect to a person reached through a switchboard. The mechanism of the 'general bureaucracy' by which such a person was reached permits him to 'intuitively grasp that this is not a phony setup,' i.e. to discount the likelihood of the applicant's manipulation of the situation. The information was delivered through organizational channels, hence it may be counted trustworthy by virtue of the occupational obligations implicitly assumed to be operating.

G. B. has yet to establish as factual the applicant's 'diligent' search for employment. Another call is placed revealing that the firm has no record of Mr A.'s application. G. B. remarks, 'I imagine he has gone there but the gentleman I spoke to didn't have the information.' When asked why he concluded that, he replied:

You generally ask what the procedure is. This one seemed to have records of other people. He (Mr A.) may have just inquired to see if there were any openings, in which case, they wouldn't have a record. So we will just check some of the other places because it is not too likely that a client would say he went to a place and get the address and manufacture the results of the interview and put it down when he knows it is going to be subject to verification. That is very unlikely.

Given that a procedure for the production of such a record was in existence, G. B. invoked the conditions under which a record might none the less not be produced. By so doing, G. B. is apparently 'taking into account' the conditions under which the applicant's contact with an organization might not routinely produce a record. By doing so, he is raising a challenge, the character of which will be seen shortly.

At this point, it should be made clear that such 'contingencies' are often appreciated, particularly by workers. By proposing that the procedures of the agency rely on the 'orderly processes of the society' it is not implied that 'the society' is taken by such officials as simply a well-oiled, infallible machine. However, from the perspective of the immediate task and its constraints, it may have to be treated *as if* it were for all practical organizational purposes. That is, should this resource fail to produce the requisite information, the matter may often be treated as indeterminate, however much the contingencies may be appreciated.

Returning to the case under consideration, the worker placed another call, remarking that 'this is one of the problems in these AFDC cases when there is an employable parent – *checking* – it takes an awful lot of time. In an OAA case, there are practically no phone calls.' The phone call produced the same results as the preceding one – there would have been a record if he were there, but there was no record of his applying. G. B. commented: 'Two places had no record. It may be that if they just weren't hiring anyone so that it would be pointless to make an application.'

It is important to emphasize again that G. B.'s treatment of the results of the phone call rests upon at least two considerations: (1) the places contacted were found to routinely keep records of job applicants, and (2) the invocation of contingencies by G. B. which might intervene between an inquiry into employment and the production of a record of that inquiry, that is, the actual taking of an application.

G. B. then approaches his supervisor, A. B., to report on the outcome of the checking procedure.

I am trying to verify his search for employment, I've had no luck. (Referring to form) no record ... no record ... will call back. This one they didn't know definitely, but the person said they had no record of it. But he might have gone down to another department or something.

Thus, G. B. repeats to the supervisor what he had already stated to the observer: the check has failed, but he is willing to grant a 'reasonable' explanation of the failure.

To this, the supervisor proposes:

No record of him even being there even. Well, you see, a lot of these places ... have you ever applied at one of these places? They have a record of you even if you go through the gate to apply.

I've walked the streets (looking for work) unfortunately, at a lot of firms in this area, and I'm well aware of it. They just don't let you in. For instance, if you go to Jordans, they won't let you in without taking your name. They have a record of some kind and they keep it for a certain length of time and then they destroy them.

She has formulated for the purposes of the issue at hand the typical way in which job applicants are processed at the type of firm where the applicant claimed to have sought employment. Her account does not detail the specific procedures, nor does it deal with the contingent factor of how, organizationally speaking, the request for information might be satisfied. But it does fashion from the particulars of the situation the vague but weighty procedural guarantee that if a certain event took place, a record of it would be available.

By so constructing the matter on this occasion, the efficacy of the verification procedure and of the document it produces is preserved. By readily admitting to the contingency posed by the worker that 'he might have gone to another department or something' the procedure would have been rendered indeterminate. To allow such a supposition routinely would be consequential for the requirement of filing a case within thirty days.

The issue is the weight to be given to the 'contingencies' of a process of record keeping (perhaps there were no job openings and the applicant did not bother to apply) compared to the force of the verification procedure to decide the issue. Taken in the context of the emphasis on case load reduction and meeting processing time requirements, strong organizational reasons exist for protecting the determinateness of such procedures. Hence, the caseworker's attempt to provide a 'reasonable' account of how it might be that the applicant had actually sought employment even though no record of it was available is set aside in favor of the organizationally more compelling interpretation that he had not, in fact, diligently sought employment.

In this case, however, the applicant was allowed a 'second chance' on this issue. The worker's willingness to entertain 'reasonable contingencies' may be a factor in such 'second chances'.[10] It is highly probable that had the failure to verify search for employment been taken at its face value, the worker could have denied the application and not been challenged, particularly by this supervisor. How 'far' a worker will go with an applicant in dealing with problems of verification appears to depend on how willing a worker (and, more crucially, a supervisor) is to accept the the 'risks' that accompany extended case processing.

The applicant as a course-of-action

The conference between the supervisor and the worker proceeded (the matter of verification of the applicant's job seeking dropped for the moment) with the specification of further details of the applicant's situation. Observe what is made of the information about the applicant's occupation:

A. B. A. is a contractor? An independent contractor? [Yes] Did you look at his income tax? [No] I'd like to see how he rates himself on an income tax declaration. I really would before I'd make a decision. . . . Does he have a license, and all of this? What's his equipment valued at? You would need all of this. What kind of a contractor is he, cement?

10. The author's presence should not be discounted as a factor in the granting of a 'second chance'. On several occasions, the author learned that administrative personnel had 'adjusted' their conduct – presumably in accordance with their conception of his prejudices – only to change it later in his absence.

G. B. Masonry. He does landscaping type of stuff and gardening.

Note that from the single fact of occupation, the supervisor has now generated as pertinent facts for investigation, a number of features of his circumstances (and that she has specified the documents pertinent to them). A. B. continues:

I think the only thing you can do probably is one grocery order while you go on with your investigation and then check out everything as fast as you can, including the value of his personal, his business equipment. I would like to look at his income tax form last year, and why, if he's a landscape gardener, this just doesn't make sense, that he couldn't get a job this time of year. It doesn't make sense.

The notion of 'what contractors do' has now generated a set of instructions for the worker which he will have to satisfy in order to act on the case. The features evoked are investigatable matters. That is, some document may be secured or produced which would, presumably, decide the matter. That he is also a gardener, given what is presumed to be the market of gardeners, also generates skepticism about the applicant, i.e. the remark, 'it doesn't make sense' is roughly equivalent to 'he isn't acting in the way he should', or, 'his motivations are unclear given who he is'. The worker attempts to make sense of his actions:[11]

G. B. I think he sold his stuff, *and that makes sense of that.* On income tax you want to know if he considers himself self-employed or. . . .

The supervisor replies to this and raises further matters for investigation:

A.B. I'd like to take a look at it if you don't mind. You take a look at it too, then I'll take a look at it. You make up your mind, then show it to me, and I'll make up mine and we'll talk about it, and you want to know, does he have a business phone, does he have a phone exchange, how does he get jobs? You see, these are the kind of things you're going to have to know. *How does he get a job?* You don't become . . . get contracts out of the Department of Employment, you bid on them. Just suppose you had a service to sell, put yourself in his place, as to how you were going to do it. You are not going to get it by going into the Department of Employment.

11. Yet another consequence of the matter of detailing the applicant's circumstances is assessing his motivation or at least, his good cause in applying through providing typical alternative courses of action a 'person like him' would usually have available. That gardeners are assumed to be able to get jobs raises the question, why isn't he gardening?

Another aspect is to be noted: extensive detailing, which opens a number of avenues of investigation, heightens the saliency of the time-limited character of the process. Keeping in mind that there are numbers of cases to be processed by any one worker, the multiplication of aspects of the investigation multiplies the demands placed on both worker and client, multiplies the number of contacts between them, and makes the filing of the case 'in time' a difficult matter.

In turn, the worker provides other possible situations for the applicant by saying:

G. B. I imagine he gets to a certain extent by word of mouth. He does small jobs, homes, and what not.[12]

She indicates a certain 'suspicion' she entertains:

I have a feeling in my heart, I can't prove this you understand, that the only reason I can think of that he would come here is that it would sound real good at the [Labor Law Commission] hearing.

As indicated above, Mr A. will be given a further opportunity to demonstrate his willingness to seek employment as required by the A F D C-U program. This 'second chance' will be structured in such a way that subsequent failure of attempts to verify this search will be taken as definitive grounds upon which to deny the application. In the meantime, the investigation will proceed along the lines suggested by the supervisor, as witness the subsequent phone call to the applicant by the caseworker:

G. B. (To the author) Well, we have about twelve things to check out. . . . (He phones Mr A.) Hello, Mr A.? Yes, I've discussed your case with the supervisor and uh, we're going to issue a grocery order, but there's a little bit of information I'd like to get regarding your situation, and one is your garden tools. You have garden tools right now? Gardening tools, yeh, for landscaping and stuff. You have them huh, you have? Let me see . . . hedge clippers, electric hedge clippers? Manual. You have a lawn mower? You have what else? What else, Mr A.? You have a hose? Right, shovels? Okay, and you still have those, right? Now, your truck is broken, right? What kind of truck is that? 1947, what kind of truck, pickup? and where is that parked and what's wrong with it? Threw a rod? Well, how much will it take to be repaired? $45? Who told you that? What's the name? And when did the truck break down? What day in October? Around the middle . . . the last part of September. Yeah? It was the last part of September. Do you have your income tax statements . . . ? I mean for you as a business owner? You don't keep business records? Okay, you started in business six months ago. Self-employed. When were you told about, eh, yeh, by the tax man what to do? When

12. This counter-typification also has structural connections. Recall that the detailing of the applicant's life through the proposing of 'the way it must be' in that kind of circumstance is taken as the basis for a course of investigation. Each instance of such imputation, in the absence of information to substantiate the applicant's claim, reinforces the doubt that the applicant is a person worthy, as well as eligible, for assistance. Given merely the information that the applicant is a self-employed contractor who also does gardening, a typified pattern of action for a person of *that sort* is constructed, the verification of which would establish his claims to be a good person in a fix. Such constructions, taken as 'probably the case' in the absence of further information, became an issue to be resolved by investigation. The worker's attempt to 'make sense' of an apparent discrepancy in the instance of his 'inability to secure' gardening work, and of the method by which he secures his work, may be the attempt to uncomplicate the case.

does he want you to file a business return, do you know? How do you secure your jobs, Mr A.? Yes, word of mouth, huh? Mr G. saw you work at the doctor's. What was that doctor's name? Dr R., I think I have it down someplace, and how did you get the job with the doctor? Through your house . . . at your house. Did you have jobs before that? Did you work for anybody else? Do you have a car? In other words, you have to rely on public transportation. . . .

A review of the relevant features of this case is in order. First, both the worker and the supervisor were oriented to the essentially problematic character of the applicant's claim, albeit in different ways and in differing degrees. Similarly, both accepted the essentially unproblematic character of official documents, again with some differences. The essential differences between them lay in the extent to which the contingencies of action were treated as relevant considerations in assessing the authority of a particular verification procedure, and hence, of the document resulting from it. The supervisor's account made the sources of information pertinent to the applicant's search for employment visible as organized, procedure-bound enterprises that could be counted on to have a record of the applicant's inquiry if he in fact made one. The assertion of 'contingencies' is a challenge, the response to which is an account which suppresses such contingencies as matters eligible for consideration.

The difference between the worker and the supervisor in the depth of skepticism concerning the applicant's story is worth comment. The supervisor employed the occasion (as they were often observed to do) to probe the case further and issue instructions for further investigation. These instructions made the applicant's circumstances accountable as courses-of-action which, if typically motivated and typically executed, could be expected to produce records serviceable for the task of deciding eligibility. Over the course of this exchange the worker introduced a variety of contingencies which could serve to rationalize departures from what the supervisor depicted as the ordinary course-of-action to be expected from someone like the applicant.

This case was eventually approved. The primary interest in it here, of course, has been the process of investigation – particularly in the way the applicant's claims are rendered problematic and challenges to the 'plain fact' of documentary procedures and their outcomes responded to. The end result is a 'documented' case that both indicates the approved or disapproved status of the applicant, and provides a record of justification for the action taken, i.e. its accountably rational character.

Concluding remarks

It has been observed that for personnel in the agency studied, documents often had an obvious character. They were seen by personnel as obviously factual reports about a variety of circumstances relevant to the determination of eligibility, and equally important, as factual depictions of the organization's conduct of its affairs. Personnel trafficked in such facts – they collected them, generated them, and used them in consequential ways.

Yet, as noted at the beginning of the chapter, not any piece of paper with any set of entries would do. And although certain other pieces of paper did routinely 'do' there are many occasions in which the authority of documents required demonstration.The persistent theme of the chapter, then, emerges as the continual interplay between the routine and the problematic, the taken-for-granted use of documents and the occasioned accounts which make their use observable as rational procedure.

The taken-for-granted use of documents, as analysed by accounts given in the setting, is dependent on the document user's sense of an ordered world of organizations, and an ordered world of the society-at-large. When simply taken for granted, the features of these ordered domains are matters of mere recognition for which no accounts are called for or given. Indeed, such routine recognition, and the action and inference proceeding from it, is the mark of the competent worker.

When a document is rendered problematic in a given case, the document-producing activities of which it is a part are made accountable as orders of necessary motives, necessary actions, and necessary procedures which may be used to analyse the features of the case and reach a determinate and warrantable decision. It is the artful accomplishment of personnel that they are able to provide such accounts which sustain the organizationally required use of documents over the manifold contingencies of everyday investigations. It is through that artful accomplishment, some features of which were examined in this chapter, that records achieve the impact they are ordinarily taken to have.

References

GARFINKEL, H. (1967), *Studies in Ethnomethodology*, Prentice-Hall.

ZIMMERMAN, D. H. (1966), 'Paper work and people work: a study of a public assistance agency', unpublished Ph.D. dissertation, University of California, Los Angeles.

ZIMMERMAN, D. H. (1969), 'Tasks and troubles: the practical bases of work activities in a public assistance agency', in D. A. Hansen (ed.), *Explorations in Sociology and Counselling*, Houghton Mifflin.

13 D. Lawrence Wieder

Telling the Code

Excerpts from D. Lawrence Wieder, *Language and Social Reality: The Case of Telling the Convict Code*, Mouton, The Hague, in press.

The convict code as an explanation of deviant behavior

The convict code is the classical or traditional explanation of those forms of deviant behavior engaged in by inmates, convicts, or residents of rehabilitative organizations. In traditional analyses of deviant behavior, some subversive or contraculture normative order is searched out by the analyst and utilized by him as an explanation for the behavior patterns he has observed. In the case of prisons and related organizations, the 'convict code' is typically encountered by the researcher and employed as such an explanation.

The code as an explicitly verbalized moral order

My participant observation detected a code which was operative at halfway house.[1] My principal resident informants, whom I came to know over a period of several months, and with whom I had at least several conversations a week and often several a day, spoke readily of a code. They called this code *the code* and told of a set of activities that they *should* and *should not* engage in. They also spoke of 'regular guys' (followers of the code) and said that every one of the residents at the halfway house was a regular guy. They explained to me that everyone there had 'done a lot of time' and had even learned the code much earlier than their prison experiences, as hypes on the street.

The code and explicitly verbalized sanctions

Residents of the halfway house, like inmates as they are described in the literature on prisons, spoke clearly about the ways in which the code was enforced. As traditionally reported, and as I observed in the case of the halfway house, enforcement of the code by inmates or residents is closely related to the use of social types. The code is generally enforced by inmates through their application of a label or social-type name to those inmates who are seen by members of the group as deviating from the code.

In the case of the halfway house, the only deviant types or labels that I

1. An intendedly rehabilitative facility for narcotic-addict felons on parole [Ed.].

regularly heard were 'kiss ass', 'snitch', and 'sniveler'. To be called a 'kiss ass' meant that one was too close to staff. The title 'snitch' was employed to designate another as an informer. 'Sniveler' was employed to designate another resident as one who chronically complained to staff and pleaded with staff for better treatment. Residents spoke of kissing ass, snitching, and sniveling as clearly moral matters which required their attention and intervention.

Sanctions directed against the sniveler were minor when compared with the measures taken against the snitch and kiss ass. A sniveler would be spoken of as a 'fool' and 'not like one of us'. Sanctions directed against kiss asses and snitches, while more potent, were spoken of with less clarity and uniformity. At times, residents said that kiss asses would be frozen out of contact with the other 'guys' and that immediate violence would be done against snitches. At other times, residents spoke of the 'fact' that violations of the code would be remembered and dealt with later. That is, the reprehensible one would, like all other residents, at some time return to the 'joint' (prison). In the joint, his reprehensible reputation would be spread, and at that point he would not be trusted by the other cons and would be suspected by the other cons on each occasion in which they thought someone had snitched.

The specifics of the code at halfway house

The code was often spoken of by residents as containing a set of maxims. While a specific resident could not recite all of the maxims, what residents said about the code can be formulated in that fashion. As a set of maxims, the code in its specifics is as follows:

1. Above all else, do not snitch. Informing was regarded as an act directed not simply against an individual, but against the whole collection of deviant colleagues. Snitching would permanently jeopardize a resident's standing with other hypes, residents, and inmates. His reputation would be spread throughout the whole deviant community, and he would find that he could no longer operate with other deviants. There was only one actual case in which I observed snitching or possible snitching as a real issue (as compared to a potential or hypothetical issue) at halfway house. And the only reason this case was observable to me was because a resident who was fearful that others regarded him as a snitch told the following story to his parole agent, who in turn told me. 'Pablo' came to his parole agent, telling him of his anxiety about a parolee who was about to move into the halfway house. Years before, the two men had used and sold drugs together. Both were arrested, but charges were dropped against Pablo, while the other man was tried. Pablo said that the other man thought Pablo had informed on him, though Pablo told him he had not. Now Pablo wanted release from the halfway house because of what that man might do and how the other residents might treat him if the other man ever talked about him. Except for this incident, I observed no cases of residents being identified as snitches.

2. Do not cop out. That is, do not admit that you have done something illegal or illegitimate. Someone who turned himself in willingly would be regarded as strange, 'not like us', dumb, and probably not trustworthy, because to 'cop out' was a form of defecting to the other side. To turn oneself in could be viewed as a form of defection, because it implied agreement with the standards that one had violated. To turn oneself in to a parole agent when one was about to be caught anyway or when one was 'tired of running' and likely to get caught by the police, however, was not talked about as 'copping out'.

3. Do not take advantage of other residents. This maxim was principally directed against thievery among residents. However, if a resident had something stolen from him, it was his own responsibility to take care of the thief. Unlike the case of the snitch, a resident could not count on others to sanction the thief negatively. Residents were prohibited by the code from appealing to staff for assistance in locating the stolen goods.

4. Share what you have. A regular resident should be relatively generous with other residents in terms of his money, clothes, and wine. If he used drugs, he should offer a 'taste' to others that were around when he 'geezed'. He should share drugs with his closest friends and sell drugs to others, if he had more than he needed. He should share his 'fit' (syringe and spoon) with others and 'score' (purchase drugs) for those who could not find a connection (source of drugs).

5. Help other residents. This maxim was principally a directive to help one's fellows avoid detection and punishment. It included 'standing point' for them (being a lookout for staff or the police when the other was involved in a compromising activity, such as injecting drugs), warning them about suspicions that staff had, telling staff that they were ignorant about the activities of other residents, so as not to help staff indirectly investigate another guy,[2] arguing with staff on the behalf of another resident, providing cover stories for other residents, helping another resident sneak into the house after curfew, etc.

6. Do not mess with other residents' interests. A resident should not prevent others from enjoying their deviance, should not disapprove of it, and should not in any way draw staff's attention to it. This includes not 'bringing the

2. Also included generally under the rule, 'do not snitch'.

heat' by engaging in suspicious actions or by getting into an unnecessary altercation with staff. For example, one could 'bring the heat' by leaving evidence of drug use around the house which would lead staff to suspect everybody.

7. *Do not trust staff – staff is heat.* This maxim simply says that in the final analysis staff cannot be trusted, because one of staff's principal occupational duties is to detect deviance. Anything a resident might let them know about himself or others could, in some presently unknown fashion, be used by them to send him or someone else back to the joint. So, if a resident has anything deviant going for him at all (like having a common law wife, occasionally using heroin, having user friends in his house, or even using marijuana), he is well advised not to let his agent know his real residence and to give his mother's address instead. In this way he avoids letting his agent know anything that might lead to the discovery of his deviant doings. This advice holds even if a resident is on the best of terms with his agent.

8. *Show your loyalty to the residents.* Staff, in fact, is 'the enemy', and a resident's actions should show that he recognizes this. He should not 'kiss ass,' do favors for staff, be friendly to staff, take their side in an argument, or accept the legitimacy of their rules. Any of these acts can be understood as a defection to their side, and makes a resident suspect of being the kind of 'guy' that would snitch. It is not that being friendly to staff or complying with staff's regulations is intrinsically illegitimate, but these matters indicate what kind of person one is and that one, thereby, may not be trustworthy in protecting residents and their interests. If a resident makes it clear in other ways (as, for example, in his private dealings with other residents) that he indeed is on the residents' side, these signalizing activities may then be understood in other ways by the other residents. They may be understood as efforts to manipulate staff in some concrete way, for example, a resident wants them to give him the best jobs they have, or wants to make the kind of impression on his parole agent that will lead the agent away from suspecting him when he otherwise might.

The code as explanation for resident behavior

Treating the rules of the code as maxims of conduct that residents follow and enforce upon one another provides a traditional sociological explanation for the regular patterns of deviant behavior that were observed in the halfway house. The rules account for that behavior in the following specific ways.

If residents comply with the maxim, 'Show your loyalty to the residents', then they would be motivated to avoid spending time with staff, avoid lively conversation with staff, and, by the use of Spanish and other conversational devices, would exclude staff from their conversations. The injunction against trusting staff, not letting staff know about residents' doings as a way of protecting other residents, and even the injunction against 'snitching'[3] are also fulfilled (in part) in the avoidance behavior 'doing distance'.

Further, residents can show their loyalty to each other by displaying a lack of enthusiasm for what staff proposes in group, by not paying attention in group, by verbally demeaning the program in group, and by not staying around after group to talk with staff about the program. That is, showing where one's loyalties are can be accomplished by displaying the behaviors 'disinterest and disrespect'. Similarly, by complying with no more than what staff demands and explicitly sanctions ('passive compliance') and by attempting to get staff to do what they hope a resident will do for himself ('demands and requests'), one can, thereby, also show his loyalties by doing as little as possible for 'the enemy' and taking him for whatever he can get.

Patterns of lying and generally being a bad informant, which left staff ignorant of what was actually happening at the moment, ignorant of what a resident would do, and ignorant of whether or not he would do as he had promised, are provided for in the maxims, 'Do not snitch', 'Do not cop out', 'Do not trust staff', 'Help other inmates', and 'Do not mess with other residents' interests'. The maxim, 'Do not snitch', directs the resident to avoid letting staff share any of his knowledge of other residents. 'Do not cop out' directs him to prevent staff from knowing about his own activities. These same maxims would lead residents to prevent staff from hearing anything about what residents were doing, including who is friends with whom, who is physically in the house, that drugs are being used – which is different from snitching, which would be that 'Jones' is using drugs – and often whether or not one resident even knows another.

Patterns of violating rules and routines are protected, supported, and encouraged by the code, though they are not directly prescribed. While there is nothing in the code which says 'miss group', 'be late for curfew', 'bring wine into the house', or 'use drugs', any of these activities, especially the use of drugs, is a relatively clear sign of one's loyalties. Residents sometimes told me that they took drugs that were offered to them, because refusing would indicate that they disapproved of drug use or were 'taking to heart' staff hopes that they would not use drugs.

Patterns of deviant behavior were protected by maxims of the code which required that (a) other residents help those who chose to violate the 'rules' and 'routines', (b) other residents cover for those who needed it [standing

3. The relationship of 'doing distance' to 'snitching' requires further explanation. Residents explained to me that being aloof from staff, which can be accomplished by 'doing distance', indicates to others that one would not snitch. If one did not stay aloof, then special effort would be required to retain the trust of other residents.

point, providing excuses and alibis, sneaking them into the house when the 'night watchman' (SPA) was not looking, etc.], and (c) no resident let staff verbally know about deviant activities. Deviant activities were further supported by the set of rules which said that residents should let each other do whatever deviant (from staff's point of view) thing they chose, and if they were to engage in deviant consumption of wine and drugs, that these should be shared with others.

In this fashion, the code as I found it at halfway house would explain the patterns of deviance that I observed there. The code provides the motivations to engage in those patterns, to sanction those patterns positively, and not to interfere with those patterns even if a resident were to find it in his own interest to do so. This form of explanation is traditional in the analysis of correctional organizations and has its direct analog in traditional analyses of others forms of deviant behavior. [. . .]

Some features of staff's use of the code

The dialogues between staff and researcher show that staff not only knew the code, but knew how to use it as well. It was used as a wide-reaching scheme of interpretation which 'structured' their environment.

Like residents and sociologists, staff 'told the code' to identify or name individual acts and patterns of repetitive action and to collect diverse actions under the rubric of a single motive and, in turn, to name them as the same kind of act. They rendered resident action sensible or rational by noting the ways in which resident action was rule-governed and directed toward achieving goals that were specified by the code. In this way staff offered a folk version of Weber's adequate causal analysis by showing that the typical patterned actions of residents followed from a 'correct' course of reasoning. Staff portrayed the reasonable character of resident action by using the code and its elements to define the residents' situation. By 'telling the code' as the residents' definition of their situation, staff showed that patterns of resident action had Durkheim's social-fact properties of exteriority and constraint. Residents' actions were reasonable in the sense that they had no choice but to behave in the fashion that they did.

In 'telling the code', staff implicitly and explicitly used a wide range of social scientific conceptions, for example rule-governed action, goal-directed action, the distinction between the intended and unintended outcomes of action, the distinction between normatively required and normatively optional means of achieving a morally valued end, roles, role-bound behaviors, and definition of the situation. The use of these ethno-social scientific conceptions in 'telling the code' structured staff's environment. It did this by identifying the meaning of a resident's act by placing it in the context of a pattern. An equivocal act then becomes 'clear' in the way that it obtains its sense as typical, repetitive, and more or less uniform, i.e. its sense as an *instance* of the kind of action with which staff was already familiar. Staff's environment was also structured by the flexibility of 'telling the code', which could render nearly any equivocal act sensible in such a way that it was experienced as something familiar, even though the act might not be 'expected' or 'predicted' in any precise meaning of those terms. For example, when the parole agent portrayed a diverse collection of actions – a resident's ridiculing the agent and other group members in a committee meeting, being late to the meeting, giving inadequate excuses, never siding with staff on any issue, and playing one staff member off against another – as instances of a familiar pattern of behavior (demonstrating one's opposition to staff as a display of one's loyalty), he made them parts of an already known pattern, even though the specific behaviors might not have been predicted. 'Telling the code' also structured staff's environment by *connecting* a given act to its possible goal or to some specific consequence of the act among its many consequences. For example, one staff member identified a case of a resident's (possibly accidental) burning his own mattress as an attack on staff. This consequence was only one among many consequences, for example, it created much smoke that would bother his dorm mates, and it could have served as a 'cover' for some illegitimate activity. By seeing the potential code relevance of the act as an attack on staff, the staff member identified 'the' specific meaning of the act. Acts were also rendered sensible by connecting them to the activities of others (especially staff) in terms of role-bound reciprocities.

'Telling the code' rendered residents' behavior *rational* for staff by placing the acts in question in the context of a loose collection of maxims which compelled their occurrence and by portraying the consequences for those residents who did not comply with these maxims. By describing resident conduct in terms of the normative order which generated it, staff depicted residents as reasonable, acting like Anyman would act under the circumstances. Staff's 'telling the code' also rendered important features of staff's environment *trans-situational* and non-situation specific in character. It rendered parts of staff's environment trans-situational by depicting them as recurrent and produced by a constantly operative set of motives (provided by the code) which were acted upon in every staff–resident encounter. Non-situation specificity was an accompaniment of trans-situationality, for in staff's hands, 'telling the code' drew attention away from the specific features of the situation of an act (for example that it was *this* resident acting toward a specific staff member who had treated him in a particular way), while giving it a trans-situational explanation. By explaining the varieties of unpleasant gestures that residents directed toward them in terms of 'the (trans-situational) principles by which these men live', staff 'avoided' the possible interpretation of those unpleasant actions in such situation-specific terms as 'getting back at a staff member for the way he treated the resident the day before' or 'responding to an obvious attack on the resident's integrity'.

As a useful and flexible explanation, 'telling the code' was an attractive, plausible story about the varieties of trouble staff encountered. 'Telling the code' was useful to staff by converting problematic acts of residents into instances of a familiar pattern, into acts which were connected to plausible ends and other activities, into acts which were rational or reasonable, and into acts whose occurrence was not dependent on the specifics of any given staff–resident encounter or relationship. In this fashion, 'telling the code' gave staff a describable environment which was sufficiently structured so that they could rationally adapt to it, i.e. they could rationally adapt to it in the sense of generating plausible strategies for dealing with residents and plausible justifications for their own actions. For example, staff's description of residents as avoiding cooperating with staff in order to comply with the code requirement that they show their loyalty to one another justified staff's ordering residents to do things that would otherwise be 'voluntary' in the quasi-democratic environment of halfway house. 'Telling the code' provided staff with a useful way of talking about residents and themselves which portrayed both teams as more or less reasonable and more or less helpless to change the character of the relationship between the teams, because of the social-fact character (in Durkheim's sense) of the regularities made available by 'telling the code' which were none of anybody's specific doing or responsibility. [. . .]

It would appear that one *could* speak of the code as an 'oral tradition' which was employed to instruct outsiders (like myself and staff) as to the organized character of what they had seen, were seeing, or would see. That is, one *could* say that residents employed this narrative to point out that an event, or 'our relationship', or the behavior of that other resident, or the resident's own behavior were instances of patterns which were long-standing, which had been seen before, and which would be seen again. One would also then say that residents were telling the code in showing, or perhaps to show, that the particular event under consideration would have been enacted by 'any resident', because persons who were residents were morally constrained to act in that fashion. That is, the code was employed to explain why someone had acted as they had and that that way of acting was necessary under the circumstances. In brief, one would be saying that the code was employed by residents to analyse for outsiders and perhaps for themselves the 'social-fact' character of their circumstances, for they were noting particular occurrences as instances of regular-patterns-of-action-which-are-produced-by-compliance-to-a-normative-order. [. . .]

While one *could* propose such an analysis of the code as an exegetical organizing narrative, that would be something like a narrative which is offered by the tour guide of a museum or the narration for a travelogue film, to do so would be misleading. Such an analysis, if it simply left the matter here, would be misleading in precisely the ways that a travelogue narrative differs from the 'telling of the code'. Since I find the travelogue narrative helpful by contrast, let me indicate what I understand as its features. In the travelogue story of a voyage, one encounters the story shown on the screen and the identifications, explanations, and descriptions of the narrative heard over a loud speaker as discrete occurrences – narrative and picture. One hears the narrative as an outside commentary on the events depicted visually. In the case of 'purely narrative films', the sound track never cuts to ongoing conversation or other sounds of events shown visually. Whatever talk comes over the loud speaker, and all of that which comes over the loud speaker, is narrative. The narrative begins with the beginning of the film and 'completes itself' by the end. Whoever speaks on the sound track is doing narration. Typically, explanations are temporally juxtaposed to the scenic occurrences they explain. Finally, one listens to the narration and sees the film passively as a depicted scene for one's enjoyment or edification, not as an object that one must necessarily actively encounter and immediately deal with. Coupled with the feature of the passive audience, the narrator speaks for whoever listens. The parties hearing him are unknown to him, do not act upon his fate, and indeed have no involvement with him beyond their listening.

'Telling the code' contrasts with each of the above enumerated features of the travelogue narration. The crucial difference is that the code was not encountered 'outside' the scene, it was purportedly describing, but was told within that scene as a continuous, connected part of that scene by being manifested as an active consequential act within it.

The talk occurring in the halfway house that invoked the code, referred to the code, or relied on the code for its intelligibility, then, was not simply or merely a description of life in a halfway house. Instead, this talk was at the same time part of life in the halfway house, and it was a part that was itself included within the scope of things over which the code had jurisdiction. It is in this sense that talk involving the code was reflexive within the setting of its occurrence.

Persuasion and reflexive formulation

'Telling the code' as simultaneously formulating many aspects of the scene and having many consequences within that formulated scene

'Telling the code' was not heard as a 'disinterested' report delivered in the manner of a narrator who was speaking to unknown and distant persons about matters upon which they could not act. Instead, the code was being 'told' about matters which were critical to hearer and listener, because 'the telling' formulated and fed into their joint action. In contrast to that sort of narrative which is a description of the events displayed on a screen, the code was often 'told' about the immediate behavior of the hearer and teller. It was multi-formulative and multi-consequential in the immediate inter-action in which it was told and multi-formulative and multi-consequential in and for the occurrence of that interaction as an aspect of the social organization of the halfway house.

As a first step in explicating this multi-consequential and multi-formula-tive character of 'telling the code', let us examine the range of 'work' that a single utterance can accomplish. When talking with residents, staff and I often had a relatively friendly line of conversation terminated by a resident's saying, 'You know I won't snitch.' Hearing such an utterance functioned to re-crystalize the immediate interaction as the present center of one's experi-ential world. 'You know I won't snitch', multi-formulated the immediate environment, its surrounding social structures, and the connections between this interaction and the surrounding social structures.

1. It told what had just happened, for example, 'You just asked me to snitch.'

2. It formulated what the resident was doing in saying that phrase, for ex-ample, 'I am saying that this is my answer to your question. My answer is not to answer.'

3. It formulated the resident's motives for saying what he was saying and doing what he was doing, for example, 'I'm not answering in order to avoid snitching.' Since snitching was morally inappropriate for residents, the utterance, therefore, formulated the sensible and proper grounds of the re-fusal to answer the question.

4. It formulated (in the fashion of pointing to) the immediate relationship between the listener (staff or myself) and teller (resident) by re-locating the conversation in the context of the persisting role relationships between the parties, for example, 'For *you* to ask *me* that, would be asking me to snitch.' Thus saying, 'You know I won't snitch', operated as a re-enunciation, or a reminder of the role relationships involved and the appropriate relations be-tween members of those categories. It placed the ongoing occasion in the context of what both parties knew about their overriding trans-situational relationships.

5. It was *one more* formulation of the features of the persisting role relation-ship between hearer and teller, for example, 'You are an agent [or state re-searcher] and I am a resident-parolee. Some things you might ask me involve informing on my fellow residents. Residents do not inform on their fellows.

We call that snitching.' Besided reminding the participants of a trans-situational role relationship, the features of that trans-situational role relationship were originally and continuously formulated through such utterances as, 'You know I won't snitch.'

Beyond the multi-formulative character of this single utterance, it was also a consequential move in the very 'game' that it formulated. As a move in that field of action which it formulated, it pointed to the contingencies in that field as they were altered by *this* move. Furthermore, the utterance as a move obtained its sense and impact from those altered contingencies. Much of the persuasiveness of 'telling the code' consisted in its character as a move in the field of action which it also defined. By saying, 'You know I won't snitch,' (1) the resident negatively sanctioned the prior conduct of the staff member or myself. Saying that the question called for snitching was morally evaluating it and rebuffing me or the staff. The utterance (2) called for and almost always obtained a cessation of that line of the conversation. It was, therefore, consequential in terminating that line of talk. In terminating that line of talk, it (3) left me or staff ignorant of what we would have learned by the question had it been answered. And it (4) signalled the consequences of rejecting the resident's utterance or the course of action it suggested. By saying, 'You *know* I *won't* snitch', the resident pointed to what he would do if the staff persisted. He 'said' he would not comply, irrespective of the staff's wishes. He thereby warned that the conversation would turn nasty if staff or I did not retreat from the question. He also pointed to the staff's obligation (or my obligation) to be competent in the affairs of residents. To refuse to acknowledge the sense and appropriateness of the resident's response was to risk being seen as incompetent in the eyes of all other residents and staff. Finally, by noting that what was being requested was *snitching*, a resident pointed to the consequences for himself if he were to go ahead and answer the question. The potential consequences for him could include beatings and even death. Since staff was obliged to protect residents, this fate was also consequential for them. The potential consequences of refusing to accept the credibility of the resident's response made that response persuasive.

The details of the consequential persuasive character of 'Telling the code'

Staff regularly encountered residents' 'telling the code' as a way in which their questions and suggestions were answered. Residents explained why they had done something, what they would 'have to do' under various circumstances, and why they could not do what staff had asked of them by 'telling the code'. In group and in private encounters, staff was told by residents that, for example, 'I can't tell you that; that would be snitching.' And, for example, when one resident was asked to find another (his friend) who was absent from the house, he replied, 'It's not safe for me to interfere with someone's life; I can't be my brother's keeper.' When a staff member suggested that a resident organize a pool tournament, the resident answered, 'You know I can't organize the pool tournament, because it would look like I'm kissing ass.' Or, when several agents and I were discussing street prices of marijuana with a resident, he stopped the conversation by saying, 'I don't think that I had better tell you any more about the marijuana market, 'cause it would look like I'm joining your side.'

Replies to staff's suggestions and questions which were phrased in this way were interactionally sufficient to terminate the request, i.e. staff did not pursue the matter further. On the many occasions in which I heard residents make replies of this sort, I never saw staff question the relevance, legitimacy, or factual character of the reply, while I often saw staff question other kinds of replies in just those terms. When a resident proposed that he did not want to do something because it was an inefficient use of his time, or that he had some other obligation which he had to meet instead, or that he preferred to do something else, etc., staff often challenged the relevance and/or truthfulness of the resident's story.

Thus, a resident's naming of a proposed act (such as the act of telling staff something or the act of participating in something) as a code-relevant event was a practically adequate answer to staff's requests, i.e. it effectively countered a request or demand in such a way that the resident was not required by staff to justify his refusal further. Moreover, on many occasions, staff not only 'heard the code' and accepted it, but also acceded to residents' requests when the code was offered as grounds for action. This is illustrated in the following observations.

On many occasions, I saw residents attempt to obtain release from the halfway house before they had met the conditions for release, i.e. before they had obtained a job and paid their bill. Residents told their agents and house staff that they could save money by living elsewhere. They complained that they found it difficult to abstain from using drugs when others around them were using. Some black residents complained that the chicanos would have nothing to do with them and that they were, therefore, very uncomfortable at the house. Other residents argued that they could get a job more quickly if they lived with their relatives, who would lend assistance and supply transportation in finding a job. Staff did not acknowledge these grounds as acceptable. However, when the resident Pablo told his agent that he was afraid that another resident thought that he was a snitch, stemming from an incident some years before, the agent had Pablo released from halfway house in light of Pablo's fears about what the other resident would do, even though he had no job and had not yet paid his bill. When the agent spoke about the incident with other staff members and with me, he insisted that we understand that Pablo was not really a snitch.

Whenever 'telling the code' occurred, it was consequential. [Earlier], we saw that when a staff member 'told the code' to other staff members, he did so as a method of managing his relationships with his colleagues. It served to relieve staff members of some of their responsibilities for motivating residents to participate in the program. It tempered staff's obligation to be knowledgeable about the affairs of residents, since they could explain their ignorance by referring to residents' unwillingness to cop out or snitch. A staff member could defeat a proposal for the program by 'telling the code' to show that the proposal was 'unrealistic'. 'Telling the code' served to defend staff and staff ideas against the complaints of residents. It was also consequential in justifying staff's control over residents and staff's unwillingness to trust or give responsibilities to residents.

When residents 'told the code' to staff, it had a similar consequentiality. In the cases we have just examined, one resident avoided looking for his friend, many avoided answering staff's questions, another avoided organizing a pool tournament, and Pablo obtained release from the halfway house without getting a job and without paying his bill.[4] In each of these cases, the specifics of the 'telling of the code' *could* have been motivated by the anticipated consequences, and 'plainly' the consequences occasioned the *fact* of the telling. For example, the resident who told staff that organizing the pool tournament would have been an act of 'joining their side' might have elaborated, perhaps even invented, a provision of the code to deal with the contingency of being asked by staff to do something for other residents, when he 'actually' chose not to organize the pool tournament because he believed that that activity would be personally unrewarding. A resident might have alluded to the code's prohibition against snitching in terminating a conversation with me in a bar, not because I had inadvertently asked him to snitch, but because he had pressing business with others there and wanted to be rid of me. One might imagine that these contingencies were so standardized as to have been well 'codified' and required the residents to turn down the requests. Nevertheless, the fact that they were confronted by a request and

4. Even the consequences have consequences. By offering such accounts of their behavior and their circumstances to staff, residents effectively dealt with staff demands that they say more about what they and their fellows were really doing. These accounts effectively dealt with staff demands that residents willingly participate in staff-sponsored activities and that they become involved in planning and carrying out the program. In general, the accumulation of incidents in which 'telling the code' defeated staff's plans and staff's tendency to foresee such defeats meant that staff's actual demands for resident participation were reduced well below the level called for in the program plan. This was so to such an extent that the actual round of activities at halfway house only vaguely resembled the program plan.

wanted or 'needed' to turn it down occasioned 'telling the code' in the fashion that it was actually told.

Even when the code was being told 'neutrally' in a situation in which what was being talked about was not an issue, as was the case when I or a novice agent probed a parolee about the code in general, the fact of the telling was itself an event which, when understood in terms of the code, was special and meant that the parolee was being friendly by 'telling the code'. Furthermore, the telling was of generalized consequentiality in the ways that it informed me or the agent of the proper limits of our action.

The visible consequentiality of 'telling the code' and its 'open, flexible structure' (which gives it the capacity to explain a very wide range of events) raises the possibility that what was being told in 'telling the code' was manufactured by the teller for the occasion in order to bring about just those consequences. From the standpoint of the teller, the visible consequentiality and the 'open, flexible structure' of 'telling the code' *invite* the free invention of the specifics of a given instance of 'telling the code' in order to bring about some set of consequences. This suggestion might be countered with the argument that neither the staff nor I were so naïve as not to suspect that possibility and would not have permitted ourselves to be 'led down the primrose path' quite so easily. At the very least, we made a judgement about the story as told and its 'fit' with what we had learned about the code thus far. Yet, as we have seen, 'telling the code', like every other collection of rules in use, had an open, flexible structure or, in Garfinkel's terms, had an etcetera clause.[5] It did not consist of a fixed set of maxims, nor did any given maxim (i.e. stated at a given time) have a definite scope of application. In every case in which the code was mentioned (literally 'heard to have been mentioned', since the mentioning was not usually named as such), it was up to the hearer to identify the 'telling of the code' as 'telling the code' and to search out and discover the linkages between 'this telling' and what he understood to be the code. Moreover, the hearer was in the position of having to depend on this same telling and others of no more definite character to tell him of what the code consisted in the first place. The hearer was not in a position to make 'harsh judgements' about the relevance of any specific telling to what he understood as a proper 'telling of the code'. This is not to suggest that any proposal whatsoever would have been acceptable, but just how such judge-

5. The etcetera clause refers to an unspecified condition of rules-in-use wherein present occurrences which were 'unforeseen in' or 'unpredicted by' some prior formulation of a rule or agreement are none the less brought under the auspices of that rule or agreement and are seen by witnesses to the occurrence as being in compliance with that rule or agreement. Etcetera and other 'ad hocing' practices have been an important theme of ethnomethodological research. See Bittner (1963), Garfinkel (1967, chs. 1 and 3), Wieder (1970) and Zimmerman (1970).

ments would have been rendered is, at the least, open to considerable manipulation, since the open, flexible structure of the code precludes the possibility of comparing some present story with what is definitely known about what a 'telling of the code' should consist of.

The thesis that residents actively manipulated staff's understanding of what was going on around them cannot be easily defeated.[6] It does not require that we imagine that the residents told one 'line' to the staff and the researcher while holding in reserve some hidden knowledge of what the code 'really' after all consisted. The ways in which residents learned the code may well be of the same character as the ways in which staff and researcher learned that code. What can be supposed about such matters on the basis of what has been observed suggests that this would be precisely the case. Moreover, when inmates or criminals do 'tell the code' to each other, it would have a parallel consequentiality. In every case of 'telling the code', the teller may have been motivated to formulate it so that it furthered his immediate interactional interests.

Since 'telling the code' was taken seriously (by me and by staff) as an active part of the environment, it did not simply describe, analyse, and explain the environment, but was as well a way in which residents (and staff, when they 'told the code') guided conduct through effective persuasion. The code operated as a device for stopping or changing the topic of a conversation. It was a device for legitimately declining a suggestion or order. It was a device for urging or defeating a proposed course of action. It was a device for accounting for why one should feel or act in the way that one did as an expectable, understandable, reasonable, and above all else acceptable way of acting or feeling. It was, therefore, a way of managing a course of conversation in such a way as to present the teller (or his colleague) as a reasonable, moral, and competent fellow. The code, then, is much more a *method* of moral persuasion and justification than it is a substantive account of an organized way of life. It is a way, or set of ways, of causing activities to be seen as morally, repetitively, and constrainedly organized.

This means that inasmuch as the way that alter's activity appears to ego as coherently organized and meaningful is dependent on the ways alter talks about what he is doing, ego's sense for what alter is doing is contingent upon whatever 'goals', 'projects', or 'interests' alter attempts to realize in or through his interaction with ego. For example, the fact that a resident's activity appears to a parole agent as a more or less clear instance of 'refusing to participate as a means of showing other residents that one is trustworthy' depends on the talk that this or other residents have done. That they talked

6. The thesis that staff members manipulated each others' understanding in the attempt to justify their own actions, strategies, or proposals is subject to the same kinds of argument.

in the way they did and in turn caused the agent to have that impression was dependent on what they were trying to accomplish in their interaction with the agent, for example trying to avoid participation or present themselves as 'good parolees'. Guided perception through description has the character of being subject to 'interests' in this way, because the same explanatory and descriptive utterances often are, and always can be, sanctions, justifications, or urgings of some course of action in the relationship between hearer and speaker. [...]

'Telling the code' as a guide to perception: the inner structure of social reality

That form of detailed ethnographic reportage upon which [earlier sections] were based shows *that* 'telling the code' created a social reality for persons who heard it and shows some of the ways in which 'telling the code' was persuasive and consequential. To show *how* 'telling the code' was productive of a social world of real events and to show *how* talk could be heard as 'telling the code', however, requires a closer look at experience than ethnographic reportage as ordinarily practiced can provide. It requires a description of how some participant at the halfway house went about the task of understanding what he heard and saw as he was hearing and seeing it. We turn to my own experiences as such (in contrast to the scenes, objects, and persons that I experienced), because there is no other place to go if we need access to an ongoing course of direct experience. That is, it requires a turn from a description of those objects which were experienced by the ethnographer to a description of the course of experiencing those occurrences *as* objects.

The code as a reflexive self- and setting-elaborative device

To further the discussion of the properties of each instance of 'telling the code', a return to a contrast between 'telling the code' and the travelogue narrative will be helpful. Unlike the travelogue narrative which, as the sound track of a film, is quickly recognizable as a commentary on that film, the recognition that some utterance was a 'telling of the code' often required active discovery on the part of the hearer. Only occasionally was an eligible utterance explicitly identified by the teller as 'telling the code'. The fact that one sometimes heard a title (The Code) only promised that there was a code to be discovered and that somehow it would have general patterns of behavior associated with it, i.e. general patterns in contrast to the particular concrete event the teller was describing or explaining. The code, as I found it, was told 'piecemeal', came from many sources, and was not necessarily temporally juxtaposed with the objects that it was purportedly about. Moreover, when residents were self-announcedly 'telling the code', they also explicitly said or implied that there was more to it than was being told at that time. Thus, in several ways, what the talk was 'about' and what further instances of that talk were, were for the listener to discover. The discovery of the organized and coherent sense of the residents' behavior, though even persuasively assisted by the residents' talking, was the task of finding particulars or instances for a title. Showing just how this is the case requires an even more detailed consideration of the way in which I, as a sociologist, formulated my description of the convict code.

The documentary method of interpretation

Equipped with what I understood to be a preliminary and partial version of the residents' definition of their situation (which was contained in the title, 'The Code', and several maxims), I saw that other pronouncements of residents were untitled extensions of this same line of talk. I used whatever 'pieces' of the code I had collected at that point as a scheme for interpreting further talk as extensions of what I had heard 'up to now'. Garfinkel (1967, p. 78), following Mannheim, calls this kind of procedure 'the documentary method of interpretation', describing it in the following terms:

The method consists of treating an actual appearance as 'the document of', as 'pointing to', as 'standing on behalf of' a presupposed underlying pattern. Not only is the underlying pattern derived from its individual documentary evidences, but the individual documentary evidences, in their turn, are interpreted on the basis of 'what is known' about the underlying pattern. Each is used to elaborate the other.

An example of the use of this method is provided by the interpretation of a remark I overheard during my first week at halfway house. I passed a resident who was wandering through the halls after the committee meetings on Wednesday night. He said to staff and all others within hearing, 'Where can I find that meeting where I can get an overnight pass?' On the basis of what I had already learned, I understood him to be saying, 'I'm not going to that meeting because I'm interested in participating in the program of halfway house. I'm going to that meeting just because I would like to collect the reward of an overnight pass and for no other reason. I'm not a kiss-ass. Everyone who is in hearing distance should understand that I'm not kissing up to staff. My behavior really is in conformity with the code, though without hearing this (reference to an overnight pass), you might think otherwise.' I thereby collected another 'piece' of talk which, when put together with utterances I had heard up to that point (which permitted me to see the 'sense' of this remark) and used with utterances I had yet to collect, was employed by me to formulate the general maxim, 'Show your loyalty to the residents.'

The scope of the maxim concerning loyalty was further elaborated a month or so later, when I attended a Monday night group. A resident had suggested that a baseball team be formed. He was then asked by the group leader (the program director) to organize the team himself. He answered, 'You know I can't organize a baseball team.' The program director nodded, and the matter was settled. Using my ethnography of the code as a scheme of interpretation, I heard him say, 'You know that the code forbids me to participate in your program in that way, and you know that I'm not going to violate the code. So why ask me?'

In this fashion, I employed my collection of 'pieces' as a self-elaborating schema. Each newly encountered 'piece' of talk was simultaneously rendered sensible by interpreting it in terms of the developing relevancies of the code and was, at the same time, more evidence of the existence of that code. Furthermore, the interpreted 'piece' then functioned as part of the elaborated schema itself and was used in the interpretation of still further 'pieces' of talk.

At each step, the interpretation was based on what was known thus far. If I had not had the general idea of the code as an interpretive device for translating utterances into maxims of a moral order, I could not have collected those utterances together as expressions of the same underlying pattern. Seeing an utterance as an expression of an underlying moral order depended on knowing *some* of the particulars of that underlying order to begin with. In the case of the convict code, having the title, 'The Code', as supplied by residents and a statement of several maxims, also supplied by residents, provided enough material initially to formulate a tentative schema. This tentative schema 'elaborated itself' as I used it to identify and elaborate the sense of objects and events in the setting. The self-same perceptual-analytic procedure simultaneously elaborated the code and the setting as the code was employed by me as a schema. Since the use-of-the-code-as-a-schema *was* the procedure, the code was self- and setting-elaborative. In this sense, it is much more appropriate to think of the code as a continuous, ongoing process, rather than as a set of stable elements of culture which endure through time. In Zimmerman and Pollner's (1970) terms, the code is an *occasioned corpus* of 'cultural elements', rather than a *stable set* of itemizable elements which reoccur in, or endure through, a collection of successive occasions.

Code events and code accounts as indexical expressions which operate as 'parts' of a Gestalt-contexture

A further feature of this method of 'fact gathering' or 'reality production' is the fact that the 'pieces' collected by means of this method were indexical expressions (Garfinkel, 1967, pp. 4–7; Garfinkel and Sacks, 1970). To say that the pieces were indexical expressions is to say that their meaning was relative to such contextual matters as (a) who was saying it (e.g., that it was a resident); (b) to whom it was being said (e.g., to a staff member or, e.g., myself being treated as an auxiliary of the staff); (c) where it was being said (e.g., in the halfway house); (d) on what kind of occasion it was being said (e.g., in a meeting attended by both staff and residents); (e) the social relationship between teller and hearer (e.g., a parolee speaking to his parole agent); and so forth. My understanding of these utterances depended as well on their association with behaviors that were seen as referents of this talk, but this matter will be taken up after these initial determinations are clarified.

If the remark, 'You know I can't organize the baseball team', had been uttered by one staff member *vis-à-vis* another staff member, I would have heard the remark as something else entirely. Depending on *which* staff member was talking and *which* staff member was listening, the remark could have been heard as, 'You know that it is your job, since you are on the recreation committee and I am not.' Had it been a case-carrying parole agent who was on the recreation committee speaking to the program director, I would have heard (and presume that the program director would have heard) the remark as, 'You know that I am already putting more time into the program than I can afford as it is; I couldn't possibly do more.'

Or, had the remark been uttered by a resident to a staff member outside the context of their staff–resident relationship (as might be the case if both belonged to some other organization and were talking to each other as members of that organization), the remark could easily have been heard as, 'I don't know enough about baseball or organizing to organize the baseball team.' If I had known nothing about the code, the remark might well have been heard in just the same way it would have been heard 'outside the context of the setting'. These hypothetical examples show that each and every one of the utterances upon which the code (or *any* code) was based has no single sense. This means, in turn, that they have no self-evident or self-explanatory sense. Instead, the utterances as 'pieces' have a sense as constituent parts of the setting in the manner that a constituent part of a Gestalt-contexture has functional significance. Gurwitsch (1964, pp. 134–5) writes:

Since each part of a Gestalt-contexture is defined and qualified by its functional significance, and since the functional significance of each part essentially refers to those of other parts, there is thoroughgoing *interdependence* among all parts or constituents of a Gestalt-contexture. To be integrated into a contexture of Gestalt-character, a constituent must exist at a certain locus within, and have a certain function for, the contexture. . . . Between the parts or constituents of a Gestalt-contexture, there prevails the particular relationship of *Gestalt-coherence* defined as *the determining and conditioning of the constituents upon each other* [with respect to the meaning of each constituent]. *In thoroughgoing reciprocity the constituents assign to, and derive from, one another the functional significance* [meaning] which gives to each one its qualification in a concrete case. In this sense, the constituents may be said to exist through each other; each retaining its qualified existence only if and as long as the others have theirs. The existence of any constituent of a Gestalt-contexture relies upon other constituents or, to put it differently, each constituent has its existence only within a *system of functional significances* which all complement and fit with, one another. . . .

From the interdependence and interdetermination of the parts of a Gestalt-contexture, it follows that if a part is extracted from its contexture and transformed into an element . . . the part may undergo most radical modifications. Since its functional significance is no longer determined by references to other constituents, the extracted part may cease to be what it phenomenally was.

Each utterance upon which my analysis of the code was based was meaningful in the ways that it was said-socially-in-a-context. Each utterance gave sense to the context and obtained sense from its place in that context in exactly the same way that a part of a Gestalt-contexture (e.g., the left-hand member of a pair of dots) obtains its sense (e.g., as a left-hand member rather than as an isolated dot) by its perceived relationship to the other parts of the contexture (e.g., the right-hand member) while giving those other members their sense through their perceived relation to it. We have already seen that an instance of 'telling the code' (e.g., 'You know I won't snitch'), in being uttered, defined the present phase of the relationship between staff and residents, while obtaining its clear sense (for each participant) from its place in that same relationship as it had developed, an understanding of which was partially formulated through prior similar utterances and acts and further elaborated and fulfilled by the present utterance. In this context it should be noted that the mutual elaboration of 'underlying pattern' and 'documentary evidence' within the documentary method of interpretation has the same formal structure as the mutual determination of meaning (the functional significance) of parts of a Gestalt-contexture.

For the present argument, the most interesting determining and conditioning of constituents upon each other exists between the 'behavior patterns' that the code was understood to be describing, analysing, and explaining, on the one hand, and an instance or formulation of 'telling the code', on the other. The embedded character of members' talk and the embedded character of instructions or guides to perception can be most clearly seen in the analysis of this 'referential' Gestalt-contexture. [. . .] Here we can see that our perception or analysis that members are acting in patterned and motivationally coherent ways is dependent on an instructed seeing of those ways of behaving. The 'instruction' is accomplished from within a setting for an observer who attends to the ways that members talk about their affairs. The mutual dependencies and determination of the parts of a Gestalt-contexture are apparent in the ways that attending to someone's talk as 'instruction' is itself dependent on seeing, in actual perception, the referential objects of their talk for that talk to be identified as a 'course of instruction' and identified for its specific sense.[7] On the other hand, what those objects are that the talk is about depends in turn on the ways that one is 'instructed' to see them.

The relative determinacy of sense of code events and code accounts

The ways a course of observation is involved in and relies upon these mutually determining dependencies can be seen in a detailed consideration of the way in which I arrived at portions of my formulation of the convict code and by hypothetically 'extracting' the data (utterances and behaviors) from their contexture and transforming them into elements. By use of this adaptation of the phenomenological method,[8] it will be seen that had I been unable to rely on the reflexive, embedded character of accounts (upon which I based my formulation of the code), many unresolvable problems of analysis would have been encountered. We shall see that:

1. Had I attempted to formulate the code on the basis of resident talk alone,[9] I could not have decided which parts of their talk were 'telling the code'.

2. If I had observed the same setting, but was deprived of the talk within it, I could not have seen which behaviors went together as 'instances' of the same pattern of behavior and which were being produced by compliance to the same rule.

7. It may well be the case that the full circle of dependencies of talk and its objects is a characteristic of the social world in ways that are not the case for what we typically regard as the physical world. One could argue that order and meaning in the social world is always dependent on the observability of motivated action. Motives are necessarily hidden in ways that no element of the physical world is hidden. This means that the ostensive showing of a motive cannot extend beyond the plausible connection between some kind of statement of a goal and a visible action.

8. The procedure is referred to in the phenomenological literature as the method of free variation (see Spiegelberg, 1960, vol. 2, pp. 655–701).

9. The proposal has a potentially unclear sense if it is interpreted as meaning that an observer with a transcript would fit the conditions of the proposal. This would not always be the case, since conversationalists attend to each other's utterances as actions and sometimes 'formulate' what they are doing in talking in those terms. In such cases, the observer might find the 'referents' of the talk in the transcript itself. Garfinkel and Sacks (1970, p. 346) provide an example:

JH Isn't it nice there's such a crowd of you in the office?
SM (You're asking us to leave, not telling us to leave, right?)

In the parenthesized sentence, the 'referent' is in the previous conversationalist's utterance. I mean to exclude such cases in the proposal such that the observer examines a transcript or hears a tape in only a 'referential' way, listening to what the conversationalists are talking about and excluding from his attention the varieties of ways that the same talk can be understood as interactional acts, for example in the fashion that Bales might treat it.

3. If I had somehow developed all of the maxims of the code, but otherwise was deprived of the talk within it, I could not have seen which behaviors went together as 'instances' of the same pattern of behavior and which were being produced by compliance to the same rule.

4. If I had somehow developed all of the maxims of the code, but otherwise was ignorant of the setting, I could not have deduced or derived a description of a single set of behavioral outcomes that would be the product of complying with those maxims, but instead would have produced many such competitive sets.

5. If I had somehow developed a description of all of the behaviors analysed as to types of behavior (for example 'doing distance' or 'doing passive compliance'), I still could not have inferred a *single* set of rules which would analyse those behaviors as the outcome of complying with that set of rules, but instead would have produced many competitive sets of rules.

These circumstances can be examined by returning to the remark, 'You know I can't organize the baseball team', and the rule it was seen to express, 'Show your loyalty to the residents.' The remark is seeable as 'telling the code' in its discovered juxtaposition with some fulfilling, associated behaviors, i.e. behaviors which can be understood as complying with the rule that the remark expresses. In this particular case, the remark, in fact, was uttered in a Monday night group in which residents did respond, when asked, with suggestions for program modifications and additions. With overwhelming typicality, however, residents did not volunteer or even agree to take part in the organizational work that any additions to the program would imply. When the remark in question was uttered in that behavioral context, it was seeable as an expression of the underlying rule, 'Show your loyalty to the residents.' The rule, thereby, not only accounted for the refusal of this particular resident to volunteer at this time, but also accounted for the general pattern of not volunteering. I had tentatively assembled the rule before this point and had already observed that it seemed to prohibit residents from helping staff with their work. In this instance, volunteering to assist in resident-oriented programs and even resident-initiated programs was seen to fall under the auspices of the general rule. That is, hearing the remark served to specify some of the applications of the rule, 'Show your loyalty....'

Had I not witnessed a series of Monday night group sessions, however, I could have alternatively imagined that residents typically did volunteer to organize recreational activities, or at least their own recreational activities. Such a possibility could not have been dismissed by merely attending to what the residents were talking about on the particular Monday night in question. In light of this possible and plausible context of volunteering, the remark could be heard as a statement of a personal exemption, rather than as an expression of a rule, for example, 'You know that I cannot volunteer to organize the baseball team.' In the latter interpretation, the expression implies that the person spoken to (but not necessarily other persons hearing the remark) knows something about the speaker which makes it inappropriate for him to organize the baseball team.

In the absence of the prior observations about volunteering, either understanding of the remark is equally plausible. Equipped with a collection of prior observations, however, the hearer is led or guided to hear the remark as a statement of a rule.

The observer's work of transforming remarks into statements of rules, or the task of simply hearing talk as expressions of rules, depends on the observer's discovery of some set of behaviors which are the fulfillment of those rules.[10] In that juxtaposition, utterance and behavior obtain their sense as a statement-of-a-rule and an instance-of-a-pattern-of-behavior. That is, one can see an utterance as a rule with a determinate sense by locating those behaviors which would be the outcome of complying with such a rule.

The observer's collection of actual instances of behavior into categorized types of behavior is dependent on hearing members' talk. Through the residents' talk, I was able tentatively to formulate what their 'rules' might be. The preformulated or tentatively formulated rules which were based on residents' talk permitted me to see what motives any particular behavioral display was likely to be 'expressing'. This permitted me (and would permit any other observer) to organize particular behaviors into coherent, classifiable types of behavior. That is, knowing something of the rules by means of resident talk would tell an observer something of the kinds of motives he would encounter in the setting. On knowing what kind of motives he might find, an observer would then be able to see the meanings of behaviors he had encountered. Without supposing something about typical motives, the particular concrete behaviors are equivocal in their sense, i.e. any particular display could be cogently depicted as contrastive kinds of acts.

If one motivational scheme is replaced with another, the perceptual field is potentially altered in such a way as radically to recompose the perceived organization of the scene. Two disparate behaviors which had heretofore been seen as going together as instances of the same behavior, because they

10. The discovery of the behaviors which give an utterance its rule-like character need not occur simultaneously with the utterance itself. In the example that I propose, the utterance was retrospectively used, i.e. the behaviors had occurred before the utterance. It could just as well have occurred prospectively such that the observer would find that he had previously uncovered a remark that was a rule on the occasion of observing behaviors which could be seen as that remark-as-a-rule's fulfillment. The temporal features of this kind of discovery are treated in Garfinkel's discussion of the documentary method of interpretation (Garfinkel, 1967, pp. 89–90). Further empirical investigation of these features may be found in McHugh (1968).

were both expressions of the same underlying motive, might no longer have a 'perceptual affinity' for one another and be seen as expressing two different motives. Similarly, two disparate behaviors which were heretofore seen as instances of two different patterns might now be seen as instances of the same pattern. [. . .] Thus, how the behaviors are seen as motivated conduct is dependent on some supposed motivational scheme (in cases like this, one supplied by rule) which is itself dependent for its determinacy on hearing talk.

If the list of maxims which made up the code were 'extracted' from their contextural juxtaposition with the behaviors they explain, one could not theoretically generate (1) a set of behaviors which matched the observed behaviors and justify not generating others that were, in fact, not observed, and (2) could not generate a *single* complementary set of behaviors and justify this 'prediction'. If one simply knew that residents were supposed to show their loyalty to other residents as an 'in-group' opposed to the 'out-group' of staff, he could plausibly 'predict' that they would thereby:

1. Assume a distinctive style of dress and talk which set them apart from staff and any others,

2. Take every opportunity to show their distaste for staff through, e.g., impoliteness,

3. Never talk to staff,

4. Not engage in attacks on one another either verbally or physically, or attack one another's property, as in stealing,

5. Not inform on one another.

These plausible 'predictions' would be correct with respect to informing, would be partially correct with respect to 'not attacking one another' in terms of verbal and physical abuse, but would not be correct with respect to stealing from one another. The other plausible predictions would be wrong.[11]

If some of the behaviors actually proposedly encompassed by this rule are examined, the nonpredictability of the behaviors is even more dramatic. From the rule, 'Show your loyalty to the residents', how should an analyst propose that residents would sit at group? Would they be 'tense and hostile' in their posture, or would they be so relaxed as to appear disinterested? How should he expect them to respond to requests put forth by the staff? Would they be very resistant to direct orders and less resistant to permissively given

11. While it was the case that staff and residents did dress differently, inasmuch as residents dressed like other working class Mexican-Americans in the neighborhood and staff dressed in coat and tie, when residents had occasion to 'dress up' as they did for Mexican Independence Day, they did not dress in ways that distinguished them from staff.

suggestions that they do something, or would they undertake no action unless they were 'forced' to do so? In both of these instances, either chosen alternative would be equally plausible interpretations in terms of the same rule, even though the alternatives propose opposite actions. This means that while one could take the rule and a set of actually occurring concrete behaviors and see that those behaviors could have been produced as outcomes of compliance with that rule, the rule in itself does not tell the investigator what to expect. Instead of 'predicting' behavior, the rule is actually employed as an interpretive device. It is employed by an observer to render any behavior he encounters intelligible, i.e. as coherent in terms of patterned motivation. However, in their 'natural' contextural location among the behaviors they explain, rules are *experienced* as predictive. Perceived behaviors are immediately rendered intelligible and *familiar* in their seen juxtaposition with an already known rule. This experienced predictiveness of the rule, which renders unforeseen behaviors familiar, is a consequence of the 'open, flexible structure' of (or the etcetera clause of) codes of conduct.

Conversely, if the descriptions of resident behaviors which were already analysed and classified as to types were 'extracted' from the context of surrounding talk, a *single* set of rules which would analyse and explain these behaviors could not be inferred. Instead, the analyst would find that he could produce a variety of plausible and competitive sets of rules. This can be seen by considering the behaviors I have classified as 'doing disinterest and disrespect'. This collection of behaviors included the typical patterns of slouching at group, dressing for group with extreme casualness, directing one's attention away from the topic of the group by eye movements, being unresponsive to inquiries and suggestions of the group leader, holding side conversations, shining one's shoes, moving in and out of the group, and verbally degrading the goals of the group. In my analysis, I explained these behaviors as a means to realizing the code's injunction, 'Show your loyalty to the residents.' In that analysis, one's loyalty to the resident group is demonstrated by a rejection of the staff group by 'doing disinterest and disrespect' toward staff programs and proposals. However, by depriving ourselves of the guidance of resident talk in formulating plausible rules (in this case, 'Show your loyalty . . .'), we could just as plausibly propose, among a variety of possibilities, that 'doing disinterest and disrespect' was action in compliance with the stylistic maxim, 'Be cool.' Compliance with the maxim, 'Be cool', requires that one show his dominance over his circumstances by suppressing any show of affect and interest in occurrences in his situation. Persons complying with such a rule do so out of motivations to obtain the *respect* and *admiration* of their fellows, in contrast to motivations to obtain the *trust* of their fellows, which is the motivation to comply with the maxim, 'Show your loyalty to the residents.'

Moreover, an analyst who was open to other kinds of explanations of the described and classified behaviors besides their possible contra-cultural production could easily discover and portray those aspects of the halfway house regime which would produce apathy or depression in the residents. For example, the residents' material circumstances were degrading when compared to those of their non-parolee friends; their occupational prospects were not bright; the program could be represented as dull and uninteresting; etc.

To reiterate, an analyst faced with the task of inspecting an array of classified behaviors of residents in order to generate theoretically a set of rules or conditions which would produce those patterned behaviors could easily do so. He would find, however, that without the guidance of resident talk, he could have many competitive sets of rules and conditions, and he would have no way of arguing which single set among the many were, in fact, operative in the setting. [...]

The theory of interests reconsidered

The facts that the accounting work of 'telling the code' defined the immediate environment of hearer and teller, that it was interactionally consequential in that environment, and that it had an open, flexible structure invited its manipulation by the teller. He could, after all, pursue his immediate interests in the interaction by freely inventing a clause to, or a particular interpretation of, the code in a specific 'telling'. 'Telling the code' masked what was 'really going on' at the halfway house – what was 'really going on' was residents' pursuing their immediate interests by fabricating instances of 'telling the code' which deceived me and the staff.

While the theory of interests may be appealing in its potential for debunking sociological theory, methods, and findings, any specific 'theory of interests' cannot be stronger than the 'theory of the convict code'. For, as I shall now argue, any attempt to specify interests is subject to the same equivocalities as specifying the maxims (or a maxim) of the code and would be accomplished through the same formal apparatus as employed in specifying the convict code. The crucial point is that while the 'open, flexible structure of the code' permits the possibility that in any particular case, the staff (or an observer) could have been manipulatively taken in by a 'false' statement of the code, 'interests' have an open, flexible structure as well. This means that in every particular case of 'telling the code', some assertion specifying the underlying 'interests' or underlying maxim of the code could be discovered – limited only by the inventiveness of the observer. Just as it is so that in every particular case of 'telling the code' it can be shown that 'telling the code' *in one way or another* advances a resident's interests, it can be shown as well that he was merely speaking consistently with what had been said by others about the code 'thus far'.

These stubborn equivocalities do not arise from the substance of 'interests' or the 'maxims of the code'. We encounter them, rather, by reason of our methods of understanding talk and action, i.e. by reason of the character of our use of embedded instructions (or any other scheme of interpretation employed within the documentary method of interpretation). The way in which we see that someone is acting or speaking consistently with the code has many formal properties in common with the way in which we see that someone is acting or speaking consistently with his interests. [. . .]

Any explicit, i.e. codified, 'theory of interests' generated either within or outside the setting could serve the same interpretive functions. In its use as a scheme of interpretation, such a theory would have the same properties. It would be employed to identify instances of some type of conduct and to connect one form of conduct to another, and in that use, its own meaning would be fulfilled, modified, and elaborated as well. Thus, analysing action by reference to 'interests' is formally identical to an analysis which is accomplished by reference to 'telling the code'. The character and adequacy of explanations having this form is [our next] topic. Though the argument concerns verbalized moral orders such as the convict code, a vision of social reality like that entailed in the 'theory of interests' is subject to all the same considerations as soon as someone conceives of and verbalizes it. Choosing between the two theories finally becomes a matter of preference, for a strong, empirically based choice between them is, in principle, unavailable, even though each is 'demonstrable-for-all-practical-purposes'. [. . .]

As a sanctioned method of interpretation, the code differs from a 'scientific' explanation of actual patterns of resident conduct in several important respects. Its employment simultaneously identifies and 'explains' the particular events it renders observable. In using the code as an explanation, parties to the setting interactionally identify the sense of a particular event as an intersubjectively recognized occurrence by effectively asserting that the event stems from adherence to the convict code. The particular occurrence has its sense as part of a pattern, because it can be explained as stemming from constantly operating motivational sources.

The code, and by extension any other normative order, cannot be an adequate explanation of patterns of action under the requirements of a deductive theory, because in its explanatory uses, situations, actions, and rules are not independent elements. The utterances and behaviors upon which the code (or any other normative order) is based have no self-evident or self-explanatory sense in isolation from one another. Instead, they have a relative definite sense as constituent parts of an actually witnessed, concrete setting in the way that each is a constituent within a system of functional significances. That is, situations, actions, and rules determine one another's sense as constituent parts of a Gestalt-contexture.

Also in this connection, situations, actions, and rules cannot be literally described, because the clear sense that each achieves in its contexture is contingent upon the concrete, historical, and ongoing course of experience of some particular observer. Part of the contexture of any present display is located within the accumulated prior experience of the observer and is known by him in a largely implicit and indefinite fashion. This fact would undercut any effort to specify definitively the explicit features that are sufficient conditions for classifying occasions or behaviors as members of the classes of situations and actions. Thus, the requirement of literal description for deductive theory cannot be met.

With respect to descriptions of the convict code and the behaviors it 'explains', every maxim and every list of maxims, as well as every 'explained' behavior and every list of 'explained' behaviors, are offered as illustrative of the kinds of maxims and kinds of behaviors that the code explains.[12] What sociologists describe as the convict code in their writings is one further *instance* of the product which results from the practices of 'telling the code'. Such accounts have the same logical status that 'telling the code' has in the very settings in which the code is told. Further, to the extent that social scientists' accounts are read and treated as a source of advice or justification by persons in those settings, their accounts have the same phenomenal status as well.[13]

Thus, 'telling the code', and any particular instance of formulating the code, *exhibits*, rather than describes or explains, the order that members achieve through their practices of showing and telling each other that particular encountered features are typical, regular, orderly, coherent, motivated out of considerations of normative constraint, and the like.

The problems encountered in describing and explaining social action hinge in part on the notion that, on the one hand, there is an event in the world, a social action, and on the other, another event which is the description of that action and the method of producing that description. This dualism – which is an instance of the subject–object dualism – generates the issue of the veridicality of the description and, in the context of science, the necessity of literal description.

The abandonment of the dualism leads to the single phenomenon, an

12. The code, thus, has the features that Garfinkel has elaborated at length in his unpublished discussions of 'a collection of instructions' and their properties, P, and that Zimmerman and Pollner (1970, pp. 93–9) describe as an 'occasioned corpus'.

13. It seems likely that many sociologists' accounts of prison culture and the convict code have, in fact, been read in this way. It is clear that Clemmer's *The Prison Community* has been. Gill (1965), writing as a prison administrator, cites Clemmer as providing a cogent formulation of what prison life is really like and employs that formulation to argue with his colleagues for changes in prison organization which might alter that way of life.

account-of-social-action, or an accounting-of-social-action. 'Telling the code', and more critically the work of 'telling the code', is in this view a course of accounting which yields an account-of-resident-behavior which, on the occasion of constructing the account, makes that occasion, the behaviors in it, and the normative order 'behind it' observable and reportable as patterned, recurrent, and connected instances of motivated actions in socially standardized situations.

Accountings-of-social-action, for example, 'telling and hearing the code', are methods of giving and receiving embedded instructions for seeing and describing a social order. The interpersonal existence of social orders and their availability to perception and description is the achievement of the various methods entailed in an accounting-of-social-action.

References

BITTNER, E. (1963), 'Radicalism and the organization of radical movements', *American Sociological Review*, vol. 28.

GARFINKEL, H. (1967), *Studies in Ethnomethodology*, Prentice-Hall.

GARFINKEL, H., and SACKS, H. (1970), 'On formal structures of practical actions', in J. C. McKinney and E. A. Tiryakian (eds.), *Theoretical Sociology: Perspectives and Development*, Appleton-Century-Crofts.

GILL, H. (1965), 'What is a prison community?', *Federal Probation*, vol. 29, pp. 15–18.

GURWITSCH, A. (1964), *The Field of Consciousness*, Duquesne University Press.

McHUGH, P. (1968), *Defining the Situation*, Bobbs-Merrill.

SPIEGELBERG, H. (1960), *The Phenomenological Movement. A Historical Introduction*, Martinus Nijhoff, The Hague.

WIEDER, D. L. (1970), 'On meaning by rule', in J. Douglas (ed.), *Understanding Everyday Life*, Aldine.

ZIMMERMAN, D. H. (1970), 'The practicalities of rule use', in J. Douglas (ed.), *Understanding Everyday Life*, Aldine.

ZIMMERMAN, D. H., and POLLNER, M. (1970), 'The everyday world as a phenomenon', in J. Douglas (ed.) *Understanding Everyday Life*, Aldine.

14 Kenneth Stoddart

Pinched: Notes on the Ethnographer's Location of Argot

First published in this volume.

A commonplace byproduct of sociological investigations of subcultures, institutions, etc., *removed* by their character from the realm of 'ordinary life', is the discovery and description of an *argot* or 'specialized language' local to the community in question. Numerous studies of such worlds have revealed that a significant portion of the talk of their members *as* members is conducted via terms and usages possessed of a sense often *impenetrable* to 'outsiders' (cf. Maurer, 1940, 1964; Sykes, 1956). The argot displayed in *The Professional Thief* (Sutherland, 1937), for example, is considered sufficiently opaque to warrant the inclusion of a *glossary* – presumably as a resource for readers wishing to remedy the strangeness of the thief's talk.

This essay reports on the discovery of an element of the argot used during 1967–8 (and likely before and since that date) by heroin users resident in a large Canadian city. Here, however – and in contrast to 'traditional' studies dealing focally or tangentially with argot – interest in the discovered element *itself* is suspended in favour of an interest in *the methods by which it was located or recognized as an instance of argot in the first place*. Such a suspension entails a deliberate *indifference* to any and all substantive matters relating to the element: its potential as an addition to the existing corpus of argot in general and heroin users' argot in particular, its possible heuristic value to ethnographers investigating communities similar to the one from which it was derived, and *all* ways of asserting its importance as a 'finding' are specifically disattended here. The element is attended solely as furnishing the opportunity for explicating the methods whereby it was located. In a very real sense, then, the essay is *not* 'about' argot but the procedures involved in the everyday business of hearing and understanding talk – whether 'opaque' or 'transparent'.

An interest in the methods employed to locate instances of argot may be actualized in the following manner:

1. Suspend the assumption that an argot and the elements that comprise it exist as entities in and of themselves, independent of the course of inquiry that made them observable. (Observe that the suspended assumption is

tacitly endorsed as a matter of fact by sociologists and others interested for theoretical or practical reasons in argot and its elements).[1]

2. Render the constitution of any collection of items problematic.

Via the following of these 'instructions' the assembly of a collection of items identifiable as elements of an argot comes to be seen as the researcher's *accomplishment*. He finds that the course of members' talk yields the production of terms and usages that are identifiable as instances of argot. This essay examines the methods by which such findings are accomplished.

Pinched

The sociological study of argot invariably involves the enumeration of the terms comprising the argot together with an elaboration of their sense. *How* the researcher comes to see that these are terms ascribable to a community of users remains unreported and unexamined, i.e. the condition of practical accomplishment is suppressed, detached from the 'findings' themselves. In order to display these unexplicated conditions *in a particular case* I hereby present a biographical reporting of some ethnographic work conducted amongst heroin users. Over the course of that work I came to see the term 'pinched' as an instance of the argot local to the community under investigation. As well, I managed to explicate the *sense* of the item. The *how* of these accomplishments is reported below.

In doing the particular ethnography under discussion I employed a technique of covert participant observation, i.e. I sought to 'pass' as someone conversant with the community of heroin users. That I was in fact researching the activities of community members was therefore not observable to those members I encountered.

Research conducted via 'passing' requires that the researcher be seen by members as already possessing what it is he is there to determine, i.e. what every competent member knows. That I was seen by members *as* a member

1. One demonstration that sociologists honour this assumption is their formulation of their task as the discovery and description of the members' distinctive lexicon. Note further that Polsky's (1969) formulation of argot as a constraint upon researchers' talk stands as another. 'Most important when hanging around criminals – what I regard as the absolute "first rule" of field research on them – is this: initially, keep your eyes and ears open *but keep your mouth shut*. At first try to ask no questions whatsoever. Before you can ask questions, or even speak much at all other than when spoken to, you should get the "feel" of their world by extensive and attentive listening – get . . . some sense of *their* sense of language (not only their special argot . . . but also how they use ordinary language). . . . Until the criminal's frame of reference and language have been learned, the investigator is in danger of coming on too square, or else of coming on too hip (anxiously overusing or misusing the argot)' (pp. 121–2). In a sense, much of the data displayed in this paper was produced via my naïve breaching of what Polsky regards as the 'first rule' of field research among criminals.

was problematic in interesting and serious ways. To what extent, for example, could I treat the opacities and obscurities I encountered in their talk and activities as legitimate points of inquiry? The mere asking of questions became a somewhat 'risky' matter: to ask after the sense of something could be seen by a 'natural' member of the heroin-using community as evidence of my naïveté. I could not have known at the beginning of my research what would have transpired to have been evidence of my exclusion from the community and thus as grounds for some members to *doubt* the bona fide character of my presence in the scene of their activities. My own activities therefore stood as prospectively fateful with respect to the outcome of the research. I *commonsensically* saw that any evidence of naïveté could invalidate my appearance as a legitimate participant and thus truncate the research at a point not of my choosing.

The problem was compounded by the fact that not everything heroin users do and say is *unique* to them: in fact, many of the things that heroin users did and said appeared to me as things that might be done or said by 'anyone', i.e. *independent* of location *vis-à-vis* the heroin-using community. The usage 'pinched' initially appeared to me in this way. As the following field-note demonstrates, I heard and responded to that usage *not* as an element of the heroin users' argot but as a usage familiar to me by virtue of my participation in another domain, i.e. 'conventional society'.

In the course of a conversation with Hughie I queried him regarding the whereabouts of Harry, a heroin user I'd met in the cafe. Hughie told me he'd 'been pinched'. I asked Hughie what he'd been arrested for and he replied: 'For junk. What did ya think?'

Seeing that 'anyone' might understand 'been pinched' to mean 'been arrested' it seemed to me that a proper inquiry might be one into the *reason* for the arrest, i.e. for *what* had Harry been arrested? That there would be anything investigable about the expression 'pinched' did not occur to me at the time of my asking the question of Hughie. I saw my asking of what seemed to me a routine question as a way of obtaining information on the kinds of dealings for which heroin users might be apprehended. Hughie's response to my query stands therefore as grounds for my reconsidering my question and finding that it was naïvely asked. Hughie's remarks suppose that the character of Harry's arrest is determinable from the pronouncement 'he's been pinched'. I concluded that for Hughie when one is pinched one is arrested for the possession of narcotics. His initial use of the term was not recognized by me as an instance of argot – but his response to my routinely produced query indicated that in some sense 'pinched' might have an 'unconventional' use. Furthermore, I found that an instance of conduct retrospectively realized as evidence of my naïveté did not appear to Hughie as such: it seems that 'naïve remarks' when produced by someone presumably taken as a genuine member of a community can be treated by other members as playfulness, foolishness, and the like. Thus Hughie proposes that I knew what he meant and that his reminding would tell me so.

It was at this time the prospect that the expression 'pinched' might be includable in a heroin users' argot occurred to me. The retrospectively demonstrated opacity of Hughie's talk then appeared to me as *possibly* not merely an idiosyncratic feature of *his* talk but an instance of a practice that would be standard for persons of the type he represented.

The discovery of the opacity of Hughie's talk encouraged me to reconstruct my orientation to the talk of others I saw as inhabiting the same community. Any occurrence of the expression 'pinched' could *now* be seen as another instance of a practice.

However, the *sense* of the term remained to be determined – as I discovered. Supposing *now* that 'pinched' referred to an arrest for possession of narcotics I thought that it might be warrantable to inquire into the nature of such an arrest: instead of asking for *what* one was pinched I could ask *how* one was pinched. The following field-note displays the posing of that question:

Earlier in the evening I'd heard that John had been arrested for possession of narcotics. I mentioned this to Robbie: 'I hear John's been pinched.' 'Yeah, so I hear', she said. I asked 'How did it happen?' and Robbie replied: 'What the fuck do you mean, how did it happen? The same way they all happen, I guess.'

Again the retrospectively naïve nature of my question was not so viewed by the native. It was treated as the occasion for a correction, for the provision of a sense I might have seen all along. For me, however, Robbie's 'correction' was seen as a further specification of the sense of 'pinched'. Robbie's remarks were heard as presuming an organization of arrests attended to as typical for the place and period: any particular arrest might be presumed without further inquiry to have been accomplished via standardized ways. Having this further specification of the sense of 'pinched' I could then attend to subsequent talk of arrests-for-possession-of-narcotics with an eye to the possibility that *unusual* ones would be remarkable and properly talked about. The following field-note demonstrates that I found this to be the case.

About a dozen people were in the cafe. Two addicts, Joe and Freddie, were talking near the rear of the counter. Joe stood up and in a very loud voice said: 'Hey. Did anybody hear what happened to Shorty last night?' Without waiting for a reply he proceeded to describe a rather unusual incident of arrest that had taken place the evening before. . . . It appeared that Joe's remarks were attended to by most of those present. Several made comments like: 'For Christ's sake' and 'How about that', etc. A few minutes later a male drug user entered the cafe and sat at the counter. Another approached him and said: 'Did y'hear about Shorty?' After receiving a negative reply he related the details of Shorty's encounter with the police.

On the basis of that observation I decided that only when members were pinched in some *other than routine* fashion were the details tellable. I was further convinced of my decision when I discovered that the relating of a 'normal' arrest's details was censured by a known member.

Freddie came to the office just as Joey, a neophyte drug user whom I'd been interviewing, was leaving. I asked Freddie if he knew Joey; he replied that he did and added the following: 'That is one asshole I don't care if I ever see again for the rest of my fuckin' natural life.' He proceeded to explain that two evenings ago Joey had spent '. . . about an hour and a half' relating to him '. . . all the fuckin' details of a pinch he took. It must've been his first one. He said: "Well I figure the cops must've been watching' me", and "Jeez, they broke the door right down." ' He added: 'Nobody wants to hear that shit.' I asked him why this was so and he replied: 'Because it's so fuckin' *boring*. Same old story all the time. Everybody knows how the bulls work.'

Notice that for me this posed the problem of deciding between alternative characterizations: e.g. Freddie's remarks could be seen as confirming evidence of what I took to be the ways of the community or it might be that Freddie himself was displaying incompetence. Freddie's negative comments could stand to be rebutted by a co-member. They could find that after all Joey had been warranted in telling the story. In the absence of any response on the part of some community member that I could use as grounds for my own decision I had to conclude that Freddie's negative comments were instances of sanctioning violation of an extant and accepted rule. The decision to treat Freddie's remarks in that way turned upon my already having the feeling that there was such a rule. How any concrete instance would be handled depends upon the temporal placement of its occurrence. Had the encounter between Freddie and Joey been the first talk about arrests that I had encountered among heroin users then I might not have attended to it in any particular way. Had I given it attention *then* it might have been grounds for suspicion that there was some normative regulation of talk about arrests rather than as the kind of confirming evidence that it in fact became.

It is possible to idealize the nature of field research. One can find that whatever one did in the course of one's research could be subsumed under some standardized model of the proper course of sociological investigation. I could find that subsequent things that I did in relation to the notion of 'pinched' were done as applications of 'proper' research procedures such as hypothesis testing. Having formulated the idea that the expression 'pinched' was part of an argot with a determinate and communally accepted sense, I *could* report my own uses of that expression as attempts on my part to test the ideas that I had tentatively formulated. The following field-note, for example, could be seen as a report on such hypothesis-testing-in-the-field.

During the course of a conversation Hughie asked me if I'd been to the Family Cafe recently. I replied that I had and he asked 'Anybody been pinched?' Earlier in the week I'd heard that Lynn, a lesbian of our mutual acquaintance, had been arrested for vagrancy. I thus replied: 'I heard Lynn was.' Hughie expressed some surprise and said: 'Jeez, I didn't even know she was using.' I told him what she'd been arrested for and he said 'Oh, I meant for junk.'

I *could* propose that my reply to Hughie's question be seen as an ethnographer's artful use of what Sacks has termed the 'correction-invitation device': that is, I could propose that the remark was made in full awareness of the possibility that it would stand to be corrected. Seen in this way, my announcement of Lynn's arrest becomes an intentional *testing* to see if such an announcement would pass as an adequate response to the query 'anybody been pinched'. That it would *not* be acceptable as such would not entail the uselessness of the remark, for its very rejection by the member would provide me with a sharper conception of the boundaries that delimited the applicability of the element of argot in question. On the basis of the results of such a 'test' I could presume that being 'pinched' does not describe or refer to the type of arrest of which vagrancy is an instance.

I cannot, however, claim that the last cited field-note reported on the testing of a provisional hypothesis. In the course of field research there will occur to the researcher conceptions of the ways in which he will eventually handle the materials he is collecting. And there will occur, too, feelings that this or that occurrence could be considered as providing the materials out of which a sociological problem may be generated. It cannot be *realistically* claimed, however, that these ideas or feelings remain *continuously* in the researcher's mind or that he wittingly designs *all* his activities so as to provide occasions upon which those ideas, etc. may be expanded, elaborated, or tested. The researcher's capacity to *remember* all of the things that occur to him over the course of his investigations may be doubted – and it may take an occurrence of the kind reported in the previous field-note to bring those ideas, etc. to mind. Thus, my announcement of Lynn's arrest can be seen as yet *another* unwittingly naïve remark which – when responded to in the way the native *did* respond – returned to mind those earlier ideas, etc. and occasioned a review of my field-notes for previous instances of the 'same thing'. It would nevertheless be possible for me to report the event cited above as having been for all practical purposes 'identical' to a thoughtfully designed experimentation with the parameters of a notion that had become and remained problematic.

Some concluding remarks

The burden of this brief report on a field study has been to describe the location of an element of argot as a practical accomplishment. The prospect that such an element may be available for description occurred to me when I encountered some talk of members *as* members that was initially unintelligible. The members' presumption that I should have seen the sense of the talk led me to the view that the term 'pinched' could be found to have a definite sense amongst *some* community of users. The elaboration of that sense, however, was only possible because of the extended nature of the investigation and the naturally generated recurrences of usages that I saw to be relevant. My management of these recurrences could be reported as having been designed planfully under the auspices of a standardized research procedure – but reporting them in that fashion would misrepresent the ways my *actual* hearings, talkings, and recallings occurred.

It seems reasonable to suppose that the ways in which *I* came to see and grasp the sense of 'pinched' as an element of heroin users' argot would be ways in which *members*, too, come to be so acquainted with the term. Furthermore, it seems warrantable to suppose that members are under some constraints similar to those that the 'passing' researcher encounters, i.e. on their first encounter with the 'strangeness' of that expression they could suppose that inquiries as to its sense might be seen as evidence of a naïveté that they would not want recognizably competent members to ascribe to them.

References

MAURER, D. (1940), *The Big Con*, Bobbs-Merrill.
MAURER, D. (1964), *Whiz Mob*, College and University Press, New Haven.
POLSKY, N. (1967), *Hustlers, Beats and Others*, Aldine.
SUTHERLAND, E. (1937), *The Professional Thief*, University of Chicago Press.
SYKES, G. (1965), *The Society of Captives*, Princeton University Press.

15 Robert W. Mackay

Conceptions of Children and Models of Socialization

Robert W. Mackay, 'Conceptions of children and models of socialization', in Hans
Peter Dreitzel (ed.), *Recent Sociology*, no 5, Macmillan, 1973, pp. 27–43.
Revised by the author for this volume.

Introduction

In sociological writings characterized as normative[1] the term socialization
glosses[2] the phenomenon of change from the birth of a child to maturity or
old age.[3] To observe that changes take place after birth is trivial, but the
quasi-scientific use of the term socialization masks this triviality. In fact, the
study of these changes as socialization is an expression of the sociologists'
common-sense position in the world, i.e. as adults.[4] The notion of socialization leads to theoretical formulations mirroring the adult view that children are incomplete beings. Investigators have consequently been distracted
from the important area of study which is adult–child interaction and the
underlying theoretically important problem of intersubjectivity implied in
such interaction. Writing about the process of socialization, then, has become for me an occasion for exploring the interaction between adults and
children.

In this paper I first examine what the normative sociological study of
socialization implies both for the study of adult–child interaction and the
development of sociological theory. I then examine the interpretive approach
demonstrating that *all* interaction is based upon underlying interpretive
competence. This competence is not acknowledged within the normative
approach because the study of socialization takes the views of the dominant
culture (adult) and proposes them as scientific findings. It ignores the interactional nature of adult–child relationships. Finally through the analysis of
adult–child interaction I show the interpretive competence of the child and

1. Here I follow the formulations of normative found in Cicourel (1970a) and Wilson
(1970).

2. I use the concept gloss throughout this paper in opposition to the concept explicate. I follow the usage found in Garfinkel (1967, p. 33).

3. Persons concerned with adult socialization see all of life as a process of socialization. For instance see Brim (1968).

4. What I am suggesting here is the same as Alan Blum has elegantly formulated,
that 'Through theorizing the theorist searches for his self, and his achievement in
theorizing is a recovery of this self' (Blum, 1970, p. 304).

the paradoxical nature of interaction between adults and children where competence is simultaneously assumed and interactionally denied.

To be – is to be socialized: the normative perspective

Children are incomplete – immature, irrational, incompetent, asocial, acultural depending on whether you are a teacher, sociologist, anthropologist or psychologist. Adults, on the other hand, are complete – mature, rational, competent, social, and autonomous unless they are 'acting-like-children'.[5] Introductory texts (e.g., Broom and Selznick, 1968; Horton and Hunt, 1968) in the social sciences suggest that without language and culture new born infants are not human because 'language creates minds and selves' (Broom and Selznick, 1968, p. 96). An implication is that children who are profoundly retarded or severely brain damaged are never human.

For the sociologist, to be human is to be socialized. To be socialized is to acquire roles (see, e.g., Brim, 1968; Clausen, 1968; Elkin, 1960; Inkeles, 1966; Parsons and Bales, 1955). To be (human) is transformed by sociologists into, to be (roles). But such theorizing is not an indifferent practice. As I have suggested in the Introduction and footnote 4, it is the formulation of the writer's own view of the world (i.e. his self). Considered thus, to conceive of being human as being roles is to conceive an eviscerated view of life. The consequence of this is that, under the auspices of current formulations of socialization the conception of children as essentially deficient vis-à-vis adults has, in practice, led to no research into children qua children and it has served to, scientifically, warrant common-sense conceptions of children as incomplete. When adult–child interaction is formulated as the process of socialization, children as a phenomenon disappear and sociologists reveal themselves as parents writing slightly abstract versions of their own or other children.

Socialization is a gloss (see footnote 2) which precludes the explication of the phenomenon it glosses, i.e. the interaction between adults and children. This glossing is characteristic of normative sociology's reliance on the common-sense world as both topic and resource.[6] As Zimmerman and Pollner (1970, p. 82) indicate, 'Sociology's acceptance of the lay member's

5. The problem with children is that they don't think like adults or so it seems in the vast literature on socialization, child rearing and its popular, and usually more empirical, variants in Spock, Ginst, etc. But then not thinking like adults could be applied to other large segments of the world – the people next door, this or that group. There is an extensive literature on how to *train* children, I suppose because they are smaller and less powerful. A similar argument could be applied to the poor, mental patients and prisoners, a similar literature supports this view. Incomplete socialization, deviance, etc. are particular sociological ways of indicating this.

6. An excellent paper which makes this distinction clear is Zimmerman and Pollner (1970).

formulation of the formal and substantive features of sociology's topical concerns makes sociology an integral feature of the very order it seeks to describe. It makes sociology into an eminently *folk discipline* deprived of any prospect or hope of making fundamental structures of folk activity a phenomenon.' This confounding is illustrated in the following quotation.

In other words both the *practice and study* of child socialization are 'forward looking.' It seems *obvious*, furthermore, that of the various later stages which socialization looks forward to, it is the personally relatively enduring and *socially important adult* stage which is the *critical one* to consider. Therefore, a central task of the study of socialization is to enquire into the effects which the experience of the child has on the shaping of the adult (Inkeles, 1968, pp. 76–7; emphasis added).

The terms adults and children are borrowed from the common-sense world by sociologists, but if they are viewed as theoretical formulations, then a very serious problem emerges. That is, to suggest theoretically that there are adults and children is to imply that to pass from one stage to the other is to pass from one ontological order to another.[7] The passage from one ontological order to another is also suggested in the formulation of the world as static[8] and as constituted by successive discrete stages – childhood and adulthood, incompleteness and completeness, lack of agreement and shared agreement (see footnote 1). If each of these ontological orders implies, on the level of social life, different communicative competencies, then the traditional formulations of socialization make communication between adults and children impossible, since they are assumed not to share common interpretive abilities.

I am suggesting that in the socialization literature the confounding of the common-sense world as topic and resource has resulted in the unavailability for sociologists of interaction between adults and children as a phenomenon of study. The phenomenon of study is adult–child interaction and how it is accomplished.

The interpretive perspective

For two days I watched some sixty children between the ages of three and six joyfully writing stories of their own, making up poems, exploring the typewriter key-

---

7. This formulation is based upon a footnote to be found in Merleau-Ponty (1964).

8. Both theory and measurement in sociology formulate the world as *static*. For example, ideal types and questionnaires take a moment in time and freeze it. If the world was not *dynamic* this would be adequate but since change is constant the models of the world and their concomitant measurement systems are inadequate. Often what passes for theory in sociology are only high level abstractions from which anything can be deduced through the application of anyone's common-sense knowledge of the world. Measurement systems are misconceived in any event because they do not measure but constitute the phenomenon. Consequently measurement is by fiat and the world remains to be described.

board and reading paragraphs based on their own conversations. They did this as spontaneously as young children ask questions. I realized then that I had stumbled onto something more important than the mechanical ability to read a few words. Evidently tiny youngsters could reason, invent and acquire knowledge far better than most adults suspected. If they could learn this much through exposure to the talking typewriter for only half an hour a day, the potentialities of preschool children were almost limitless (Pines, 1966, p. ix; emphasis added).

I take this quotation to represent what might be sociologists' similar surprise at the ability of children to 'reason, invent and acquire knowledge', that is, at their interpretive competencies. In contrast to the study of socialization suggested by normative sociology (discussed in the previous section) work in interpretive sociology (see, e.g., Cicourel, 1970b; Garfinkel, 1967; Holt, 1969; Labov, 1972; Neill, 1960; Schutz, 1962) restores the interaction between adults and children based on interpretive competencies as the phenomenon of study.[9] Without reviewing the literature in this area (see especially Cicourel, 1970, 1972; Garfinkel, 1967), the interpretive perspective posits interpretive and surface rules,[10] the reflexive articulation of which enables people to assign meaning to the world. The complexity of the world and its orderliness is seen to rest on persons' (adults and children[11]) interpretive competencies. The focus of investigation is *how* persons display the meaningfulness of the world.

A demonstration of children's interpretive competencies can be found in research conducted in a grade one classroom.[12] After completing a state-wide reading test designed to measure reading and inference skills, children were asked by researchers how they had decided on answers. The children often linked the stimulus sentence and the answer in ways which the test constructor had not 'meant' but which demonstrated their inference/interpretive skills in providing reasonable accounts of the world. For example, the stimulus sentence of one test item was about an animal that had been out in the rain. The 'correct answer' was a picture of a room with dotted wallpaper walls and a floor imprinted with a trail of animal tracks. When the child was asked what the picture was about, she replied, 'It's snowing.' When questioned about the design on the wallpaper – 'Do you know what these are?' – she replied, 'sprinkles'. The child had perceived the picture to be the exterior of a house with snow falling rather than the interior of a house covered with dotted wallpaper. Because of this 'misperception' she had

9. This perspective implies a notion of liberation and as such offers the intellectual possibility of freeing children as political prisoners. See especially the writings of Holt, Labov and Neill.

10. This formulation is particularly Cicourel's based on his critique of Chomsky.

11. Particularly important to the discussion of children is Cicourel's article mentioned above (Cicourel, 1970b).

12. For a fuller report of the work referred to see Mackay (1974).

chosen an answer which while it was reasonable within the frame of reference was the wrong answer. While the child demonstrated the inference/interpretive skills that were claimed to be 'measured by the test', no credit was given for this item. This research[13] makes clear that children possess interpretive competencies undiscerned in standard research. The interpretive perspective makes available, then, children as beings who interpret the world as adults do. By revealing the child's competencies, it transforms a theory of deficiency into a theory of competency.

In addition to suggesting that children are competent interpreters in the world, I want to suggest that they are also in possession of their own culture or succession of cultures. Although the evidence for this is only fragmentary, the Opies have presented the most convincing case for the existence of separate cultures.[14] Ariès (1965) also points to the possibility of separate children's cultures and their changing particularity over time (see also Plump, 1971).

If the two claims are correct, that children are competent interpreters of the social world and that they possess a separate culture(s), then the study of adult–child interaction (formerly socialization) becomes substantively the study of cultural assimilation, and theoretically the study of meaningful social interaction.

Adult–child interaction[15]

I have suggested that adult–child interaction is problematic because of cultural differences. Hall (1959) has documented that problems arising out of poor cultural translation can have serious practical outcomes (i.e. misunderstandings, breaches). Teachers and other adults remain cultural strangers to the world of children and their interaction with children often results in the generic type of misunderstandings that Hall describes.[16] I have argued on

13. For further demonstration of children's competencies see Mehan (1971), Roth (1972) and a related work by Labov (1969).

14. Opie and Opie (1959). The idea of separate children's culture was suggested by Harvey Sacks in a lecture at a conference on 'Language, society and the child', Berkeley, 1968. Also see Speier (n.d.).

15. The data reported here is part of a larger study that was supported by a Ford Foundation Grant, Aaron V. Cicourel Principal Investigator. Although this research was conceived in part to study children's communicative competencies, the videotapes which were taken focus on the teacher's face with the result that often the children have their backs to the camera. In the segment reported on in this paper the teacher's face is clear but when the child looks at the teacher his back is to the camera. This is in part, I would suggest, because of the ubiquity of the adult view of the world mirrored in the organization of the classroom which makes shooting videotapes towards the children almost impossible.

16. Hall (1959, pp. 9–13). It should also be noted here that culturally different persons who are serious about understanding each other spend long periods of time working

two fronts, first that understanding between two separate cultures requires adequate translation and second that *all* human interaction rests on the participants' interpretive abilities. On a theoretical level, however, there is no difference between these two.[17]

I turn now to an analysis of a specific occasion of interaction between an adult and a child which indicates how understanding based on interpretive abilities is built up through the course of the interaction. The teacher treats the child as a cultural stranger while relying on his 'adult' competencies to understand the lesson and review. The following excerpts [18] are from a written transcript of the audio portion of a videotaped interview between a grade one teacher and one child in her class. In the interview, which took place at the end of the lunch hour, the teacher is asking the child about the assignment distributed earlier in the morning. This assignment was to sequence a series of dittoed sentences which were either taken verbatim or paraphrased from the story read before lunch. In the lesson and assignment the teacher had been concerned with introducing the concept of sequencing to the children. The interview was carried out at the request of the researchers to find out how the child would describe his understanding of the lesson and assignment.

Instruction: understanding as the location of the 'correct' answer

Given the working assumption that children are *tabula rasa* beings on which to etch programmes, teachers and other adults ignore the fact that understanding rests upon an ongoing reflexive, constructed, convergence of schemata of interpretation (see Garfinkel, 1967; Schutz, 1962). In the transcript it can be seen that the teacher acts as though the world is a static (i.e. not dialectical) place in which she can move the child cognitively from point A to point B while ignoring the child's contributions. In the lesson and review her concern was with moving him from a state of not knowing the concept of sequencing to a state of knowing the concept of sequencing. The teacher thus treats the child as empty of knowledge (i.e. correct answers) and moves him from this state of emptiness to a state of fullness (i.e. knowledge), a process she accomplishes by asking questions and reformulating them until the child gives the 'correct' answer. In some instances the teacher not

out the translation problems. A good example is an anthropologist doing field work. I can think of no similar attempts on the part of teachers and other adults to understand children.

17. Cultural differences may add an element of practical difficulty created by the problems of doing adequate translation but this is not a principled difference. I am following Cicourel's formulation of interpretive abilities as invariant. Under this formulation culture differences are surface rules. See Cicourel (1970b).

18. The reader is asked to consult the full transcript presented in the appendix in order to locate the excerpts in the larger context of the interview.

only asks the questions but also finally *gives* the 'correct' answers (see Teacher 39, page 192). Instruction is the occasion for adults to exercise their preference for a certain meaning of the world for the child. The child as more or less passive in the situation is involved only in so far as he is conceived to be an organism capable of memory.[19] The child can/must *remember* the instructions (i.e. in this case the lesson).

Children's interpretive competence

I am using interpretive competence in an analytic sense to refer to the ability to use interpretive procedures to assign meaning to the world (Cicourel, 1970b, esp. pp. 147–57; Garfinkel, 1967, esp. ch. 1). I demonstrate in the following sections that children possess the same interpretive abilities as adults do.

Competence as the teacher's assumption

The teacher assumes the child's interpretive competence in doing lessons and reviews. One example of this assumption of interpretive competence in the transcript is when the teacher (Segment Teacher 14) asks Tom '. . . see if you can find the sentence that tells best . . .' where 'best' implies the careful evaluation of the total situation, i.e. the exercise of those abilities she herself uses to decide which is 'best'. This assumption by adults of children's interpretive competence can be found even in situations where children are considered unlikely ever to be competent. For example, in one research study (Mayer, 1967) with mentally retarded children (measured I.Q. between 50 and 75) the researcher administered a measure which consisted of a list of twenty-two personality traits. The children were to rank themselves on a five point scale for each item. The format was:

I am	happy	not at all	not very often	some of the time	most of the time	all of the time
	clean					
	lazy					
	etc.					

The researcher assumes that these children have interpretive competence if he assumes that they are able to reflect upon their personalities-as-traits and then rate them on a five-point scale. After the measurement is completed it is assumed that the aggregated measure of self-concept is of persons unable to reason well – they are, *after all*, mentally retarded.

The teacher assumes the child's interpretive competencies at every point. In the transcript this is especially clear in the segments following.

19. A persistent feature of the common-sense world seems to be a 'trust in memory'.

TEACHER 39 Umhum, so you understood the story and it didn't make any difference about that word did it because the idea was that it fell on Chicken Little and it was really a nut instead of ah a piece of the sky. Thank you very much Tom.

The above segment was uttered at about 1:05 p.m. The segment below was said by the teacher about 10:45 a.m. the same morning in reference to the story of Chicken Little she was about to tell them.

TEACHER My story might be a little bit different from the way you heard it, the names might be different but the ideas are the same.

In both segments she is assuming that what she is saying is obvious, i.e. she does not elaborate, ask if it is clear, etc. She is asserting that ideas subsume many different words and names and in doing so eliminates what appears to be a difference. It is important to note that this is a more complex notion to grasp than the one that she makes the topic of the lesson – a concretized presentation of sequencing. What I am proposing is that she is assuming in an analytic sense the interpretive procedures which define competence. The following describes one aspect of interpretive competence and it is clear in the above segments that the teacher assumes this ability of the child.

A corollary of this property (reciprocity of perspectives) is that members assume, and assume others assume of them, that their descriptive accounts or utterances will be intelligible and recognizable features of the world known in common and taken for granted (Cicourel, 1970b, p. 147).

When the two segments are considered together it can be seen that she is also assuming that the child can *remember* the earlier utterance and find the principle of consistency in the lesson, assuming that her use of the word 'idea' in the later utterance is a tacit reference back to the earlier utterance as a way of finding the mistake to be irrelevant to the sense of the lesson. (The 'mistake' is discussed more fully below.) Here the teacher has assumed further interpretive competence, viz. the ability to search retrospectively (Cicourel, 1970b, p. 149) for the sense of the present utterance.

I offer the following segment as a final example of the child's interpretive competence.

TEACHER 32 Humm this is interesting. What did it say in the story that Chicken Little ah where the nut fell on Chicken Little.
TOM 28 At the tree.
TEACHER 33 Umhum what part of his body did it land on did it say?

Tom has formulated the correct answer to the question 'where was Chicken Little when the nut fell?' i.e. the location of Chicken Little was the scheme of interpretation. While this is a correct interpretation of her question the teacher treats it as 'incorrect' by invoking her own scheme of interpretation 'where on the body of Chicken Little did the nut fall?' While interpretive ability is demonstrated by Tom in that he articulates the particular words of the teacher with a frame of reference which allows a reasonable answer to the question, what is also demonstrated is that adults can pre-empt the inter-action with children for their own purposes without explanation. For ex-ample, the teacher might have said to another adult 'Oh no, what I meant was where on Chicken Little's body.' The teacher not only has the power to ignore reasonable answers but also assumes more competence of the child than of an adult, i.e. that he can figure out both that and why his answer was wrong and the other answer correct.

Understanding as evidenceable

The paradigmatic example of verifying a child's understanding is found in Socrates' encounter with the boy in *The Meno* (see Rouse, 1956, pp. 48–9):

SOCRATES Very well. How many times the small one is the whole space.
BOY Four times.
SOCRATES But we wanted a double space, don't you remember?
BOY Oh, yes I remember.
SOCRATES Then here is a line running from corner to corner, cutting each of the spaces in two parts.
BOY Yes.
SOCRATES Are not these four lines equal and don't they contain this space within them?
BOY Yes that is right.

The verification of the boy's understanding is in the answer 'yes'. *The Meno* can be read as a monologue and the 'yes' answer by the boy as Socrates' own production. A similar example is found in the transcript, beginning with Teacher 32 and ending at dismissal of Tom. The segment begins with the teacher's recognition that she has made a mistake 'Humm this is interesting.' She has incorrectly written the sentence on the assignment sheet to read that the nut fell on Chicken Little's head while in the story it fell on his tail. The rest of the segment is the teacher's attempt to find out if the error made any difference in Tom's understanding of the lesson. What is important, how-ever, is that beginning at Tom 32 it is absolutely clear that Tom no longer has any part in the interaction (i.e. it becomes a monologue); perhaps he no longer even knows what is going on although at the end the teacher seems convinced that Tom understood.

TOM 31 Ya but I always thought.
TEACHER 37 In some stories it does fall on his head so it didn't bother you that it said head?

TEACHER 38 Have you ever heard a story where it falls on Chicken Little's head
. . . instead of his tail?

TOM 33 Ya.

TEACHER 39 Umhum, so you understood the story and it didn't matter about
that word did it because the idea was that it fell on Chicken Little and it was
really a nut instead of ah a piece of the sky. Thank you very much Tom.

A viewing of the videotape[20] reveals that Tom's sentence 'Ya but I always
thought' did not end unfinished because the teacher interrupted but was a
complete utterance. What is evident from the tape is that Tom turns his eyes
from looking at the teacher down to the desk in front of him when he con-
cludes the utterance. He continues to look down in this manner until the end
of the interview. When he utters 'Ya' (Tom 33) it is softly and he does not
look up. This is in marked contrast to the rest of the interview where he
meets the eyes of the teacher whenever he gives an answer. The teacher, however, continues to find his understanding even though he is no longer a participant. The teacher appropriates the interaction and asserts the child's
understanding. In doing this she provides for both speakers and suspends
the possibility of the child's use of his interpretive competencies in the interaction, i.e. the child is treated as incompetent. The teacher asserts that Tom
has understood '. . . you understood . . .' and points out why '. . . because
the idea . . .', not the word, was what mattered. The assertions imply the
teacher's assumption of the child's interpretive competence to figure out the
sense, i.e. understand.

Thus, throughout the interview, the teacher guides the child to the correct
answers and finds in the answers the sense of the lesson which constitutes the
evidence of its success, i.e. that the child understood. What is equally important is that the teacher finds both her own competence *qua* teacher and
the child's understanding in the pre-constituted structure of the lesson, i.e.
there are no surprises.[21]

20. For a discussion of the methodological consequences of the use of videotape, see
Cicourel (1972).

21. This observation has strong implications for the educational system. Learning
for the teacher is to find evidence of its accomplishment *now* (i.e. during the lesson and
review). When later on (i.e. grade 5) the child demonstrates the ability covered in the
grade one lesson it is assumed that the genesis of the ability was in the lesson and not in
his ability to learn it *somewhere*. By referring to somewhere, I mean to point out that
the child has competencies to figure out the world in a variety of different ways and in a
variety of settings. The assumption of the importance of the lesson provides the *raison
d'être* for formal instruction to be located in organizations called schools. If the focus
in schools is on the practical organizational activities *here* and *now*, how can these
activities produce children committed to the pursuit of knowledge in a larger and more
temporally extensive sense? Practically, how is it possible under these circumstances to
get children to see that the material 'learned' in schools applies beyond its walls?

The paradox

The analysis has revealed the paradoxical[22] nature of adult–child interaction. On the one hand, the teacher relies on the child's interpretive competencies to understand the lesson but, on the other, treats him throughout as incompetent (i.e. she creates or gives the 'correct' answers). The child is treated as deficient as he is under the normative sociological view of children. The sociological view and the teacher's view are characterized by the fact that they are eminently common-sensical. As such, sociological writings on adult–child interaction are not theoretical but part of the very order that was intended for description (Garfinkel, 1967, ch. 1). Seeing the child's interpretive competencies implies that the interpretive theory applies to both adult–adult and adult–child interaction. Differences between the two types of interaction are not theoretical but substantive. Substantively, the phenomena of study are (a) the ways in which adults attribute incompetence to children and create situations for its manifestation, and (b) the structure of children's culture. Theoretically, the phenomenon of study is the interpretive basis of intersubjectivity.

Appendix
Interview[23]

TEACHER 1 Pick out the ones that should come first. Which one would come first in the story? Why did you choose that?

TOM 1 Because that's the first one.

TEACHER 2 Why is it the first one?

TOM 2 Whack something fell on Chicken Little's . . . head I guess.

TEACHER 3 Umhum. When you read the story in the book was that the very first sentence? Was it exactly like that in the book?

TOM 3 No.

TEACHER 4 No but the this does tell what happened first. Find the sentence which would tell what happens next.

TEACHER 5 Why did you choose that one?

TOM 4 Because I guess that's was what happened (next).

TEACHER 6 What, who was the first animal in the story?

22. A major assumption of this paper is that phenomena maintain a transparency of being more than one thing at once. Although the phenomenon is unitary the various parts seem sequential when talked or written about. For some phenomenologists (Merleau-Ponty, 1962) this is regarded as the perspectival nature of experience and for the Zen monk the unity of experience. One of the most dramatic examples of a phenomenon being two things at once is Carlos Castaneda's experiences using 'smoke' (reported in Castaneda, 1971).

23. During the interview the teacher is seated at her desk looking sideways into the camera, the boy is standing beside her between her and the camera. The sentences to be sequenced are in front of him on her desk.

TOM 5 Chicken Little.

TEACHER 7 And the next?

TOM 6 Henny Penny.

TEACHER 8 And who came next?

TOM 7 Goosey Loosey.

TEACHER 9 No, not quite, somebody else came after Henny Penny,

TOM 8 $\left\{\begin{array}{l}\text{some}\\\text{Cocky Locky.}\end{array}\right.$

TEACHER 10 Cocky Locky.
And then?

TOM 9 Henny.

TEACHER 11 Goosey Poosey. And then, then what?

TOM 10 Turkey Lurkey.

TEACHER 12 Ya in the flannel board who came story who came last?

TOM 11 Foxy Loxy.

TEACHER 13 Who was not in the book that was in the flannel board story?

TOM 12 Foxy Loxy.

TEACHER 14 Alright, good, alright see if you can find the sentence then that tells best what happened after Henny Penny went with Chicken Litttle.

TEACHER 15 Why didn't you choose this one it's got Henny Penny and Chicken Little in it.

TOM 13 Ah. Umm. Henny Penny. Cocky Locky and Chicken Little. Cocky Locky and Goosey Poosey he he isn't here yet.

TEACHER 16 That's right.

TOM 14 Here Goosey Poosey, here boy.

TEACHER 17 That's fine Tom, just tell me quietly please you don't have to act it out right now. There are times for acting but this is not one of them, 'k.

TOM 15 They all met Goosey Poosey.

TEACHER 18 Alright. Why did you choose that 'Four animals met Turkey Lurkey' next?

TOM 16 Because he's the last one they ( ) met.

TEACHER 19 How do you know he's . . . all the other animals like Henny Penny and Cocky Locky are there it doesn't give their names?

TOM 17 Because. . . .

TEACHER 20 What does it say?

TOM 18 'The four animals met Turkey Lurkey.' There wasn't four animals.

TEACHER 21 Weren't there?

TOM 19 One.

TEACHER 22 Right.

TOM 20 Two.

TEACHER 23 Henny Penny is

TOM 21 One.

TEACHER 24 Cocky Locky $\left\{\begin{array}{l}\text{is}\\\text{two}\end{array}\right.$

TOM 22

TEACHER 25 Two.

TOM 23 Three . . . four.

TEACHER 26 See there are you are forgetting about Chicken Little he has met three people but Chicken Little's there too so that makes an extra one ( ). Alright what comes next? The animals have seen Turkey Lurkey what would come next?

TEACHER 27 Craig would you please take your seat.

TEACHER 28 Why did you choose that. Will you read it to me please.

TOM 24 Turkey Lurkey saw a nut under a big tree.

TEACHER 29 Why did you choose that ⎰ instead of
TOM 25 ⎱ because

TEACHER 30 That one.

TOM 26 Because th the sky is not falling. He can't say it because he doesn't know yet.

TEACHER 31 Umm. Did Turkey Lurkey know all the time that it was a nut that fell on his head – that fell on ah Chicken Little's tail?

TOM 27 I guess so, I don't know.

TEACHER 32 Humm this is interesting. What did it say in the story that Chicken Little ah where the nut fell on Chicken Little?

TOM 28 At the tree.

TEACHER 33 Umhum what part of his body did it land on did it say?

TOM 29 Tail.

TEACHER 34 Read the first sentence.

TOM 30 Whunk.

TEACHER 35 Whack.

TOM 31 Whack something fell on Chicken Little's head ( )

TEACHER 36 Did you notice that when you were putting the sentences together?

TOM 32 Ya, but I always thought.

TEACHER 37 In some stories it does fall on his head so it didn't bother you did it that it said head?

TEACHER 38 Have you ever heard a story where it fell on Chicken Little's head . . . instead of his tail.

TOM 33 Ya.

TEACHER 39 Umhum, so you understood the story and it didn't matter about that word did it because the idea was that it fell on Chicken Little and it was really a nut instead of ah a piece of the sky. Thank you very much Tom.

References

ARIÈS, P. (1965), *Centuries of Childhood*, Random House; Penguin, 1973.

BLUM, A. (1970), 'Theorizing', in J. Douglas (ed.), *Understanding Everyday Life*, Aldine.

BRIM, O. G. (1968), 'Adult socialization', in J. Clausen (ed.), *Socialization and Society*, Little, Brown.

BROOM, L., and SELZNICK, P. (1968), *Sociology*, 4th edn, McGraw-Hill.

CASTANEDA, C. (1971), *A Separate Reality*, Simon & Schuster.

CICOUREL, A. V. (1970a), 'Basic and normative rules', in H. P. Dreitzel (ed.), *Recent Sociology*, vol. 2, Macmillan.

CICOUREL, A. V. (1970b), 'The acquisition of social structure', in J. Douglas (ed.), *Understanding Everyday Life*, Aldine.

CICOUREL, A. V. (1972), 'Ethnomethodology', in T. S. Sebeok *et al.* (eds.), *Current Trends in Linguistics*, vol. 12, Mouton.

CLAUSEN, J. (1968), 'Introduction', in J. Clausen (ed.), *Socialization and Society*, Little, Brown.

ELKIN, F. (1960), *The Child and Society*, Random House.

GARFINKEL, H. (1967), *Studies in Ethnomethodology*, Prentice-Hall.

HALL, E. T. (1959), *The Silent Language*, Faucett Pubns.

HOLT, J. (1969), *The Underachieving School*, Dell Publishing; Penguin, 1971.

HORTON, P. B., and HUNT, C. L. (1968), *Sociology*, 2nd edn, McGraw-Hill.

INKELES, A. (1966), 'Social structure and the socialization of competence', *Harvard Educational Review*, vol. 36, no. 3.

INKELES, A. (1968), 'Society, social structure and child socialization', in J. Clausen (ed.), *Socialization and Society*, Little, Brown.

LABOV, W. (1969), 'The logic of nonstandard English', *Georgetown Monographs on Language and Linguistics*, vol. 22.

LABOV, W. (1972), 'The logic of nonstandard English', in P. P. Giglioli (ed.), *Language and Social Context*, Penguin.

MACKAY, R. (1974), 'Standardized tests: objective and objectified measures of competence', in A. V. Cicourel *et al.* (eds.), *Language Use and School Performance*, Seminar Press.

MAYER, C. L. (1967), 'Relationships of self-concepts and social variables in retarded children', *American Journal of Mental Deficiency*, vol. 72.

MERLEAU-PONTY, M. (1962), *The Phenomenology of Perception*, Humanities Press.

MERLEAU-PONTY, M. (1964), 'The child's relations with others', in M. Merleau-Ponty (ed.), *The Primacy of Perception*, Northwestern University Press.

MEHAN, H. (1971), 'Understanding in educational settings', unpublished Ph.D. dissertation, University of California, Santa Barbara.

NEILL, A. S. (1960), *Summerhill*, Hart Publishing; Penguin, 1962.

OPIE, I., and OPIE, P. (1959), *The Lore and Language of School Children*, Oxford University Press.

PARSONS, T., and BALES, R. F. (1955), *Socialization and Interaction Process*, Free Press.

PINES, M. (1966), *Revolution in Learning*, Harper & Row.

PLUMP, J. H. (1971), 'The great change in children', *Horizon*, vol. 8, no. 1.

ROTH, D. (1972), 'Children's linguistic performance as a factor in school achievement', unpublished Ph.D. dissertation, University of California, Santa Barbara.

ROUSE, W. H. D. (trans) (1956), *Great Dialogues of Plato: The Meno*, New American Library.

SCHUTZ, A. (1962), *Collected Papers: I. The Problem of Social Reality*, Martinus Nijhoff.

SPEIER, M. (n.d.), 'The child as conversationalist: some culture contact features of conversational interactions between adults and children', unpublished.

WILSON, T. P. (1970), 'Normative and interpretative paradigms in sociology', in J. Douglas (ed.), *Understanding Everyday Life*, Aldine.

Part Four
Methodical Bases of Interaction

The first three papers in this section are devoted to the analysis of conversational materials. In the words of Schegloff and Sacks, 'they are part of a program of work undertaken . . . to explore the possibility of achieving a naturalistic observational discipline that could deal with the details of social action(s) rigorously, empirically and formally'. The exploration of the orderliness of conversation has indicated that the concerted character of the organization of talk will stand up to analysis in fine detail. These papers share with earlier Readings in this volume the noticing of and emphasis upon members' practical accomplishments, in this case the accomplishment of the orderliness of (conversational) interaction. Thus, Schegloff and Sacks insist that 'in so far as [conversational materials] exhibited orderliness, they did so not only for us . . . but for the co-participants who had produced them'. In line with this claim these four papers are concerned with locating and describing ways in which co-participants to interaction produce displays of orderliness, analyse over its course the displayed orderliness of co-participation, and exhibit the results of their analysis to one another as a further feature of the production of concerted activities.

Reading 19 by Ryave and Schenkein is particularly interesting in that it suggests that the framework developed first out of a consideration of specifically conversational materials may well be viable also for research on so-called 'paralinguistic' or 'non-verbal interaction', in this case walking. Tentative as their paper is, it invites further research upon non-exotic materials available to any student of interaction.

16 Roy Turner

Words, Utterances and Activities*

Roy Turner, 'Words, utterances and activities', in Jack Douglas (ed.), *Understanding Everyday Life*, Aldine, 1970, pp. 165–87.

It is increasingly recognized as an issue for sociology that the equipment that enables the 'ordinary' member of society to make his daily way through the world is the equipment available for those who would wish to do a 'science' of that world.[1] This might be formulated as the sociologist's 'dilemma', but only so long as a notion of science is employed that fails to recognize the socially organized character of *any* enterprise, including the enterprise of doing science. A science of society that fails to treat speech as both topic and resource is doomed to failure. And yet, although speech informs the daily world and is the sociologist's basic resource, its properties continue to go almost unexamined. Linguistic models have had some recent influence on the development of sociolinguistics, but it is still not at all clear that any specifically linguistic properties of talk can be related to central sociological concerns. If we take sociology to be, in effect, 'a natural history of the social world', then sociologists are committed to a study of the *activities* such a world provides for and of the methodical achievement of those activities by socialized members.

In 1955, the British linguistic philosopher J. L. Austin set foot on sociological territory when he claimed a concern with the 'business' of any utterance considered as a piece of talk. In the course of beginning to map out the configurations, Austin identified an important class of utterances which he termed *performatives*.[2] A crucial test an utterance must meet to gain mem-

* Work on this paper was supported by grants from the Canada Council and The Foundations' Fund For Psychiatry.

1. Some particularly relevant discussions of this issue are to be found in Blum (1970), Cicourel (1964), Garfinkel (1967), Garfinkel and Sacks (1970) and Moerman (1972).

2. Austin's work on performatives is treated at great length in Austin (1965) and more briefly in 'Performative utterances' in Austin (1961). This is the place to acknowledge my great indebtedness to Austin's writings. In developing a critique of his concept of performative utterances here, I am biting the hand that has fed me for several years. I would like to make it quite clear that my perfunctory treatment of Austin's concept, in the service of elaborating some tools useful for conversational analysis, does no justice to the power and richness of *How To Do Things with Words*. The book is a sociological gold mine, waiting for prospectors.

bership in that class is described as follows: 'If a person makes an utterance of this sort we should say that he is *doing* something rather than merely *saying* something.' Austin (1961, p. 222) gives the following examples of what would count as performative utterances.

Suppose for example, that in the course of a marriage ceremony I say, as people will, 'I do' – (sc. take this woman to be my lawful wedded wife). Or again, suppose that I tread on your toe and say 'I apologize'. Or again, suppose that I have the bottle of champagne in my hand and say 'I name this ship the *Queen Elizabeth*.' Or suppose I said 'I bet you sixpence it will rain tomorrow.'

This sounds like a promising beginning, in that it sets out to provide some rigorous connection between talk (utterances) on the one hand, and activities (doing) on the other. More than that, it suggests that at least some talk can be analysed *as* the doing of activities, thus taking us at once beyond the naïve view that perhaps at best talk merely 'reports' activities. If Austin substantiates his claims, then, the links thus established between utterances and activities are very much the business of sociology. In this chapter I shall consider Austin's treatment of performative utterances in some detail, although I shall not do so in the spirit of providing an exposition or critique of Austin's work as an end in itself. My concern, rather, is with the elaboration of arguments that may underpin some actual procedures – primitive though they may be – for 'taking apart' stretches of talk in the examination of its constituent activities. Later in the chapter I shall provide some transcribed talk as data and attempt a brief demonstration of how such materials may be analysed in a sociologically relevant way so as to elucidate commonplace and recurrent activities. Indeed, very briefly I shall try to indicate how 'substantive findings' may be derived from such an analysis, but let me emphasize that the point of the chapter is not so much to present a set of findings as to demonstrate and discuss possible procedures for 'analysing utterances into activities'.[3]

I. Before looking further into Austin's treatment of performatives, let me suggest what might be their potential importance for sociological analysis in purely formal terms. Suppose for a moment that an exhaustive list of performative 'verbs' could be constructed, and that a formula could be provided to identify a performative utterance constructed out of an appropriate verb form; for example, if 'to bequeath' were an item in the list of performative verbs, then a corresponding utterance might be constructed along the following lines:

3. I borrow the phrase from the unpublished lectures of Harvey Sacks. Although I have tried to keep the record of specific borrowings straight, I have taken too much from Sacks to hope that a few footnotes will be an adequate measure of his writings as a resource.

I bequeath+[object name] to [person, kin or organization term] yielding, for example,
I bequeath [my watch] to [Jehovah's Witnesses].

If such a list and such a set of formulas could be provided, we should have achieved the following: *we should be in a position to scan transcripts of talk and formally identify items as instances of activities, where the name of the activity would be derivable from the performative verb* (for example, the activity of bequeathing). I assume this would be a significant sociological achievement in that it would provide the analyst with a tool with which he could systematically analyse transcribed conversations into at least one class of their constituent activities and identify mechanically some of the things persons *accomplish* through 'talk'. Indeed, presumably such a resource would provide the ultimate in contemporary sociological validation of methods, in that it could be fairly readily computerized.

Unfortunately, Austin's own elaboration of performatives provides at least two grounds on which such a procedure must fail. An examination of those grounds will, I believe, enable us to grasp both the fundamental usefulness of the notion of performatives and the ultimate failure of Austin's treatment to come to terms with social-organizational parameters of activities. I shall discuss briefly each of these grounds in turn.

The existence of 'implicit' and 'primitive' performatives

The development of a mechanical procedure for the extraction of performative utterances from a transcript, and hence the mechanical identification of a set of activities, depends upon both the 'listable' character of performative verbs (which would therefore need to be finite in number) and the ability to generate an unambiguously identifiable formula from any item in the list. Leaving aside the problem of constructing such a list, this requirement fails on the grounds that the formulaic appearance of a suitable verb form is not a necessary condition for the identification of a performative utterance. Thus Austin (1965, pp. 32–3) notes:

It is both obvious and important that we can on occasion use the utterance 'go' to achieve practically the same as we achieve by the utterance 'I order you to go': and we should say cheerfully in either case, *describing subsequently what someone did* [emphasis added], that he ordered me to go. It may, however, be uncertain in fact, and so far as the mere utterance is concerned, is always left uncertain when we use so inexplicit a formula as the mere imperative 'go', whether the utterer is ordering (or is purporting to order) me to go or merely advising, entreating or what not me to go. Similarly, 'There is a bull in the field' may or may not be a warning, for I *might* just be describing the scenery and 'I shall be there', may or may not be a promise. Here we have primitive as distinct from explicit performatives; and there may be nothing in the circumstances by which we can decide whether or not the utterance is performative at all. Anyway, in a given situation, it can be open to me to take it as *either* one or the other. It was a performative formula – *perhaps* – but the procedure in question was not sufficiently explicitly invoked. Perhaps I did not *take it as* an order or was not anyway *bound* to take it as an order. The person did not *take it as* a promise: i.e. in the particular circumstance he did not accept the procedure, on the ground that the ritual was incompletely carried out by the original speaker.

So much, then, for the mechanical recognition of performative utterances. But there is more to be learned from this discussion than the mere fact that no mechanical recognition procedure can be derived from Austin's analysis. Consider, for instance, the precise form of the initial condition for admission of an utterance to the class of performatives, as quoted earlier in the chapter: 'If a person makes an utterance of this sort *we should say* [emphasis added] that he is *doing* something rather than merely *saying* something.' The situation invoked here is not that of the doer of the activity but of the potential reporter of the activity and what he 'should' say in giving such a report. Similarly, in elaborating the problems of implicit and primitive performatives, Austin again, as a test of the character of the original utterance, appeals to the situation of 'describing subsequently what someone did'. In terms more familiar to sociologists, it appears that Austin is preoccupied with the giving of *warranted accounts* of events. Thus, I take it that the following hypothetical example is in the spirit of Austin's analysis.

A, returning from church, where he has just heard B utter the words 'I do' at the appropriate moment in a wedding ceremony, meets C, an old friend of both A and B. A tells C he has just seen B, and C asks, 'Oh, what was he doing?' Now, according to Austin, it would be 'odd' for A to reply, 'He was just saying a few words', *under the condition that it could be said,* 'He just got married.' I assume that it is indeed a basic fact of daily life that 'reports' or 'descriptions' are so constrained, and that behavioral or technical descriptions of events would frequently be treated as bizarre, humorous, in bad taste, or in some way incompetent. Nevertheless, there is a deeper issue here that I must briefly explore. In order to do this I want to make some changes in my hypothetical example.

A reads in the newspaper that B has recently married. He meets C (who has been out of town) on the street and says, 'Say, B just got married.' Now given that A was not present at the wedding – and indeed may never have been present at any wedding, being quite vague as to the structure of such an occasion – he certainly cannot be *reporting* on an utterance he did not hear. In this case we might be inclined (to use Austin's own criterion) to say that A was 'bringing C up-to-date', 'announcing' that B had got married, or whatever. Announcing, after all, is surely plausible business for an utterance to do.

Austin himself, in a classic paper, has provided for the possibility of an utterance's constituting an act of 'excusing' or 'justifying', where one condition of the utterance's doing that work is that *it occurs in the context of following upon an 'accusation'*. Thus:

You dropped the tea-tray: Certainly but an emotional storm was about to break out: or, Yes, but there was a wasp (1961, p. 124).

Suppose, then, that in the face of an accusation a person answers, 'He ordered me to do it.' Austinian logic would require us to treat such an utterance as *doing* the activity, 'excusing' or 'justifying'. What then of his treatment of utterances like 'He ordered me to do it' as derived from, dependent upon, and reporting on an earlier employment of a performative? In looking at some piece of talk as the 'later' report which serves as evidence for the 'earlier' existence of a performative utterance, Austin appears to claim that utterances can be treated as reports or descriptions *without reference to the interactional location of the utterance in question*.

Consider, then, the following difficulty which seems to be entailed by Austin's treatment of performatives.

We should find it 'odd' to say that Jones had 'uttered a few words' in the circumstances that what Jones did could be seen as 'getting married'. Should we not also find it odd to say that A was 'describing' some earlier talk of B's as a performative, in the circumstance that what A was doing was 'providing an excuse'?

In short, Austin's treatment of 'explicit' performatives as model forms to which other (related) utterances are to be assimilated as 'implicit' or 'primitive' varieties leads him to overlook the 'business' (the character *as an activity*) of utterances that he is inclined to treat as reports or descriptions of other utterances. 'Context' and 'convention', which are invoked to characterize the work of explicit performatives and as criterial for seeing other utterances as 'weaker' forms of performatives, cannot be permitted to go off duty when we seek to analyse other classes of utterances. Indeed, Austin himself is finally led to take explicit notice of describing as an activity, itself to be seen as a *located phenomenon*, when he argues that

The total speech act in the total speech situation is the *only actual* phenomenon which, in the last resort, we are engaged in elucidating (1965, p. 147).

It may be, of course (as I shall discuss in some detail in the data sections of the chapter), that *this* kind of recognition severs – or at least greatly weakens – the link between formulas for *doing* activities and the procedure whereby we decide *what* activity has been done: remember that at some point Austin's solution to the problem is simply to participalize the performative verb to locate a 'name' for the activity achieved by the performative utterance (for example, 'I apologize' is doing 'apologizing').

At this point I shall turn to the second ground (provided by Austin's own analysis) for undercutting the possibility of a 'mechanical' procedure for identifying instances of performative utterances.

The conventional supports of performatives

Recall that the issue is the possibility of locating members of a class of performative utterances (and hence activities) on the basis of developing some formula providing for their recognition. Even if the first objection to such a possibility (the existence of 'implicit' and 'primitive' performatives) did not exist, such an approach would still fail. For, as Austin notes, the successful employment (indeed, the existence) of utterances having a performative force depends upon two conditions, which we might refer to as social-organizational supports. The two conditions, as Austin states them are

(a) *There must exist an accepted conventional procedure having a certain conventional effect, the procedure to include the uttering of certain words by certain persons in certain circumstances* (1965, p. 26).
(b) *The particular persons and circumstances in a given case must be appropriate for the invocation of the particular procedure invoked* (1965, p. 34).

This seems reasonable enough, in that it argues that it is not the mere stringing together of words into utterances that automatically produces activities but that utterances are to be examined as being situated. Thus, I may say as many times as I wish, 'I bequeath the Crown Jewels to my son', but I have bequeathed nothing, and therefore have not performed an act of bequeathing, since the Crown Jewels are not mine to dispose of. Austin is fond of pointing out that utterances embedded in jokes or stage plays do not carry their normal performative force: an actor and actress do not 'in fact' become man and wife by nightly going through a representation of a wedding ceremony.

It is a sufficient objection to locating instances of performative utterances by formula, then, to note that two appearances of the 'same' utterance may not count as two instances of the 'same' activity (if one is spoken within the framework of a stage play, for example). But again, there is surely more to say about utterances and their settings than can be generated by considering how performatives may 'fail' for want of some proper 'fit' between situational elements. Thus, to mention a possibility without pursuing it in any detail, 'doing a joke' may be achieved precisely by virtue of the fit between utterance and setting; the utterance 'I promise' may come off as a successful joke, where it would be perverse to see it as merely an instance of a spoiled 'promise'.

For the sociologist, further, Austin's two conditions can be faulted on the grounds that they simply take for granted matters that persons in the society may have to decide, negotiate, or assert as premises for bringing off activities. Thus, granted that the events of a stage play do not have the force of the activities they merely depict, *that it is a stage play* must itself be made demonstrable as a framework for viewing. The 'brute fact' of being a stage play is not in itself a guarantee that at least some represented activities may not be fully consequential. Thus, to take a gross instance, if you and I decide to rehearse a scene from a script on the sidewalk downtown, wherein I press a gun in your ribs and say 'This is a stick-up', the 'brute fact' that it is, after all, a play, will not necessarily prevent my being cut down by a passing armed policeman. Even 'happenings' and other advanced forms of 'spontaneous' theater take place at announced times in announced places. Pirandellian tricks depend for their effect upon their being viewed as theatrical devices; a literal 'confusion' between depicted and 'for real' events is no part of the theater that trades upon realism and spontaneity.

I shall now provide some transcribed pieces of talk and employ them for a discussion of some elementary procedures for analysing activities. Although I still plan to travel a little further with Austin, I think the journey will be more eventful if it leads us to confront the concrete problems of dealing with actual bits of interaction.

II. Here, then, is a piece of talk pulled out of a transcript made from a tape-recorded occasion. I shall deliberately withhold any description of the occasion or the setting for the moment, since issues concerning their relevance are part of what we have to discuss.

BERT Yea, yeah, that's correct. I uh uh really did know im and uh he was with me
   in the Alexander Psychiatric Institute in in Alexander, Western Province. I I
   don't remember his name but we uh we always buddied around together when
   uh we were at the hospital and we always (( )) French. And uh I saw him out at
   Western City about three weeks ago, and I said to 'm, 'Hello, howarya doing?'
   He said 'I don't know you – who are you?' 'Well, lookit', I said, 'You *must*
   know me.' He says, 'No, I don't know you.' Now he was with another fellow
   there too – waal he didn't want to admit that he was in a mental hospital uh in a
   hospital – he didn't want to admit it to the other fellow that was with him. So
   he just walked off and that was it. He wouldn't say hello to me. He wouldn't say
   nothin!
ROB What was you view there? Do you have your own views on that? A touchy
   point.
BERT Uh.
?: (( ))
JAKE Perhaps he didn't like the idea of being in that place. Maybe he didn't
   want/
BERT Well no he had to say it – there was another fellow with him you see/

JAKE Well he didn't want to admit/
BERT Who hadn't been in a mental hospital probably, and he *was* in the hospital.
      He didn't want *him* to know.
ART You mean he
?: This other guy
COUNS But he
BERT Oh, oh never been in a hospital
BERT He didn't want to know his friends.[4]

Now, given such materials as these, the practical issue is: how might they be analysed in a sociologically relevant way – that is to say, as a demonstration of their orderliness? An initial problem seems to be that as societal members we find that such materials are often terribly obvious, if not trite (and I imagine that the reader was able to find sense in the talk on the basis of a very rapid reading, despite the fact that he has no personal knowledge of Bert and the other speakers); while as sociologists, confronted with the task of obtaining some leverage in providing an analytical description, the very same set of utterances become forbiddingly opaque. It becomes opaque, I believe, under the condition that as sociologists we suppose that we must locate instances (or indicators) of concepts posited by an explicit theory; and yet we obviously have no such theory to guide us in analysing talk in any detail. Thus an elementary problem might be formulated as: what are we to attend to as units – words, sentences, utterances?

Let us assume that we are agreed for the moment that we want to locate and look at instances of activities. The problem still remains. I take it that Austin did not doubt that we can *recognize* activities; indeed, his method of operation seems to require, first, the collection of a number of performative utterances, treated as non-problematic in itself, after it has been explained what shall count as a performative utterance, and, then, the search for formal criteria that distinguish the class of performatives from other classes of utterances. Of course, if we isolated the formal criteria, we should then have no problem in scanning further candidates of performatives to decide their membership status; but that scarcely solves the problem of how we assemble our first collection of utterances on the basis of which the formal criteria are to be derived.

As a solution to the vexed problem of the relation between the shared cultural knowledge (members' knowledge) that the sociologist possesses and the analytical apparatus that it is his responsibility to produce, I propose the following:

1. *The sociologist inevitably trades on his members' knowledge* in recognizing the activities that participants to interaction are engaged in; for example, it

4. This transcript was supplied to me by Anthony Crowle.

is by virtue of my status as a competent member that I can recurrently locate in my transcripts instances of 'the same' activity. This is not to claim that members are infallible or that there is perfect agreement in recognizing any and every instance; it is only to claim that no resolution of problematic cases can be effected by resorting to procedures that are supposedly uncontaminated by members' knowledge. (Arbitrary resolutions, made for the sake of easing the problems of 'coding', are of course no resolution at all for the present enterprise.)

2. The sociologist, having made his first-level decision on the basis of members' knowledge, must then *pose as problematic* how utterances come off as recognizable unit activities. This requires the sociologist to *explicate the resources* he shares with the participants in making sense of utterances in a stretch of talk. At every step of the way, inevitably, the sociologist will continue to employ his socialized competence, while continuing to make explicit *what* these resources are and *how* he employs them. I see no alternative to these procedures, except to pay no explicit attention to one's socialized knowledge while continuing to use it as an indispensable aid. In short, sociological discoveries are ineluctably discoveries *from within the society*.

Now leaving the programmatics aside, let me cite once again Austin's admonition that 'the total speech act in the total speech situation is the *only actual* phenomenon which, in the last resort, we are engaged in elucidating'. Supposing we decide to take this seriously, how do we bring it to bear on the data presented above? What, for example, is 'the total speech situation' of the talk recorded and transcribed?

Consider the possibility that more than one technically correct description of the occasion of the talk might be provided. Thus I could propose that a tape recording was made of Bert and a few acquaintances sitting around having an evening's chat. Another possible description of the occasion is as follows: a number of former mental patients voluntarily attended an evening group discussion sponsored by a mental health association; the discussion was in the charge of a counselor whose instructions were to help members of the group discuss their problems. As between these two possible descriptions I offer the latter as the more useful, employing the following criterion: the latter description characterizes the occasion as that occasion was organized, announced, and made available to the participants; an act of self-identification as a 'former mental patient' was any member's entitlement to attend, and his entitlement to see that his fellow participants (apart from the 'counselor') were likewise 'former mental patients.'

Why does this matter? It matters, I argue, in that it provides participants with an orientation and a set of criteria for contributing and recognizing activities. Whatever one says during the course of the evening may be treated as 'something said by a former mental patient', not on the 'technical' grounds that after all one *is* such a person but on the grounds that that identification is occasioned and thereby warranted as relevant.

Presumably this does not end a characterization of the 'total speech situation' of any unit of speech smaller than the whole conversation. Thus consider Bert's remark 'So he just walked off and that was it.' I assume that in order to see the sense of this remark it is necessary to notice its ties to at least the earlier parts of the utterance from which it is extracted. Notice, for instance, that given its position in the utterance, the 'he' in the remark 'So he just walked off and that was it' can be given a determinate reading by hearers (and now readers). Put crudely, then, one task of an analysis such as this is to make explicit just what features of the occasion and the talk are appealed to as providing for the force of an utterance or the character of an activity.

I hear Bert's remarks in this portion of the talk as constituting a 'complaint', or 'doing complaining'. In so identifying it, I am unable to locate any obvious syntactic properties that might be seen as structural correlates of complaints, nor do I have any operational means for identifying its boundaries. I take it that Bert may have begun his complaint in an utterance previous to the first utterance given here; and I further assume that Bert's last utterance given here (but not the end of the talk), 'He didn't want to know his friends', is in some sense 'part of' the complaint. I know of no *a priori* reason an activity should be expected to require so many words or so many utterances; in any piece of data being considered it will be an issue to note the boundedness of an activity.

I now want to look at the production of a recognizable complaint in some detail, to look at the resources and components of Bert's complaint. I use the term resources carefully, since I take it that there is an issue of bringing off an activity in such a way that one's hearers can bring to the talk the necessary equipment and materials to make out its intended character.

Commonsensically there is no difficulty in saying that the basis of Bert's complaints is a 'snub'. More specifically, I take it that Bert's account is of 'a former mental patient being snubbed', and thus is produced as an instance of 'the kind of thing that can happen to a former mental patient'.

Let us assume for the moment that a snub or slight, in the form of a refusal of recognition, can happen to 'anyone'. For the person to whom it has happened, such an event can presumably constitute a puzzle – that is to say, it is an event requiring an explanation. If I walk down the corridor and meet a colleague I encounter in such circumstances daily, and if we exchange greetings, then an interactional routine will have been achieved that – *for members* – is nonproblematic. Thus, if you are accompanying me at the time and you ask 'Why did that guy smile at you?' I assume that an answer such as 'He's a colleague of mine', will be sufficient, that is, that it would be 'odd' for you to persist, 'I know that, but why did he smile at you?' A snub becomes a puzzle, presumably, just because such a nonproblematic routine is breached.

Now if after being snubbed one makes that event the basis of an anecdote for others, one thing they may do, it seems, is to offer possible 'explanations' or queries directed to uncovering 'what happened'. One readily available explanation has the consequence of inviting you to reconsider the event, to see that it wasn't a snub after all, perhaps that 'there was some mistake' – that it wasn't who you thought it was. He looked remarkably like an old friend, but you caught only a glimpse, and it was probably a stranger. I mention this routine treatment because if we look carefully at Bert's first utterance we can see that Bert orients to the possibility of this being forthcoming from his hearers, and forestalls it: 'I uh uh really did know im.' The reader should notice here the interplay between common-sense knowledge offered as how I make out what is going on, and sociological concern, in that I take it as an analytical responsibility to account for the remark 'I uh uh really did know im', while having recourse to members' knowledge in providing the substance of my account.

Now if we look at Bert's first utterance as a unit, it seems that it (a) recounts the occurrence of the snub, and (b) provides an explanation for it. Nevertheless, at the same time it is via the character of the explanation that I see that Bert is constructing a complaint. In effect, this leads us to consider the 'mechanics' of doing an activity. If Bert is to bring off a successful instance of a complaint, he must build it out of components that will provide for its recognition by hearers who are presumed to be – like Bert, and like readers – 'experts' in constructing and recognizing a repertoire of activities. In looking at the talk in detail, then, we are discovering how the materials at hand are made to serve the requirements of certain invariant properties of activities. The following considerations lead me to argue that the explanation provides for Bert to be seen as 'complaining'.

1. Recall Austin's requirement for the successful achievement of a performative utterance, that 'the particular persons and circumstances in a given case must be appropriate for the invocation of the particular procedure involved'. How is that relevant to the present issue? In the first place, since we are not analysing as data the talk that took place between Bert and his acquaintance upon the occasion of the snub, we are hardly in a position to characterize that 'total speech situation' in a way that a transcript of the occasion might permit. What we have, rather, is Bert's characterization of the occasion, developed as a resource for constructing a complaint. In effect, then, we are dealing with the societal member's concern with providing for the 'appropriateness' of the 'particular persons and circumstances' as features that

will properly orient hearers to the sense of the occasion – that is, orient them to a sense of the occasion that will enable them to recognize what Bert is *now* doing. This permits us to ask: *how* does Bert provide such an orientation?

Notice first, then, that Bert does not simply tell his listeners that he was snubbed by 'an acquaintance', 'an old friend' or 'a guy I knew', although presumably any of these would have been a sufficient and proper identification of the party to allow for what happened to be seen as a snub. Bert identified the snubber as a man who 'was with me in the Alexander Psychiatric Institute'. Now I take it that this identification is not warranted simply by its literal correctness, since a range of possible 'correct' identifications is always available (in this case, for example, 'a fellow I used to know in Western Province') and it is not a matter of indifference which item of a set of possible items is selected. One thing we can note about the identification selected, then, is a relevance provided by the occasion, by the presence of this collection of hearers, in that the party mentioned is mentioned now as 'one of us'. Beyond that, the identification of the snubber as 'he was with me in the Alexander Psychiatric Institute' provides that Bert himself could be seen by the other party as a 'released mental patient'.

2. Bert tells his listeners that on recognizing the other party he said to him, 'Hello, howarya doing?' Now given that he has already indicated *that* (and *how*) they were acquainted, a greeting is seen to be in order and to require a greeting in return, since an exchange of greetings is a procedure permitted among acquainted persons; and upon one party's offering a greeting the other is taken to be under obligation to return it. In short, I take it that Bert is invoking what I have just stated in the form of a 'norm', and that it is by reference to such a procedure that it becomes 'obvious' to his listeners that 'something was wrong' when instead of the greeting the greeted party returned with 'I don't know you – who are you?' That this is the case is further provided for by Bert's remark 'He wouldn't say hello to me. He wouldn't say nothin!' As I understand Bert's remark, assumption of shared knowledge that a greeted acquaintance has an *obligation* to respond with a greeting is both a requirement and a resource for seeing how Bert is entitled to say 'He *wouldn't* say hello to me', in that he is thus enabling his listeners to find the 'absence of a greeting' as a motivated act.[5]

So far, then, all we have seen is an account of a breached norm, the norm that requires acquainted persons to acknowledge one another upon meeting face-to-face. This component of the account constitutes the occurrence of a 'trouble', in this case, a snub.

5. On the notion of 'relevant absences', see Sacks, unpublished lectures and research notebooks. Compare Schegloff's discussion of 'conditional relevance' in Schegloff (1968).

3. If we look further at the utterance we find that Bert claims to see *why* he was offered a slight by an aquaintance who owed him at least the return of a greeting. Thus, Bert remarks: 'Now he was with another fellow there too – waal he didn't want to admit that he was in a mental hospital uh in a hospital – he didn't want to admit to the other fellow that was with him. So he just walked off and that was it.'

Now the interesting question to ask is: *How does this come off as an explanation?* To set it up with heuristic naïvité, what could Bert be talking about in saying of the other party 'He didn't want to admit . . . that he was in a mental hospital?' How does the question of making an admission arise? To put the question in somewhat different form, we may ask: are there any resources that Bert's listeners (as well as ourselves) might bring to bear on this remark to see in it the sense it is presumably intended to have (as grounds for the refusal to return a greeting)? How might it be seen that a returned greeting would be, or would lead to, an 'admission to the other fellow' that he had been in a mental hospital? To put it differently, and in common-sense terms, it might be argued that it would have been entirely inconsequential for Bert's former fellow-patient to have responded, for example, 'Pretty good, thanks. How's yourself?'

I take it that Bert is able to trade upon an 'obvious' feature of 'chance encounters', namely, their informational value. The paradigm case is suggested by the following hypothetical conversation.

A Who was that guy who waved from across the street?
B Oh, just a fellow I knew in the Marines.
A Really? I didn't know you were in the Marines! When was that?

Bert's friend, then, could be depicted as motivated to refuse an acknowledgement of the acquaintance on the grounds that it might have opened him up to 'explaining' to his companion 'who' Bert was – where the relevant sense of 'who' would require a reference to the basis of their being acquainted. But beyond that, there are other norms relating to the situation of renewing acquaintance that are possibly being invoked here.

An issue in the orderly conduct of conversation may be termed 'the distribution of speaker's rights' (see Garfinkel and Sacks, 1970; Speier, 1968). Thus Sacks has pointed out with respect to questions and answers as paired units that a potentially infinite chain of utterances may be produced under the auspices of the following rule: *the questioner has a right to talk again when an answer is returned*, that is, when the answerer finishes his turn at talking the right to speak passes back to the questioner, *and the questioner has a right to ask another question* (thus providing for another answer and a further question; and so the cycle may be repeated, as court transcripts nicely indicate). Similarly, Schegloff (1968) has indicated that within the structure of a telephone call the caller may select the first topic for talk. With respect to face-to-face social contacts among the acquainted it appears to be the case that a simple exchange of greetings – 'hello', 'hello' – may constitute an adequate 'conversation', and the parties may separate without breach of the relationship. However, it further appears to be the case that the initial greeter has the right to talk again when a greeting is returned, and that he thus becomes a 'first speaker' with respect to rights of topic selection. If this is the case, then (as I take it Bert and his listeners could see), to acknowledge a greeting by returning a greeting is to open oneself up to the initial greeter's developing a conversation and to his initiating a topic. In the cited incident, Bert would have had the right to so talk, providing that his acquaintance did not attach the opening of topical talk to the utterance returning a greeting.

If we shift our attention for the moment from the initiation of talk to the issue of the *management of relationships*, conversations can be seen as having sequential properties; that is, when related parties meet, the conversational possibilities may be constrained by 'what happened last time' or by events that have intervened. Thus, persons employ opening slots in conversations to 'bring one another up-to-date', or – when the passage of time has been considerable, or 'circumstances' have changed – to talk over 'when we last saw each other', or, as in reunions, to 'talk over old times'. Notice again that I am suggesting this not as an analysis independent of members' knowledge and members' concerns but as integral to them, and I take it that it is a commonplace experience to 'look forward to' or 'avoid' persons with whom such conversations are to be expected.

In this connection it is relevant to note that Bert's development of the situation permits his hearers to see that indeed 'bringing up-to-date' might have been in order, in that this was apparently a first meeting since the hospital days, and in a city more than a thousand miles from the hospital. In short, the locational and temporal features of the occasion are not simply descriptive but are *explanatory*: a 'reunion' would have 'normally' been in order, and a reunion could be seen as precisely what a former mental patient who is 'passing' could anticipate as a threat.[6] Returning a greeting, then, is not

6. Stan Persky pointed out to me the importance, for the account, of the encounter being seen as 'the first since the hospital'. An instance of the fulfillment of such a threat is contained in the following account given me by a former mental patient, in response to my asking if he would greet 'fellow former patients' he might meet on the street:

Al: Yes I do. I stop and say hello to them and one case I came across was . . . we used to buy our groceries from the New Market Store and he was the manager – of the New Market Store. Well, he went out to State Hospital. I met him out there and I said hello to him out there and talked to him for a while. A year later I met him downtown in Western City. He was with his wife and I said, 'Oh, hello, Mr Robbins. Remember

without cost.[7] For Bert's acquaintance, the return of a greeting, carrying with it an acknowledgement of their relationship, would have entitled Bert to develop talk about what each had done 'since the hospital', etc. Thus potential conversational partners may avoid eye contacts, give signs of 'being in a hurry', or balk at the first interchange, where the 'danger' is seen to be located at some later (and unspecifiable) spot in the conversation that mutual acknowledgement may generate.

4. To recapitulate, I have suggested that the visible breach of a norm requiring acquainted persons to acknowledge one another, or at least return a proffered greeting, has constituted a trouble for Bert – he has been snubbed. Bert saw and made available to his hearers an explanation of the snub; it was by no means a case of mistaken identity but rather a matter of 'deliberate' (motivated) refusal to 'know a friend' on the part of one who might find that the cost of an acknowledgement would be disclosure to a companion that he had been a 'mental patient'.

But – and this I suppose to be crucial – it isn't the mere fact that the snubber had been a 'mental patient' that constitutes *Bert's* embarrassment or chagrin: for Bert the complaint-worthy item is presumably *that he sees that he himself had been identified as a 'former mental patient'*; the snubber's own problems stemmed from *Berts's* former-patient status.

This I take to be the feature of the account that constitutes it as a complaint, where the complaint could be formulated, for example, as 'He wouldn't talk to me because I've been a mental patient.' The complaint, then, is directed to the recurrent kinds of 'troubles' that persons can find themselves inheriting along with an unwanted categorical identification – in this case the identification that constitutes the tie between participants to the group talk and that is taken by them to generate the occasion in the first place. The complaint thus becomes a *category-generated activity*, providing for any members of the category (such as Bert's hearers) to see that 'what happened to him' could happen to 'us'.

Earlier in the chapter I mentioned briefly that the analysis of talk into activities here presented could be seen to provide for at least a suggestion of 'substantive findings'. What I have in mind is that the preceding discussion permits some comments on the traditional sociological literature on former mental patients and their 'problems', a literature which, with few exceptions beyond the writings of Erving Goffman, establishes as its framework of inquiry a set of psychiatric assumptions concerning the character of such

me out at State Hospital?' And his wife looked at me and said, 'He's never been out in State Hospital.' But there was no mistaking it. It was him. (laughs) I thought that was quite funny.

7. Compare the anecdote cited by Schegloff to make the point 'that conversational oaks may out of conversational acorns grow', in Schegloff (1968, p. 1094).

'problems'.[8] On the basis of the analysis presented here I believe I am warranted in suggesting that the categorical identification 'former mental patient' (as used by former mental patients themselves and by others) does the work of organizing and structuring accounts of persons' behavior and difficulties. That is to say, under the conditions that a person can be categorized *as* a former mental patient, such an identification can and will be used by members as explanatory and predictive of what such persons 'do'.

For persons in the rehabilitative professions, such an identification provides the auspices for searching out (and finding), for example, residual illness, bizarre behavior, having a relapse, etc. 'Former mental patients' themselves, on the other hand, make use of their membership in the category to both locate and explain a set of interactional 'difficulties' that they provide accounts of as recurrent events in transactions with friends, family, neighbors, etc. Notice that although I have constantly appealed to membership in the category 'former mental patient' to elucidate what I took it participants to the talk were orienting themselves to, I have not *as part of my own analytical apparatus* attributed any special properties to such category incumbents, on the grounds (hopefully clear by now) that the invocation of the category as part of the 'total speech situation' is the only relevant feature for my purposes.

What I want to note, then, is that a plausible view of at least one class of 'problems' of 'former mental patients' is that such problems are generated out of the same raw materials that provide for 'normal' interactional routines, in particular, the invocation of norms governing such matters as meeting an old friend. It is in finding that such norms may be breached systematically, and the breach accounted for by the identification 'former mental patient', that Bert is able to propose that 'what happened' constituted a complaint-worthy event. Further, not only is it the case that such persons may find their 'problems' cut from the same cloth that allows 'normals' to manage relationships in a satisfactory way, it also seems to be the case that 'former mental patients' employ the same standard methodical procedures for 'giving accounts', 'constructing complaints', etc., as are available to 'anyone'. Even persons who claim that their lives have been 'ruined' as a consequence of time spent in the mental hospital may still retain intact their grasp on 'how to do things with words' – *their* claims, in effect, validating *my* claim.

8. I am thinking particularly of *Stigma* (Goffman, 1963), but the structure of interactionally generated problems is a theme in all of Goffman's writings. It is interesting to note by contrast that when Freeman and Simmons (1963, p. 233), in a book-length study of the 'problems' of former mental patients, turn their attention to the issue of 'stigma' it is to note the embarrassment created for 'the family' by having a former mental patient in their midst.

III. A few concluding remarks about words, utterances, and activities. A traditional sociological approach treats speech either as a source of 'hidden' realities – such as values, attitudes and beliefs – waiting for the sociologist to uncover them, or as the reporting of members' 'perceptions' of social facts, to be verified or falsified by 'scientific' procedures. The initial value of Austin's work is that it at least brings our attention back to the fact that, as persons go about their business, some of that business is done (and not merely reported upon) *in* and *through* talk. It also helps us to see that an inventory of 'norms' or 'role expectations' fails to come to terms with the fact that members may (and do) assert, argue, hint at, deny, undercut, etc., the 'relevant' situational features of accountable actions, *upon the occasion of giving accounts*. Some recent sociological writings do stress the 'negotiated' or 'emergent' character of interaction but usually fail to demonstrate how the structure of any given piece of talk can be displayed as an interlocking set of activities. Without linked demonstrations, of course, such programmatic statements must resemble 'advice' given at a level of generality which leaves the researcher still facing the crucial problem of how to analyse the tapes or transcripts that constitute his data. Too often such theories of interaction becomes the rugs under which the data are conveniently swept. The reader who wishes to utilize such 'theoretical' writings is typically left to ask 'Now what do I do?' It is in the hope of avoiding another such exhortation that I have attempted to spell out in some detail what an analysis of talk into its constituent activities might look like.[9]

In building upon and departing from Austin's work I have argued:

9. A few sociologists have recently tried to develop models based on premises derived from transformational grammar. Despite the intrinsic interest of such work, and the cogency of the arguments, such writings differ from the work of linguists proper in one crucial respect; they fail to tie their theoretical arguments to the analysis of particular instances of data. Thus, whatever insensitivity to social structure the sociologist may find in some linguistic treatments of the deep structure of sentences, at least the linguist typically spells out in detail the steps whereby he arrives at his analysis, thus permitting his colleagues to pinpoint their criticisms and requiring them to demonstrate the basis of alternative treatments of the same data. It is for this reason that I have taken the space to spell out rather literally how I 'hear' talk in the transcript above. Readers are free to perform their own analyses of the data in alternative to mine. In this connection I cannot resist quoting Gilbert Ryle's comment (in Chappell, 1964, p. 26) on his problems in arguing the 'stock use' of an 'ordinary' expression with his colleagues: 'One's fellow-philosophers are at such pains to pretend that they cannot think what its stock use is – a difficulty which, of course, they forget about when they are teaching children or foreigners how to use it, and when they are consulting dictionaries.' The point, I take it, is that our concern in treating interaction is not to see how ingenious we can be in torturing alternative senses out of utterances, but that our task is to characterize their employment as it is located in the talk – such as we may (and do) find ourselves engaged in. Wittgenstein (1958, p. 18) might almost have had traditional sociology in mind when he spoke of 'the contemptuous attitude towards the particular case'.

1. That all and any exchanges of utterances – defining an utterance for the moment as one speaker's turn at talking – can in principle be regarded as 'doing things with words'.

2. That there is no *a priori* reason to suppose that syntactical or lexical correspondences exist between units of speech and activities.

3. That in constructing their talk, members provide for the recognition of 'what they are doing' by invoking culturally provided resources.

4. That 'total speech situations' are to be elucidated as the features oriented to by members in doing and recognizing activities, and assessing their appropriateness.

5. That in undertaking such elucidations, sociologists *must* (and do) employ their own expertise in employing and recognizing methodical procedures for accomplishing activities.

6. That the task of the sociologist in analysing naturally occurring scenes is not to deny his competence in making sense of activities but to *explicate* it.

7. That such explication provides for a cumulative enterprise, in that the uncovering of members' *procedures* for doing activities permits us both to replicate our original data and to generate new instances that fellow members will find recognizable.

I would particularly like to emphasize this last claim that the sociological apparatus that emerges from the detailed study of interaction is a set of descriptions of *methods* and *procedures* (for accomplishing and locating activities). Work that is currently proceeding along these lines suggests that the logic of the 'programming' whereby socialized members 'produce' social structure will result in a more viable central core for a 'scientific' sociology than the existing common-sense division of the discipline into 'substantive fields'. The building of this core as an empirical enterprise depends upon the sociologist's recognition that he has no choice but to reflect upon and analyse the social order to which he himself subscribes.

References

AUSTIN, J. L. (1961), *Philosophical Papers*, J. O. Urmson and G. L. Warnock (eds.), Oxford University Press, Inc.

AUSTIN, J. L. (1965), *How to Do Things with Words*, J. O. Urmson (ed.), Oxford University Press, Inc.

BLUM, A. F. (1970), 'The sociology of mental illness', in J. Douglas (ed.), *Deviance and Respectability: The Social Construction of Moral Meanings*, Basic Books.

CHAPPELL, V. C. (ed.) (1964), *Ordinary Language*, Prentice-Hall.

CICOUREL, A. V. (1964), *Method and Measurement in Sociology*, Free Press.

FREEMAN, H. D., and SIMMONS, O. G. (1963), *The Mental Patient Comes Home*, Wiley.

GARFINKEL, H. (1967), *Studies in Ethnomethodology*, Prentice-Hall.

GARFINKEL, H., and SACKS, H. (1970), 'On formal structures of practical actions' in J. C. McKinney and E. A. Tiryakian (eds.), *Theoretical Sociology: Perspectives and Development*, Appleton-Century-Crofts.

GOFFMAN, E. (1963), *Stigma: Notes on and Management of Spoiled Identity*, Prentice-Hall; Penguin, 1970.

MOERMAN, M. (1972), 'Analysis of Lue conversation: providing accounts, finding breaches, and taking sides', in D. Sudnow (ed.), *Studies in Social Interaction*, Free Press.

SCHEGLOFF, E. A. (1968), 'Sequencing in conversational openings', *American Anthropologist*, vol. 70.

SPEIER, M. (1968), 'Some conversational problems for interactional analysis', in D. Sudnow (ed.), *Studies in Social Interaction*, Free Press.

WITTGENSTEIN, L. (1958), *The Blue and the Brown Books*, Harper & Row.

17 Harvey Sacks

On the Analysability of Stories by Children

Harvey Sacks, 'On the analyzability of stories by children', in
John J. Gumperz and Dell Hymes (ed.) *Directions in Sociolinguistics:
The Ethnography of Communication*, Holt, Rinehart & Winston, 1972, pp. 329-45.

In this chapter I intend, first, to present and employ several of the more basic concepts and techniques which I shall be using. Since most of those I shall use at this point may also be found in the paper 'An Initial Investigation of the Usability of Conversational Data for Doing Sociology' (Sacks, 1972), the discussion here may be seen as reintroducing and extending the results developed there. Second, I shall focus on the activity 'doing describing' and the correlative activity 'recognizing a description', activities which members may be said to do, and which therefore are phenomena which sociologists and anthropologists must aim to be able to describe. It will initially be by reference to an examination of instances of members' describings that my attempts to show how sociologists might solve their own problem of constructing descriptions will be developed. Proceeding in the fashion I have proposed will permit a focus on several central and neglected issues which social science must face, most particularly, the problem of members' knowledge and the problem of relevance. Let us then begin.

Problems in recognizing possible descriptions

The initial data are the first two sentences from a 'story' offered by a two-year-and-nine-month-old girl to the author of the book *Children Tell Stories*. They are, 'The baby cried. The mommy picked it up'. I shall first make several observations about these sentences. Before doing so, however, let me note: if these observations strike you as a ranker sort of subjectivism, then I ask you to read on just far enough to see whether it is or is not the case that the observations are both relevant and defensible. When I hear 'The baby cried. The mommy picked up up', one thing I hear is that the 'mommy' who picks the 'baby' up is the mommy of that baby. That is a first observation. (You will, of course, notice that the second sentence does not contain a genitive. It does not read, 'Its mommy picked it up', or variants thereof.) Now it is not only that *I* hear that the mommy is the mommy of that baby, but I feel rather confident that at least many of the natives among you hear that also. That is a second observation. One of my tasks is going to be to construct an apparatus which will provide for the foregoing facts to have occurred; an apparatus, i.e. which will show how it is that we come to hear the fragment as we do.

Some more: I take it we hear two sentences. Call the first S_1 and the second S_2; the first reports an occurence O_1 and the second reports on occurrence O_2. Now, I take it we hear that as S_2 follows S_1, so O_2 follows O_1. That is a third observation. And also: we hear that O_2 occurs because of O_1, i.e. the explanation for O_2 occurring is that O_1 did. That is a fourth observation. I want the apparatus to show how we come to hear those facts also. If I asked you to explain the group of observations which I have made, observations which you could have made just as well – and let me note, they are *not* proposed as sociological findings, but rather do they pose some of the problems which social science shall have to resolve – you might well say something like the following: we hear that it is the mommy of the baby who picks the baby up because she's the one who ought to pick it up, and (you might eventually add) if she's the one who ought to pick it up, and it was picked up by somebody who could be her, then it was her, or was probably her.

You might go on: while it is quite clear that not any two consecutive sentences, not even any consecutive sentences that report occurrences, are heard, and properly heard, as reporting that the occurrences have occurred in the order which the sentences have, if the occurrences ought to occur in that order, and if there is no information to the contrary (such as a phrase at the beginning of the second, like 'before that, however'), then the order of the sentences indicates the order of the occurrences. And these two sentences do present the order of the occurrences they report in the proper order for such occurrences. If the baby cried, it ought to have started crying before the mother picked it up, and not after. Hearing it that way, the second sentence is explained by the first; hearing them as consecutive or with the second preceding the first, some further explanation is needed, and none being present, we may suppose that it is not needed.

Now let me make a fifth observation: all of the foregoing can be done by many or perhaps any of us without knowing what baby or what mommy it is that might be being talked of. With this fifth observation it may now be noticed that what we've essentially been saying so far is that the pair of sentences seems to satisfy what a member might require of some pair of sentences for them to be recognizable as 'a possible description'. They 'sound like a description', and some form of words can, apparently, sound like a description. To recognize that some form of words is a possible description does not require that one must first inspect the circumstance it may be characterizing.

That 'possible descriptions' are recognizable as such is quite an important fact, for members, and for social scientists. The reader ought to be able to think out some of its import for members, e.g. the economies it affords them. It is the latter clause, 'and for social scientists', that I now wish to attend to. Were it not so both that members have an activity they do, 'describing', and that at least some cases of that activity produce, for them, forms of words recognizable as at least possible descriptions without having to do an inspection of the circumstances they might characterize, then it might well be that social science would necessarily be the last of the sciences to be made do-able. For, unless social scientists could study such things as these 'recognizable descriptions', we might only be able to investigate such activities of members as in one or another way turned on 'their knowledge of the world' when social scientists could employ some established, presumptively correct scientific characterizations of the phenomena members were presumably dealing with and knowing about. If, however, members have a phenomenon, 'possible descriptions' which are recognizable *per se*, then one need not in the instance know how it is that babies and mommies do behave to examine the composition of such possible descriptions as members produce and recognize. Sociology and anthropology need not await developments in botany or genetics or analyses of the light spectra to gain a secure position from which members' knowledge, and the activities for which it is relevant, might be investigated. What one ought to seek to build is an apparatus which will provide for how it is that any activities, which members do in such a way as to be recognizable as such to members, are done, and done recognizably. Such an apparatus will, of course, have to generate and provide for the recognizability of more than just possible descriptions, and in later discussions we shall be engaged in providing for such activities as 'inviting', 'warning', and so forth, as the data we consider will permit and require.

My reason for having gone through the observations I have so far made was to give you some sense, right off, of the fine power of a culture. It does not, so to speak, merely fill brains in roughly the same way, it fills them so that they are alike in fine detail. The sentences we are considering are after all rather minor, and yet all of you, or many of you, hear just what I said you heard, and many of us are quite unacquainted with each other. I am, then, dealing with something real and something finely powerful.

Membership categorization devices

We may begin to work at the construction of the apparatus. I'm going to introduce several of the terms we need. The first term is *membership categorization device* (or just *categorization device*). By this term I shall intend; any collection of membership categories, containing at least a category, which may be applied to some population containing at least a member, so as to provide, by the use of some rules of application, for the pairing of at least a population member and a categorization device member. A device is then a collection plus rules of application.

An instance of a categorization device is the one called 'sex'; its collection is the two categories (male, female). It is important to observe that a collection consists of categories that 'go together'. For now that may merely be seen as a constraint of the following sort: I could say that some set of categories was a collection, and be wrong. I shall present some rules of application very shortly.

Before doing that, however, let me observe that 'baby' and 'mommy' can be seen to be categories from one collection: the collection whose device is called 'family' and which consists of such categories as ('baby,' 'mommy', 'daddy' . . .) where by ' . . .' we mean that there are others, but not any others, e.g. 'shortstop'.

Let me introduce a few rules of application. It may be observed that if a member uses a single category from any membership categorization device, then they can be recognized to be doing *adequate reference* to a person. We may put the observation in a negative form: it is not necessary that some multiple of categories from categorization devices be employed for recognition that a person is being referred to, to be made; a single category will do. (I do not mean by this that more cannot be used, only that for reference to persons to be recognized more need not be used.) With that observation we can formulate a 'reference satisfactoriness' rule, which we call 'the economy rule'. It holds: a single category from any membership categorization device can be referentially adequate.

A second rule I call 'the consistency rule'. It holds: if some population of persons is being categorized, and if a category from some device's collection has been used to categorize a first member of the population, then that category or other categories of the same collection *may* be used to categorize further members of the population. The former rule was a 'reference satisfactoriness' rule; this latter one is a 'relevance' rule (Sacks, 1972).

The economy rule having provided for the adequate reference of 'baby', the consistency rule tells us that if the first person has been categorized as 'baby', then further persons may be referred to by other categories of a collection of which they are a member, and thus that such other categories as 'mommy' and 'daddy' are relevant given the use of 'baby'.

While in its currently weak form and alone, the consistency rule may exclude no category of any device, even in this weak form (the 'may' form – I shall eventually introduce a 'must' form), a corollary of it will prove to be useful. The corollary is a 'hearer's maxim'. It holds: if two or more categories are used to categorize two or more members of some population, and those categories can be heard as categories from the same collection, then: hear them that way. Let us call the foregoing 'the consistency rule corollary'. It has the following sort of usefulness. Various membership categorization-device categories can be said to be ambiguous. That is, the same categorial word is a term occurring in several distinct devices, and can in each have quite a different reference; they may or may not be combinably usable in regard to a single person. So, e.g. 'baby' occurs in the device 'family' and also in the device 'stage of life' whose categories are such as 'baby', 'child', . . . 'adult'. A hearer who can use the consistency rule corollary will regularly not even notice that there might be an ambiguity in the use of some category among a group which it can be used to hear as produced via the consistency rule.

It is, of course, clear that the two categories 'baby' are sometimes combinably referential and sometimes not. A woman may refer to someone as 'my baby' with no suggestion that she is using the category that occurs in the 'stage of life' device; her baby may be a full-fledged adult. In the case at hand that problem does not occur, and we shall be able to provide the bases for it not occurring, i.e. the bases for the legitimacy of hearing the single term 'baby' as referring to a person located by reference both to the device 'family' and to the device 'stage of life'.

With this, let us modify the observation on the consistency rule as follows: The consistency rule tells us that if a first person has been categorized as 'baby', the further persons may by referred to by categories from either the device 'family' or from the device 'stage of life'. However, if a hearer has a second category which can be heard as consistent with one locus of a first, then the first is to be heard as *at least* consistent with the second.

Given the foregoing, we may proceed to show how the combined reference of 'baby' is heard for our two sentences, and also how 'the mommy' is heard as 'the mommy of the baby'. We shall deal with the latter task first, and we assume from now on that the consistency rule corollary has yielded at least that 'baby' and 'mommy' are heard as from the device 'family'. We assume that without prejudice to the further fact that 'baby' is also heard as 'baby' from the device 'stage of life'.

The device 'family' is one of a series which you may think of by a prototypical name 'team'. One central property of such devices is that they are what I am going to call 'duplicatively organized'. I mean by the use of that term to point out the following: When such a device is used on a population, what is done is to take its categories, treat the set of categories as defining a unit, and place members of the population into cases of the unit. If a population is so treated and is then counted, one counts not numbers of daddies, numbers of mommies, and numbers of babies but numbers of families – numbers of 'whole families', numbers of 'families without fathers', etc. A population so treated is partitioned into cases of the unit, cases for which what properly holds is that the various persons partitioned into any case are 'coincumbents' of that case.

There are hearer's maxims which correspond to these ways of dealing with populations categorized by way of duplicatively organized devices. One that is relevant to our current task holds: If some population has been categorized by use of categories from some device whose collection has the 'duplicative organization' property, and a member is presented with a categorized population which *can be heard* as 'coincumbents' of a case of that device's unit, then: Hear it that way. (I will consider the underscored phrase shortly.) Now let it be noticed that this rule is of far more general scope than we may seem to need. In focusing on a property like duplicative organization it permits a determination of an expectation (of social scientists) as to how some categorized population will be heard independently of a determination of how it is heard. It is then formal and predictive, as well, of course, as quite general.

Now, by the phrase 'can be heard' we mean to rule out predictions of the following sort. Some duplicatively organized devices have proper numbers of incumbents for certain categories of any unit. (At any given time a nation-state may have but one president, a family but one father, a baseball team but one shortstop on the field, etc.) If more incumbents of a category are proposed as present in the population than a unit's case can properly take, then the 'can be heard' constraint is not satisfied, and a prediction would not be made.

Category-bound activities

The foregoing analysis shows us then how it is that we come to hear, given the fact that the device 'family' is duplicatively organized and the 'can be heard' constraint being satisfied, 'the mommy' to be 'the mommy of the baby'. It does, of course, much more than that. It permits us to predict, and to understand how we can predict, that a statement such as 'The first baseman looked around. The third baseman scratched himself' will be heard as saying 'the first baseman of the team of which the third baseman is also a player' and its converse.

Or, putting the claim more precisely, it shows us how, in part – 'in part' because for the materials at hand it happens that there are other means for providing that the same hearing be made, means which can operate in combination with the foregoing, otherwise sufficient ones, to further assure the hearings we have observed. That will be done in the next section. Let us now undertake our second task, to show how 'the baby' is heard in its combined form, i.e. as the category with that name from both the 'stage of life' device and from the 'family' device.

Let me introduce a term which I am going to call *category-bound activities*. While I shall not now give an intendedly careful definition of the term, I shall indicate what I mean to notice with it and then in a while offer a procedure for determining that some of its proposed cases are indeed cases of it. By the term I intend to notice that many activities are taken by members to be done by some particular or several particular categories of members where the categories are categories from membership categorization devices.

Let me notice then, as is obvious to you, that 'cry' is bound to 'baby', i.e. to the category 'baby' which is a member of the collection from the 'stage of life' device. Again, the fact that members know that this is so only serves, for the social scientist, to pose some problem. What we want is to construct some means by reference to which a class, which proposedly contains at least the activity-category 'cry' and presumably others, may have the inclusion of its candidate-members assessed. We will not be claiming that the procedure is definitive as to exclusion of a candidate-member, but we will claim that it is definitive as to inclusion of a candidate-member.

It may be observed that the members of the 'stage of life' collection are 'positioned' ('baby' . . . 'adolescent' . . . 'adult' . . .), an observation which, for now, we shall leave unexamined. I want to describe a procedure for praising or degrading members, the operation of which consists of the use of the fact that some activities are category bound. If there are such procedures, they will provide one strong sense of the notion 'category-bound activities' and also will provide, for any given candidate activity, a means for warrantably deciding that it is a member of the class of category-bound activities.

For some positioned-category devices it can be said as between any two categories of such a device that A is either higher or lower than B, and if A is higher than B, and B is higher than C, then A is higher than C.

We have some activity which is a candidate-member of the class 'category-bound activities' and which is proposedly bound to some category C. Then, a member of either A or B who does that activity may be seen to be degrading himself, and may be said to be 'acting like a C'. Alternatively, if some candidate activity is proposely bound to A, a member of C who does it is subject to being said to be acting like an A, where that assertion constitutes 'praising'.

If, using the 'stage of life' categories, we subject 'crying' to such a test, we do find that its candidacy as a member of the class 'category-bound activities' is warrantable. In the case of 'crying' the results are even stronger. For, it appears, if a 'baby' is subject to some circumstances which would for such a one warrant crying, and he does not, then his 'not crying' is observable, and may be used to propose that 'he is acting like a big boy', where that assertion is taken to be 'praise'.[1]

The foregoing procedure can, obviously enough, be used for other devices and other candidate activities. Other procedures may also be used, e.g. one way to decide that an activity is category bound is to see whether, the fact of membership being unknown, it can be 'hinted at' by naming the activity as something one does.[2]

Having constructed a procedure which can warrant the candidacy of some activity as a member of the class 'category-bound activities', and

---

1. Consider, e.g. the following: 'These children are highly aware that they have graduated from the rank of 'baby' and are likely to exhibit considerable scorn of babies, whether a neighbor's child or a younger sibling. This feeling of superiority is the residue of the parents' praise for advance behaviour and their inciting the child by remarks like 'only *babies* do that. *Your're* not a baby'. The frequency of these remarks at this age, however, suggest that in adult minds, at least, there is concern lest the children lapse into babyish ways' (Fischer and Fischer, 1963).

2. The following data is from a telephone call between a staff member (S) and a caller (C) to an emergency psychiatric clinic. Note the juxtaposition of 'hair stylist' in item 4 with suspected homosexuality in the last item.

S So, you can't watch television. Is there anything you can stay interested in?
C No, not really.
S What interests did you have before?
C I was a hair stylist at one time. I did some fashions now and then. Things like that.
S Then why aren't you working?
C Because I don't want to, I guess. Maybe that's why.
S But do you find that you just can't get yourself going?
C No. Well, as far as the job goes?
S Yes.
C Well, I'll tell you. I'm afraid. I'm afraid to go out and look for a job. That's what I'm afraid of. But more, I think I'm afraid of myself because I don't know. I'm just terribly mixed up.
S You haven't had any trouble with anyone close to you?
C Close to me. Well, I've been married three times and I'm – Close, you mean, as far as arguments or something like that?
S Yes.
C No. nobody real close. I'm just a very lonely person. I guess I'm very –
S There's nobody who loves you.
C Well, I feel that somebody must someplace, but I don't know where or who.
S Have you been having some sexual problems?
C All my life.
S Uh huh. Yeah.
C Naturally. You probably suspect – as far as the hair stylist and – either go one one way or the other. There is a straight or homosexual, something like that. I'm telling you, my whole life is just completely mixed up and turned over and it's just smashed and I'm not kidding.

which warrants the membership of 'cry' and provides for its being bound to 'baby', i.e. that category 'baby' which is a member of the 'stage of life' collection, we move on to see how it is that 'the baby' in our sentence is heard in the combined reference we have proposed.

We need, first, another 'hearer's maxim'. If a category-bound activity is asserted to have been done by a member of some category where, if that category is ambiguous (i.e. is a member of at least two different devices) but where, at least for one of those devices, the asserted activity is category bound to the given category, then hear that *at least* the category from the device to which it is bound is being asserted to hold.

The foregoing maxim will then provide for hearing 'The baby cried', as referring to at least 'baby' from the 'stage of life' device. The results obtained from the use of the consistency rule corollary, being independent of that, are combinable with it. The consistency rule corollary gave us at least that 'the baby' was the category from the device 'family'. The combination gives us both.

If our analysis seems altogether too complicated for the rather simple facts we have been examining, then we invite the reader to consider that our machinery has intendedly been 'overbuilt'. That is to say it may turn out that the elaborateness of our analysis, or its apparent elaborateness, will disappear when one begins to consider the amount of work that the very same machinery can perform.

In the next section I will attempt to show that the two sentences 'The baby cried. The mommy picked it up' constitute a possible description.

Identifying possible descriptions

I shall focus next on the fact that an activity can be category bound and then on the import of there being a norm which provides for some second activity, given the occurrence of a first, considering both of these with regard to the 'correctness', for members, of 'possible description'.

Let me for the moment leave aside our two sentences and consider some observations on how it is that I see, and take it you see, describable occurrences. Suppose you are standing somewhere, and you see a person you don't know. The person cries. Now, if I can, I will see that what has happened is that a baby cried. And I take it that you will, if you can, see that too. That's a first pair of observations. Suppose again you are standing somewhere and you see two people you don't know. Suppose further that one cries, and the other picks up the one who is crying. Now, if I can, I will see that what has happened is that a baby cried and its mother picked it up. And I take it that you will, if you can, see that too. That's a second pair of observations.

Consider the first pair of observations. The modifying phrases, to deal with them first, refer simply to the possibility that the category 'baby' might be obviously inapplicable to the crier. By reference to the 'stage of life' collection the crier may be seen to be an adult. And that being so, the 'if . . . can' constraint wouldn't be satisfied. But there are certainly other possible characterizations of the crying person. For example, without respect to the fact that it is a baby, it could be either 'male' or 'female', and nonetheless I would not, and I take it you would not, seeing the scene, see that 'a male cried' if we could see that 'a baby cried'.

The pair of observations suggest the following 'viewer's maxim': If a member sees a category-bound activity being done, then, if one can see it being done by a member of a category to which the activity is bound, then: See it that way. The viewer's maxim is another relevance rule in that it proposes that for an observer of a category-bound activity the category to which the activity is bound has a special relevance for formulating an identification of its doer.

Consider the second pair of observations. As members you, of course, know that there is a norm which might be written as: A mother ought to try to soothe her crying baby. I, and you, not only know that there is such a norm but, as you may recall, we used it in doing our hearing of 'The baby cried. The mommy picked it up'. In addition to the fact of duplicative organization, the norm was relevant in bringing us to hear that it was the mommy of the baby who did the picking up. While we would have heard that it was the mommy of the baby for other pairs of activities in which the two were involved (but not any pair), the fact that the pair were relatable via a norm which assigns the mother of the baby that duty may have operated in combination with the duplicative organization to assure our hearing that it was she who did it.

Leaving aside the hearing of the sentence, we are led to construct another viewer's maxim: If one sees a pair of actions which can be related via the operation of a norm that provides for the second given the first, where the doers can be seen as members of the categories the norm provides as proper for that pair of actions, then: (a) See that the doers are such-members and (b) see the second as done in conformity with the norm.

This second viewer's maxim suggests an observation about norms. In the sociological and anthropological literature, the focus on norms is on the conditions under which and the extent to which they govern, or can be seen by social scientists to govern, the relevant actions of those members whose actions they ought to control. While such matter are, of course, important, our viewer's maxim suggests other importances of norms, for members.

Viewers use norms to provide some of the orderliness, and proper orderliness, of the activities they observe. Via some norm two activities may be made observable as a sequentially ordered pair. That is, viewers use norms to explain both the occurrence of some activity given the occurrence of another and also its sequential position with regard to the other, e.g. that it follows the other, or precedes it. That is a first importance. Second, viewers use norms to provide the relevant membership categories in terms of which they formulate identifications of the doers of those activities for which the norms are appropriate.

Now let me observe, viewers may use norms in each of the preceding ways, and feel confident in their usage without engaging in such an investigation as would serve to warrant the correctness of their usages. This last observation is worth some further thought.

We may, at least initially, put the matter thus: For viewers, the usability of the viewer's maxims serves to warrant the correctness of their observations. And that is then to say, the usability of the viewer's maxims provides for the recognizability of the correctness of the observations done via those maxims. And that is then to say, 'correct observations' or, at least, 'possible correct observations' are 'recognizable'.

(Members feel no need in warranting their observation, in recognizing its correctness to do such a thing as to ask the woman whether she is the mother of the baby,[3] or to ask her whether she picked it up because it was crying, i.e. they feel no such need so long as the viewer's maxims are usable.)

In short: 'Correctness' is recognizable, and there are some exceedingly nice ties between recognizably correct description and recognizably correct observations. One such tie which is relevant to the tasks we have undertaken is: A string of sentences which may be heard, via the hearer's maxims, as having been produced by use of the viewer's maxims, will be heard as a 'recognizably correct possible description'.

Sequential ordering

The rest of this chapter will be devoted to two tasks. I shall try to develop some further rewards of the analysis so far assembled, some consequences it throws off; and to show also how it is that the two sentences ('The baby cried. The mommy picked it up') can warrantably be said to be from 'a story'. I start with the latter task.

It ought to be apparent that the fact that the children whose talk is reported in *Children Tell Stories* were asked to tell a story is not definitive of their having done so. It is at least possible that the younger ones among

3. 'A late child was at times embarrassing to one woman who, while enjoying him, found that in public places she often overheard people saying, "They must be his grandparents" ' (Fischer and Fischer, 1963).

them are not capable of building stories, of building talk that is recognizable as a 'story', or, at least, as a 'possible story'.

It happens to be correct, for Western literature, that if some piece of talk is a possible description it is also, and thereby a possible story or story part. It appears, therefore, that having established that the two sentences are a possible description, I have also, and thereby, established that they are possibly (at least part of) a story. To stop now would, however involve ignoring some story-relevant aspects of the given sentences which are both interesting and subjectable to analysis. So I go on.

Certain characteristics are quite distinctive to stories. For example, there are characteristic endings ('And they lived happily ever after') and characteristic beginnings ('once upon a time'). I shall consider whether the possible story, a fragment of which we have been investigating, can be said (and I mean here, as throughout, 'warrantably said') to close with what is recognizable as 'an ending' and to start with what is recognizable as 'a beginning'.

In suggesting a difference between 'starts' and proper 'beginnings', and between 'closes' and proper 'endings', I am introducing a distinction which has some importance. The distinction, which is by no means original, may be developed by considering some very simple observation.

1. A piece of talk which regularly is used to do some activity – as 'Hello' is used to do 'greeting' – may not invariably be so used, but may do other activities as well – as 'Hello' is used to check out whether another with whom one is talking on the phone is still there or has been cut off – where it is in part its occurrence in 'the middle' and not 'the start' of a conversation that serves to discriminate the use being made of it.

2. Certain activities not only have regular places in some sequence where they do get done but may, if their means of being done is not found there, be said, by members, to not have occurred, to be absent. For example, the absence of a greeting may be noticed, as the following conversation, from field observation, indicates. The scene involved two adult women, one the mother of two children, ages six and ten. The kids enter and the following ensues:

WOMAN Hi.
BOY Hi.
WOMAN Hi, Annie.
MOTHER Annie, don't you hear someone say hello to you?
WOMAN Oh, that's okay, she smiled hello.
MOTHER You know you're supposed to greet someone, don't you?
ANNIE [Hangs head] Hello.

3. Certain activities can only be done at certain places in a sequence. For example, a third strike can only be thrown by a pitcher after he has two strikes on a batter.

Observations such as these lead to a distinction between a 'slot' and the 'items' which fill it, and to proposing that certain activities are accomplished by a combination of some item and some slot.

The notion of slot serves for the social scientist to mark a class of relevance rules. Thus, if it can be said that for some assertable sequence there is a position in which one or more activities properly occur, or occur if they are to get done, then: The observability of either the occurrence or the nonoccurrence of those activities may be claimed by reference to having looked to the position and determined whether what occurs in it is a way of doing the activity.

An instance of the class of relevance rules might run: To see whether a conversation included 'greetings', look to the first utterance of either party and see whether there occurs in it any item which passes as a greeting; items such as ('hello', 'hi', 'hi there', . . .). The fact that the list contains the ellipsis might be deeply troublesome were it not the case that while we are unable to list all the members of the class 'greeting items', we can say that the class is bounded, and that there are some utterables which are not members of it, perhaps, for example, the sentence now being completed. If that and only that occurred in a first utterance, we might feel assured in saying that a greeting did not occur.

Consider just one way that this class of relevance rules is important. Roughly, it permits the social scientist to nontrivially assert that something is absent. Nontrivial talk of an absence requires that some means be available for showing both the relevance of occurrence of the activity that is proposedly absent and the location where it should be looked for to see that it did not occur. Lacking these, an indefinite set of other activities might equally well be asserted to be absent given some occurrence, and the assertion in question not being discriminable from the (other) members of that indefinite set, it is trivialized.

It does seem that for stories it is correct to say that they can have beginnings, and we can then inspect the items that occur at their start to see whether they can be seen to make a beginning. Given further that stories can have endings, we can inspect the items that occur at their close to see whether they can be seen to make an ending.

While my main interest will be with the story's start as a possible proper beginning, let me briefly consider its close: 'She went to sleep'. With this the speaker would seem to be not merely closing but closing making a proper ending. It so seems by virtue of the fact that such a sentence reports an occurrence, or can be heard as reporting an occurrence, which is a proper ending to something for which endings are relevant and standardized, that very regularly used unit of orientation, the day. A day being recognized as ending for some person when they go to sleep, so a story may be recognized as closing with an ending if at its close there is a report of the protagonist's having gone to sleep. This particular sort of ending is, of course, not at all particular to stories constructed by young children; it, and other endings like it, from 'the last sleep' death unto the shutting down of the world, are regular components of far more sophisticated ventures in Western literature.

Let me turn then to the start, to consider whether it can be said to be a beginning. I shall attempt to show that starting to talk to adults is for small children a rather special matter. I shall do that by focusing on a most characteristic way that small children, of around the age of the teller of the given story, characteristically open their talk to adults, i.e. the use of such items as 'You know what?' I shall offer an analysis of that mode of starting off, which will characterize the problems such a start can be seen to operate as a methodical solution to.

The promised analysis will warrant my assertion that starting to talk is, for small children, a special matter. That having been established, I shall turn to see whether the particular start we have for this story may be seen as another type of solution to the same problem that I will have shown to be relevant.

If I can then show that another solution is employed in our problematic utterance (the sentence 'The baby cried'), I will have shown that the story starts with something that is properly a beginning, and that therefore, both start and close are 'proper' beginning and end. Such, in any event, are my intentions.

I begin, roughly and only as an assumption (though naively, the matter is obvious), by asserting that kids have restricted rights to talk. That being the case, by assumption, I want to see whether the ways that they go about starting to talk, with adults, can be most adequately seen to be solutions to the problem which focuses on needing to have a good start if one is going to get further than that. Starts which have that character can then be called beginnings.

Now, kids around the age of three go through a period when some of them have an almost universal way of beginning any piece of talk they make to adults. They use things like: 'You know what, Daddy?' or 'You know something, Mommy?'

I will introduce a few rules of conversational sequencing. I do that without presenting data now, but the facts are so obvious that you can check them out easily for yourself; you know the rules anyway. The sequencing rules are for two-party conversation; and, since two-party conversation is a special phenomenon, what I say is not intended as applying for three- or more party conversation.

One basic rule of two-party conversation concerns a pair of objects, questions and answers. It runs: If one party asks a question, when the question is complete, the other party properly speaks, and properly offers an answer to the question and says no more than that. The rule will need considerable explication, but for now, it will do as it stands.

A second rule, and it's quite a fundamental one, because by reference to it the, in principle, infinite character of a conversation can be seen as: A person who has asked a question can talk again, has, as we may put it, 'a reserved right to talk again', after the one to whom he has addressed the question speaks. *And*, in using the reserved right he can ask a question. I call this rule the 'chaining rule', and in combination with the first rule it provides for the occurrence of an indefinitely long conversation of the form Q-A-Q-A-Q-A-. . . .

Now the characteristic opener that we are considering is a question (e.g. 'You know what?'). Having begun in that way, a user who did not have restricted rights to talk would be in a position of generating an indefinite set of further questions as each question was replied to, or as the other otherwise spoke on the completion of some question.

But the question we begin with is a rather curious one in that it is one of those fairly but not exceptionally rare question which have as their answer another question, in this case the proper and recurrent answer is 'What?'. The use of initial questions of this sort has a variety of consequences. First, if a question which has another question as its proper answer is used and is properly replied to, i.e. is replied to with the proper question, then the chaining rule is turned around, i.e. it is the initial answerer and not the initial questioner who now has the reserved right to speak again after the other speaks. The initial questioner has by his question either not assumed that he can use the chaining rule or has chosen not to. (Note that we are not saying that he has not chosen to invoke the chaining rule but rather that he has instead given the choice of invoking it to the initial answerer. There are two different possibilities involved.)

Second, the initial questioner does not only not make his second speech by virtue of the chaining rule but he makes it by virtue of the first sequencing rule, i.e. by reference to the fact that a person who has been asked a question properly speaks and properly replies to it. His second speech is then not merely not made as a matter of either the chaining rule or his choice by some other means of making a second speech but it is something he makes by obligation, given the fact that he has been asked a question and is therefore obliged to answer.

Third, the question he is obliged to answer is, however, 'an open one' in the sense that what it is that an answer would be is something that its asker does not know, and further is one that its answerer by the prior sequence should know. What an answer is then to the second question is whatever it is the kid takes to be an answer, and he is thereby provided with the opportunity to say whatever it is he wanted to say in the first place, not now, however, on his own say-so but as a matter of obligation.

In that case then – and the foregoing being a method whereby the production of the question 'You know what?' may be explicated – we may take it that kids take it that they have restricted rights which consist of a right to begin, to make a first statement and not much more. Thereafter they proceed only if requested to. And if that is their situation as they see it, they surely have evolved a nice solution to it.

With the foregoing we can say then that a focus on the way kids begin to talk is appropriate, and we can see whether the beginnings of stories, if they are not made of the culturally standardized beginnings (such as 'once upon a time'), might be seen to be beginnings by virtue of the special situation which kids have *vis-à-vis* beginning to talk.

We may arrive at the status of 'The baby cried' as a proper beginning, in particular as a start that is a beginning by virtue of being a proper opener for one who has restricted rights to talk, by proceeding in the following way. Let us consider another solution to the problem of starting talk under restricted rights. I'll begin by introducing a word, 'ticket'. I can show you what I mean to point to with the word by a hypothetical example. Suppose two adults are copresent and lack rights to talk to each other, e.g. they have never been introduced, or whatever. For any such two persons there are conditions under which one can begin to talk to the other. And that those conditions are the conditions used to in fact begin talk is something which can be shown via a first piece of talk. Where that is done we will say that talk is begun with a ticket. That is, the item used to begin talk is an item which, rights not otherwise existing, serves to warrant one having begun to talk. For example, one turns to the other and says, 'Your pants are on fire'. It is not just any opening, but an opening which tells why it is that one has breached the correct silence, which warrants one having spoken. Tickets then are items specially usable as first items in talk by one who has restricted rights to talk to another. And the most prototypical class of tickets are 'announcements of trouble relevant to the other'.

Now it is clear enough (cf. the discussion of norms earlier) that the occurrence of a baby crying is the occurrence of a piece of trouble relevant to some person, e.g. the mother of the baby. One who hears it gains a right to talk, i.e. to announce the fact that it has occurred, and can most efficiently speak via a ticket i.e. 'The baby cried'. That being so, we can see then that the opener 'The baby cried' is a proper beginning, i.e. it is something which can serve as a beginning for someone whose rights to talk are in the first instance restricted.

With the foregoing we have established that the story we have been examining has both a proper beginning and a proper end, and is thus not only a story by virtue of being a possible description but also by virtue of its employing, as parts, items which occur in positions that permit one to see that the user may know that stories have such positions, and that there are certain items which when used in them are satisfactory incumbents.

References

FISCHER, J., and FISCHER, A. (1963), 'The New Englanders of Orchard Town, USA', in B. Whiting (ed.), *Six Cultures: Studies in Child Rearing*, John Wiley.

PITCHER, E. G., and PRELINGER, E. (1963), *Children Tell Stories: An Analysis of Fantasy*, International Universities Press.

SACKS, H. (1972) 'An initial investigation of the usability of conversational data for doing sociology', in D. N. Sudnow (ed). *Studies in Social Interaction*, Free Press.

18 Emmanuel Schegloff and Harvey Sacks

Opening Up Closings

Slightly abridged from Emmanuel Schegloff and Harvey Sacks, 'Opening up closings', *Semiotica*, vol. 8, 1973, pp. 289–327.

Our aim in this paper is to report in a preliminary fashion on analyses we have been developing of closings of conversation. Although it may be an intuitively apparent feature of the unit 'a single conversation' that it does not simply end, but is brought to a close, our initial task is to develop a technical basis for a closing problem. This we try to derive from a consideration of some features of the most basic sequential organization of conversation we know of – the organization of speaker turns. A partial solution of this problem is developed, employing resources drawn from the same order of organization. The incompleteness of that solution is shown, and leads to an elaboration of the problem, which requires reference to quite different orders of sequential organization in conversation – in particular, the organization of topic talk, and the overall structural organization of the unit 'a single conversation'. The reformulated problem is used to locate a much broader range of data as relevant to the problem of closings, and some of that data is discussed in detail. Finally, an attempt is made to specify the domain for which the closing problems, as we have posed them, seem apposite.

This work is part of a program of work undertaken several years ago to explore the possibility of achieving a naturalistic observational discipline that could deal with the details of social action(s) rigorously, empirically, and formally.[1] For a variety of reasons that need not be spelled out here, our attention has focused on conversational materials; suffice it to say, this is not because of a special interest in language, or any theoretical primacy we accord conversation. None the less, the character of our materials as conversational has attracted our attention to the study of conversation as an activity in its own right, and thereby to the ways in which any actions accomplished in conversation require reference to the properties and organization of conversation for their understanding and analysis, both by

1. Products of that effort already published or in press or preparation include: Jefferson (1972), Moerman (1967; 1970), Sacks (1972a, 1972b, in press), Schegloff (1968; 1972, in press), Schenkein (1972).

participants and by professional investigators. This last phrase requires emphasis and explication.[2]

We have proceeded under the assumption (an assumption borne out by our research) that in so far as the materials we worked with exhibited orderliness, they did so not only to us, indeed not in the first place for us, but for the co-participants who had produced them. If the materials (records of natural conversations) were orderly, they were so because they had been methodically produced by members of the society for one another, and it was a feature of the conversations that we treated as data that they were produced so as to allow the display by the co-participants to each other of their orderliness, and to allow the participants to display to each other their analysis, appreciation and use of that orderliness. Accordingly, our analysis has sought to explicate the ways in which the materials are produced by members in orderly ways that exhibit their orderliness and have their orderliness appreciated and used, and have that appreciation displayed and treated as the basis for subsequent action. In the ensuing discussion, therefore, it should be clearly understood that the 'closing problem' we are discussing is proposed as a problem for conversationalists; we are not interested in it as a problem for analysts except in so far, and in the ways, it is a problem for participants. (By 'problem' we do not intend puzzle, in the sense that participants need to ponder the matter of how to close a conversation. We mean that closings are to be seen as achievements, as solutions to certain problems of conversational organization. While, for many people, closing a conversation may be a practical problem in the sense that they find it difficult to get out of a conversation they are in, that problem is different from the problem of closing that we are concerned with. The problem we are concerned with sets up the possibilities of a practical problem but does not require that such practical problems occur. Our discussion should then be able to furnish bases for the existence of practical problems of closing conversations.)

The materials with which we have worked are audio tapes and transcripts of naturally occurring interactions (i.e. ones not produced by research intervention such as experiment or interview) with differing numbers of participants and different combinations of participant attributes. There is a danger attending this way of characterizing our materials, namely, that we be heard as proposing the assured relevance of numbers, attributes of participants, etc., to the way the data are produced, interpreted, or analysed by investigators or by the participants themselves. Such a view carries considerable plausibility, but for precisely that reason it should be treated with extreme caution, and be introduced only where warrant can be offered for the relevance of such characterizations of the data from the data themselves. We

2. Here our debts to the work of Harold Garfinkel surface. Elsewhere, though they cannot be pinpointed, they are pervasive.

offer some such warranted characterization of our materials at the end of this paper. The considerations just adduced, however, restrain us from further characterizing it here. [For example, they restrain us from characterizing our findings as relating to 'some general features of conversation rules in American English' – a suggestion offered by Dell Hymes (personal communication), for that suggests implicitly an ethnic or national or language identification as a relevant putative boundary for both our materials and findings. We cannot offer a warrant for asserting such a boundary and we suspect others cannot either.][3]

In addressing the problem of closings, we are dealing with one part of what might be termed the overall structural organization of single conversations. While one can certainly address other closing or completion loci, e.g., utterance completion, topic closure, etc., the unit whose closing is of concern here is 'a single conversation'. While therefore in one sense we are dealing with closing, in another we are dealing with one aspect of the structure of the unit 'a single conversation', other aspects of which include 'openings', and topical structure. As we shall see, dealing with the one aspect of the overall structural organization of conversation will require reference to other orders of conversation's organization. And because an adequate account of the order of organization 'overall structural organization' would require space far beyond that available to us, and knowledge beyond that in hand (as well as reference to other orders of organization, such as the organization of the unit 'a topic' about which not enough is now known), our account will remain in many respects indicative rather than complete. It is in that sense a preliminary account of how to deal with 'closings', and an even more rudimentary account of overall structure in general.

Not all conversational activity is bounded and collected into cases of the unit 'a single conversation'. That unit, and the structure that characterizes and constitutes it, is therefore not necessarily relevant wherever conversational activity occurs. On the other hand, other orders of organization, most notably those organizing utterances and the speaker turns in which they occur, are co-terminous with, and indeed may be taken as defining, conversational activity (though not all talk; not, for example, formal lecturing). On that account, they may be regarded as fundamental (for more compelling reasons for so regarding them, see Sacks, in press). We will return to the theme of conversational activity that does not seem to constitute instances of the unit 'a single conversation' at the end of this paper. In view of the preceding argument, however, it seems useful to begin by formulating the problem of closing technically in terms of the more fundamental order of organization, that of utterances.

3. For a discussion of unwarranted ethnic characterizations of the domain of relevance for materials and findings, see Moerman (1967) [Reading 6 – Ed.].

I. Elsewhere (Sacks, in press), two basic features of conversation are proposed to be: (1) at least, and no more than, one party speaks at a time in a single conversation; and (2) speaker change recurs. The achievement of these features singly, and especially the achievement of their co-occurrence, is accomplished by co-conversationalists through the use of a 'machinery' for ordering speaker turns sequentially in conversation. The turn-taking machinery includes as one component a set of procedures for organizing the selection of 'next speakers', and, as another, a set of procedures for locating the occasions on which transition to a next speaker may or should occur. The turn-taking machinery operates utterance by utterance. That is to say: in contrast to conceivable alternative organizations (e.g. in which the occasions of speaker transition and the mode or outcome of next speaker selections would be predetermined for the whole conversation, from its outset, by mappings into other attributes of the parties; see Albert, 1965), it is within any current utterance that possible next speaker selection is accomplished, and upon possible completion of any current utterance that such selection takes effect and transition to a next speaker becomes relevant. We shall speak of this as the 'transition relevance' of possible utterance completion. It is in part the consequence of an orientation to the feature, 'speaker change *re*curs', which provides for the *recurrent* relevance of transition to a next speaker at any possible utterance completion point (except where special techniques have been employed to modify that relevance).

These basic features of conversation, the problem of achieving their co-occurrence, and the turn-taking machinery addressed to the solution of that problem are intended, in this account, not as analysts' constructs, but as descriptions of the orientations of conversationalists in producing proper conversation. Conversationalists construct conversations in their course, and in doing so they are oriented to achieving the co-occurrence of the features cited above, and employ the turn-taking machinery to do so. We cannot here present a detailed demonstration of this claim (cf. Sacks, in press), but an indication of one direction in which such a demonstration might be pursued may be offered. If the features are normative, i.e. are oriented to by conversationalists, then the machinery for achieving their co-occurrence should include procedures for dealing with violations, and indeed should locate failure to achieve the features, singly and jointly, as 'violations', as in need of repair. A minimal requirement for this would be that the machinery locates as 'events' cases of the non-achievement of the features. That it does so may be suggested by such matters as the occurrence of conversationalists' observations about 'someone's silence' when no one in a setting is talking. The noticeability of silence reflects an orientation by conversationalists to the 'at least . . . one at a time' feature; the feature must be oriented to by conversationalists, and not merely be an analytic construct, if conversationalists do accomplish and report the noticing. The attributability of the silence reflects an orientation to the next-speaker-selection component of the turn-taking machinery that can have generated a 'some speaker's turn' at a given point in the course of the conversation, such that a silence at that point may be attributable to that 'speaker'.

E: He hadtuh come out tuh San Francisco. So he called hhh from their place, out here to the professors, en set up, the, time, and hh asked them to hh – if they'd make a reservation for him which they did cuz they paid for iz room en et cetera en he asked them tuh:: make a reservation for iz parents. En there was a deep silence she said at the other end 'e sez 'Oh well they'll pay for their own uh' – hhh – 'room an' accommodations.'

(What is reported seems to involve that the silence that was noted was dealt with by appending a clarification to the request, the silence being heard by the speaker as not his, and then being transformed into his pause by his producing such a continuation as they might then reply to appropriately. That the silence is heard as the other's, but treated as one's own for talk purposes is a delicately interesting matter.)

Similarly, there are available and employed devices for locating cases of 'more than one at a time' as events, and for resolving them, or warrantedly treating them as violations. Again, that such devices are available to, and employed by, conversationalists requires treatment of the feature 'no more than one at a time' as normative, as oriented to, by conversationalists, rather than as theorists' devices for imposing order on the materials.

It may be noted that whereas these basic features with which we began (especially the feature of speaker change recurrence), and the utterance by utterance operation of the turn-taking machinery as a fundamental generating feature of conversation, deal with a conversation's ongoing orderliness, they make no provision for the closing of conversation. A machinery which includes the transition relevance of possible utterance completion recurrently for any utterance in the conversation generates an indefinitely extendable string of turns to talk. Then, an initial problem concerning closings may be formulated: *how to organize the simultaneous arrival of the co-conversationalists at a point where one speaker's completion will not occasion another speaker's talk, and that will not be heard as some speaker's silence.* The last qualification is necessary to differentiate closings from other places in conversation where one speaker's completion is not followed by a possible next speaker's talk, but where, given the continuing relevance of the basic features and the turn-taking machinery, what is heard is not termination but attributable silence, a pause in the last speaker's utterance, etc. It should suggest why simply stopping to talk is not a solution to the closing problem: any first prospective speaker to do so would be hearable as 'being silent' in terms of the turn-taking machinery, rather than as having suspended its relevance. Attempts to 'close' in this way would be interpretable as an 'event-in-the-conversation', rather than as outside, or marking, its boundaries, and would be analysed for actions being accomplished in the conversation, for example, anger, brusqueness, pique, etc. Again, the problem is *how to coordinate the suspension of the transition relevance of possible utterance completion, not how to deal with its non-operation while still relevant*.

II. How is the transition relevance of possible utterance completion lifted? A proximate solution involves the use of a 'terminal exchange' composed of conventional parts, e.g., an exchange of 'good-byes'. In describing how a terminal exchange can serve to lift the transition relevance of possible utterance completions, we note first that the terminal exchange is a case of a class of utterance sequences which we have been studying for some years, namely, the utterance pair, or, as we shall refer to it henceforth, the adjacency pair.

While this class of sequences is widely operative in conversation, our concern here is with the work they do in terminations, and our discussion will be limited to those aspects of adjacency pair that fit them for this work. Briefly, then, adjacency pairs consist of sequences which properly have the following features: (1) two utterance length, (2) adjacent positioning of component utterances, (3) different speakers producing each utterance.

The component utterances of such sequences have an achieved relatedness beyond that which may otherwise obtain between adjacent utterances. That relatedness is partially the product of the operation of a typology in the speakers' production of the sequences. The typology operates in two ways: it partitions utterance types into 'first pair parts' (i.e. first parts of pairs) and second pair parts; and it affiliates a first pair part and a second pair part to form a 'pair type'. 'Question–answer', 'greeting–greeting', 'offer–acceptance/refusal' are instances of pair types. A given sequence will thus be composed of an utterance that is a first pair part produced by one speaker directly followed by the production by a different speaker of an utterance which is (a) a second pair part, and (b) is from the same pair type as the first utterance in the sequence is a member of. Adjacency pair sequences, then, exhibit the further features (4) relative ordering of parts (i.e. first pair parts precede second pair parts), and (5) discriminative relations (i.e. the pair type of which a first pair part is a member is relevant to the selection among second pair parts).

The achievement of such orderliness in adjacency pair sequences requires the recognizability of first pair part status for some utterances. That problem is handled in various ways; constructionally, as when the syntax of an utterance can be used to recognize that a question is being produced, or through

the use of conventional components, as when 'hello' or 'hi' is used to indicate partially that a greeting is being produced, to cite but two procedures.

A basic rule of adjacency pair operation is: given the recognizable production of a first pair part, on its first possible completion its speaker should stop
and a next speaker should start and produce a second pair part from the pair
type the first is recognizably a member of.

Two sorts of uses of adjacency pairs may be noticed. We are interested in
only one of them here, and mention the other for flavor. First, for flavor:
wherever one party to a conversation is specifically concerned with the close
order sequential implicativeness of an utterance they have a chance to produce, the use of a first pair part is a way they have of methodically providing
for such implicativeness.[4] So, if they are concerned to have another talk
directly to some matter they are about to talk to, they may form their own
utterance up as a question, a next speaker being thereby induced to employ
the chance to talk to produce what is appreciable as an answer. Such uses of
adjacency pairs occur freely in conversation. Secondly, wherever, for the
operation of some *type of organization*, close ordering of utterances is useful
or required, we find the adjacency pairs are employed to achieve such close
ordering. So, in the case of that type of organization which we are calling
'overall structural organization', it may be noted that at least initial sequences (e.g., greeting exchanges), and ending sequences (i.e. terminal exchanges) employ adjacency pair formats. It is the recurrent, institutionalized
use of adjacency pairs for such types of organization problems that suggests
that these problems have, in part, a common character, and that adjacency
pair organization is specially fitted to the solution of problems of that character. (Lifting the transition relevance of possible utterance completion being
that sort of problem, adjacency pair organization would be specially adapted
to its solution, in the form of the terminal exchange.)

The type of problem adjacency pairs are specially fitted for, and the way
they are specially suited for its solution, may very briefly be characterized as
follows. Given the utterance by utterance organization of turn-taking, unless close ordering is attempted there can be no methodic assurance that a
more or less eventually aimed-for successive utterance or utterance type will
ever be produced. If a next speaker does not do it, that speaker may provide
for a further next that should not do it (or should do something which is not
it); and, if what follows that next is 'free' and does not do the originally
aimed-for utterance, it (i.e. the utterance placed there) may provide for a yet
further next that does not do it, etc. Close ordering is, then, the basic general-

4. By 'sequential implicativeness' is meant that an utterance projects for the sequentially following turn(s) the relevance of a determinate range of occurrences (be they
utterance types, activities, speaker selections, etc.). It thus has sequentially organized
implications.

ized means for assuring that some desired event will ever happen. If it cannot be made to happen next, its happening is not merely delayed, but is made unassured to ever happen. The adjacency pair technique, in providing a determinate 'when' for it to happen, i.e. 'next', has then means for handling the close order problem, where that problem has its import via its control of the assurance that some relevant event will be made to occur.

But, it may be wondered, why are two utterances required for either opening or closing? It is plain, perhaps, why adjacency pairs are relevant to getting answers ever to happen for questions; for one thing, the parts of question–answer pairs are rather different sorts of objects. The problem of closing might, on the other hand, appear to be handleable with just one utterance. That is, if two utterances are needed, then a pair format is understandable; but why are two utterances needed?

What two utterances, produced by different speakers, can do that one utterance cannot do is: by an adjacently positioned second, a speaker can show that he understood what a prior aimed at, and that he is willing to go along with that. Also, by virtue of the occurrence of an adjacently produced second, the doer of a first can see that what he intended was indeed understood, and that it was or was not accepted. Also, of course, a second can assert his failure to understand, or disagreement, and, inspection of a second by a first can allow the first speaker to see that while the second thought he understood, indeed he misunderstood. It is then through the use of adjacent positioning that appreciations, failures, correctings, et cetera can be themselves understandably attempted. Wherever then there is reason to have the appreciation of some implicativeness made attendable, 'next utterance' is the proper place to do that, and a two utterance sequence can be employed as a means for doing and checking some intendedly sequentially implicative occurrence in a way that a one utterance sequence can not.

(The foregoing is not at all exclusive, though it is sufficient. For example, in the case of initial sequences, their paired status also permits the use of their assertion to be inspected for, in the case of telephone calls in particular, who is talking or, whether who is talking is recognizable from just that presentation.)

We are then proposing: if *where* transition relevance is to be lifted is a systematic problem, an adjacency pair solution can work because: by providing that transition relevance is to be lifted after the second pair part's occurrence, the occurrence of the second pair part can then reveal an appreciation of and agreement to the intendedness of closing *now* which a first part of a terminal exchange reveals its speaker to propose. Now, given the institutionalization of that solution, a range of ways of assuring that it be employed have been developed, which make drastic difference between one party saying 'good-bye' and not leaving room for the other to return, and one party saying 'good-bye' and leaving room for the other to return. The former becomes a distinct sort of activity, expressing anger, brusqueness, and the like, and available to such a use by contrast with the latter. It is this consequentiality of alternatives which is the hallmark of an institutionalized solution. The terminal exchange is no longer a matter of personal choices; but one cannot explain the use of a two-utterance sequence by referring to the way that single utterance closings are violative, for the question of why they are made to be violative is then left unexamined.

In referring to the components of terminal exchanges, we have so far employed 'good-bye' as an exclusive instance. But, it plainly is not exclusively used. Such other components as 'O.K.', 'see you', 'thank you', 'you're welcome' and the like are also used. Since the latter items are used in other ways as well, their sheer use does not mark them as unequivocal parts of terminal exchanges. This fact, that possible terminal exchanges do not necessarily, by their components, indicate their terminal exchange status, is one source for our proposal that the use of terminal exchanges is but a proximate solution to the initially posed problem of this paper. We turn now to a second problem, whose examination will supply some required additions.

III. In the last section we focused on one type of placing consideration relevant to closing conversation: the close order organization of terminal exchanges. By the use of an adjacency pair format, a place could be marked in a string of utterances, such that on its completion the transition relevance of utterance completion might be lifted. The second part of a terminal exchange was proposed to be such a place. The second part of a terminal exchange had its positioned occurrence provided for by the occurrence of a first part of such an exchange. No discussion was offered about the placement of the first part of terminal exchanges. Here we begin to take up that issue, and to develop what sorts of problems are involved in its usage.

While it should be experientially obvious that first parts of terminal exchanges are not freely occurrent, we shall here try to develop a consideration of the sorts of placing problems their use does involve. First, two preliminary comments are in order. (1) Past and current work has indicated that placement considerations are general for utterances. That is: a pervasively relevant issue (for participants) about utterances in conversation is 'why that now', a question whose analysis may (2) also be relevant to find what 'that' is. That is to say, some utterances may derive their character as actions entirely from placement considerations. For example, there do not seem to be criteria other than placement (i.e. sequential) ones that will sufficiently discriminate the status of an utterance as a 'statement', 'assertion', 'declarative', 'proposition', etc., from its status as an 'answer'. Finding an utterance to be an 'answer', to be accomplishing 'answering', cannot be achieved by reference to phonological, syntactic, semantic, or logical features of the utterance itself, but only by consulting its sequential placement, e.g., its placement 'after a question'. If terminal exchanges are not necessarily marked as such by their components (as was suggested above), we are well advised to consider the contribution of their placement to their achievement of that status.

Addressing considerations of placement raises the issue: what order of organization of conversation is the relevant one, by reference to which placement is to be considered? We dealt earlier with one kind of placement issue, i.e. the placement of *second* parts of terminal exchanges, and there the order of organization by reference to which placement was done and analysed was the adjacency pair, which is one kind of 'local', i.e. utterance organization. It does *not* appear that *first* parts of terminal exchanges, which is what we are now concerned with, are placed by reference to that order of organization. While they, of course, occur after some utterance, they are not placed by reference to a location that might be formulated as " 'next' after some 'last' utterances or class of utterances". Rather, their placement seems to be organized by reference to a properly initiated closing *section*, and it is by virtue of the lack of a properly initiated closing section that the unilateral dropping in of the first part of a terminal exchange is only part of the solution to the closing problem. We shall need, therefore, to concern ourselves with the proper initiation of closing sections. To do so adequately, and to understand the basis for this order of organization as the relevant one for closing, we will explore some aspects of overall conversational organization as the background for a subsequent consideration of the placement issue. In view of the 'background' character of our purpose, the discussion is necessarily minimal and somewhat schematic.

The aspect of overall conversational organization directly relevant to the present problem concerns the organization of topic talk. (The last phrase is ambiguous, being understandable both as the organization of the unit 'a topic' and as the organization of a set of such units within the larger unit 'a single conversation'. While the former of these is also relevant to closings, it is the latter that we intend in the present context.) If we may refer to what gets talked about in a conversation as 'mentionables', then we can note that there are considerations relevant to conversationalists in ordering and distributing their talk about mentionables in a single conversation. There is, for example, a position in a single conversation for 'first topic'. We intend to mark by this term not the simple serial fact that some topic gets talked about temporally prior to others, for some temporally prior topics such as, for example, ones prefaced by 'First, I just want to say . . .', or topics that are minor developments by the receiver of the conversational opening of 'how areyou' inquiries, are not heard or treated as 'first topics'. Rather, we want to note that to make of a topic a 'first topic' is to accord it a certain special status in the conversation. Thus, for example, to talk a topic as 'first topic' may provide for its analysability (by co-participants) as 'the reason for' the conversation, that being, furthermore, a preservable and reportable feature of the conversation.[5] In addition, making a topic 'first topic' may accord it a special importance on the part of its initiator (a feature which may, but need not, combine with its being a 'reason for the conversation').

These features of 'first topics' may pose a problem for conversationalists who may not wish to have special importance accorded some 'mentionable', and who may not want it preserved as 'the reason for the conversation'. It is by reference to such problems affiliated with the use of first topic position that we may appreciate such exchanges at the beginnings of conversations in which news *is* later reported, as:

A What's up.
B Not much. What's up with you?
A Nothing.

Conversationalists, then, can have mentionables they do not want to put in first topic position, and there are ways of talking past first topic position without putting them in.

A further feature of the organization of topic talk seems to involve 'fitting' as a preferred procedure. That is, it appears that a preferred way of getting mentionables mentioned is to employ the resources of the local organization of utterances in the course of the conversation. That involves holding off the mention of a mentionable until it can 'occur naturally', that is, until it can be fitted to another conversationalist's prior utterance, allowing his utterance to serve as a sufficient source for the mentioning of the mentionable (thereby achieving a solution to the placement question, the 'why that now', whose pervasive relevance was noted earlier, for the introduction of the topic).

1. (At 56 minutes into the conversation)[6]
    (15.0)

5. By 'preservable and reportable' we mean that in a subsequent conversation, this feature, having been analysed out of the earlier conversation and preserved, may be reported as 'he called to tell me that . . .'. We think that such references to prior conversation are orderly, and can be made available for criterial use, but the argument cannot be developed here.

6. Symbols used in transcriptions are as follows:

/	indicates upward intonation
//	indicates point at which following line interrupts
(x)	indicates pause of x seconds
( )	indicates something said but not transcribable
(word)	indicates probable, but not certain, transcription

KEN Well, we were on a discussion uh before Easter that we never finished on uh on why these guys are racing on the street?

     (3.0)

KEN You know. D'you remember that?

ROGER Oh, I was in a bad accident last night. My legs are all cut up. I was uh – speakina racing on the streets, picking up the subject. We were doin th'Mulholland stretch again and one guy made a gross error an' we landed in – in the wrong si(hh)de of the mountain hehh I was wearin a belt but my knees an' everything got all banged up.

2. (At one hour, thirteen minutes into conversation)

(Ken is talking about people liking to do things, but having to work hard at making it happen)

KEN Al likes to uh t- to ride sailboats or – or something
     //( )

ROGER Not any more hah hehh ah hah heh

KEN Why? What happened?

ROGER She's gone hehh

AL She is sold. She's gonna be sold.

KEN Oh. Well, he used to.

AL ⌈⌈Mm hm,

KEN ⌊⌊Or – he – he still does in – in the back of his mind probly.

ROGER Now he // likes to drive // fast Austin Healey's now.[7]

KEN Or –

KEN Or he – he – // he

AL NOT ANY MORE.

ROGER What happened?

AL IT BLEW UP.

ROGER *Did*ju really?!

     (1.0)

ROGER Whadju *do* to it?

AL The uh engine blew – I don't know, the valves an' everything went – phooh!

     (1.0)

ROGER Are you kidding?

AL There's three hundred an' fifty dollars worth of work to be done on the engine now.

---

but	indicates accent
emPLOYee	indicates heavy accent
::::	indicates stretching of sound immediately preceding, in proportion to number of colons inserted
becau-	indicates broken word.

7. Roger has sold Al the Austin Healey.

What we have, then, is that some mentionables ought not or need not be placed in first topic position, and may or are to be held off in the ensuing conversation until they can be fitted to some last utterance. There is, however, no guarantee that the course of the conversation will provide the occasion for any particular mentionable to 'come up naturally'.[8] Thus, the elements of topical organization so far discussed leave open the possibility that for some mentionable which a conversationalist brings to the conversation, no place for its occurrence will have been found at any point in its developing course. This can be serious because some mentionables, if not mentioned in some 'this conversation', will lose their status as a mentionable, or as the kind of mentionable they are, for example, they may lose their status as 'news'.

B I saw you with your uh filling out a thing for the U. of — bookstore. Does that mean you're going there?
A Oh yes. Sorry. I didn't know I hadn't told you.
B Well, oh you never tell me anything. When well //
A Well I tell you if I talk to you when something has just happened.
B I su-pose
A But I don't always remember how long it's been since I've seen people.

This being the case, it would appear that an important virtue for a closing structure designed for this kind of topical structure would involve the provision of a place in which hitherto unmentioned mentionables can be mentioned. The terminal exchange by itself makes no such provision. By exploiting the close organization resource of adjacency pairs, it provides for an immediate (i.e. next turn) closing of the conversation. That this close-ordering technique for terminating does not exclude the possibility of inserting unmentioned mentionables can be achieved by placement restrictions on the first part of terminal exchanges, for example, by requiring 'advance notice' or some form of foreshadowing.

These considerations about topical structure lead us back to one element of the placement considerations for closings mentioned before, to wit, the notion of a properly initiated closing section. One central feature of proper initiations of closing sections is their relationship to hitherto unmentioned mentionables, and some methods for initiating closings seem designed precisely for such problems as we have been discussing.

8. This is so even when the occasion for the conversation was arranged in the interests of that topic. For example, there was a report several years ago in the student newspaper of the School of Engineering at Columbia University about a meeting arranged with the Dean to air student complaints. No complaints were aired. In answer to a reporter's question about why this happened, a student who had been at the meeting replied 'The conversation never got around to that.'

IV. The first proper way of initiating a closing section that we will discuss is one kind of (what we will call) 'pre-closing'. The kind of pre-closing we have in mind takes one of the following forms, 'We-ell . . .', '*O*.K. . . .', 'So-oo', etc. (with downward intonation contours), these forms constituting the entire utterance. These pre-closings should properly be called '*possible* pre-closing', because providing the relevance of the initiation of a closing section is only one of the uses they have. One feature of their operation is that they occupy the floor for a speaker's turn without using it to produce either a topically coherent utterance or the initiation of a new topic. With them a speaker takes a turn whose business seems to be to 'pass', i.e. to indicate that he has not now anything more or new to say, and also to give a 'free' turn to a next who, in that such an utterance can be treated as having broken with any prior topic, can without violating topical coherence take the occasion to introduce a new topic, e.g., some heretofore unmentioned mentionable. *After* such a possible pre-closing is specifically a place for new topic beginnings.

When this opportunity, provided by possible pre-closings of the sort we are discussing, is exploited, that is, when another thereupon mentions a hitherto unmentioned mentionable, then the local organization otherwise operative in conversation, including the fitting of topical talk, allows the same possibilities which obtain in any topical talk. The opening which a possible pre-closing makes for an unmentioned mentionable may thus result in much more ensuing talk than the initial mentionable that is inserted; for that may provide the occasion for the 'natural occurrence' of someone else's mentionables in a fitted manner. It is thus not negative evidence for the status of utterances such as 'We-ell', etc. as possible pre-closings that extensive conversational developments may follow them. (In one two-party conversation of which we have a transcript running to eighty-five pages, the first possible pre-closing occurs on page twenty.) The extendability of conversation to great lengths past a possible pre-closing is not a sign of the latter's defects with respect to initiating closings, but of its virtues in providing opportunities for further topic talk that is fitted to the topical structure of conversation.

We have considered the case in which the possible pre-closing's provision for further topic talk is exploited. The other possibility is that co-conversationalists decline an opportunity to insert unmentioned mentionables. In that circumstance, the pre-closing may be answered with an acknowledgement, a return 'pass' yielding a sequence such as:

A O.K.
B O.K.

thereby setting up the relevance of further collaborating on a closing section. When the possible pre-closing is responded to in this manner, it may constitute the first part of the closing section.

We have referred to utterances of the form '*O*.K.', 'We-ell', etc. as possible pre-closings, intending by that term to point to the use of such utterances not only possibly to initiate a closing section, but also, by inviting the insertion of unmentioned mentionables, to provide for the reopening of topic talk. On their occurrence, they are only *possible* pre-closings because of this specific alternative they provide for.[9] But there is another sense in which they are only *possible* pre-closings. Clearly, utterances such as '*O*.K.', 'We-ell', etc. (where those forms are the whole of the utterance) occur in conversation in capacities other than that of 'pre-closing'. It is only on some occasions of use that these utterances are treated as pre-closings, as we have been using that term. To recommend that the terminal exchange solution initially sketched must be supplemented by an analysis of the placement of terminal exchanges; that the placement be seen in terms of properly initiated closing sections; that closing sections can be properly initiated by possible pre-closings; and that utterances of the form 'We-ell' can be pre-closings is not of great help unless it can either be shown (1) that utterances of the form 'we-ell' are invariably pre-closings, which is patently not the case, or (2) some indication can be given of the analysis that can yield utterances of the form 'we-ell' to be possible pre-closings. One consideration relevant to such a finding (by participants in the conversation; it is their procedures we seek to describe) is the placement of utterances of the form 'we-ell' in the conversation.

One way of discriminating the occasions on which such utterances are found to constitute possible pre-closings turns on their placement with respect to topic organization (not in the sense of the organization of mentionables over the course of the conversation which we have hitherto intended, but in the sense of 'the organization of talk on a single topic'). In brief, utterances of the form 'we-ell', '*O*.K.', etc., operate as possible pre-closings when placed at the analysable (once again, *to participants*) end of a topic.

To do justice to a discussion of this placement would require an analysis of the organization of 'talk about a topic' which cannot be developed here (work on such analysis is in progress).

The discussion in this section, it should be noted, has dealt with only one kind of possible pre-closing, and the suggestions we have offered concerning the placement which allows the analysis of an utterance as a possible pre-closing has reference only to that form. We will deal with others shortly. In regard to the form we have been concerned with, we should note that the

9. We return to the idea of 'specific alternatives' below at page 252, where it is more fully discussed.

techniques of topic bounding we have discussed are not specified for the place of a topic in the serial organization of topics. They are not techniques for first topic, fifth topic, intendedly last topic,[10] etc., but any topic (in terms of serial organization) can be so treated. That makes all the more fitting the character of possible pre-closings as specifically inviting the re-opening of topic talk. For, given that the use of an '$O.K.$' or a 'we-ell' after the close of a topic can be analysed (by co-participants) as a possible pre-closing and that is so without regard to which serial topic in a conversation has been closed, the absence of the re-opening alternative might have the consequence of systematically excluding from possible use in the present conversation the whole range of unmentioned mentionables which the participants might have to contribute. In their use of the etiquette of invitation, that is, the offering of the floor to another, possible pre-closings operate to allow a distribution of the opportunities and responsibilities for initiating topic talk and using unmentioned mentionables among various participants in the conversation. It is when the participants to a conversation lay no further claim to these opportunities and responsibilities that the potential of the possible pre-closing for initiating a closing section may be realized.

V. What the preceding discussion suggests is that a closing section is initiated, i.e. turns out to have begun, when none of the parties to a conversation care to choose to continue it. Now that is a *warrant* for closing the conversation, and we may now be in a position to appreciate that the issue of placement, for the initiation of closing sections as for terminal exchanges, is the issue of warranting the placement of such items as will initiate the closing at some 'here and now' in the conversation.[11] The kind of possible pre-closing we have been discussing – '$O.K.$', 'we-ell', etc. – is a way of establishing one kind of warrant for undertaking to close a conversation. Its effectiveness can be seen in the feature noted above, that if the floor offering is declined, if the '$O.K.$' is answered by another, then together these two utterances can constitute not a possible, but an actual first exchange of the closing section. The pre-closing ceases to be 'pre-' if accepted, for the acceptance establishes the warrant for undertaking a closing of the conversation at some 'here'.

Having seen that this kind of pre-closing establishes a particular warrant for undertaking the closing of a conversation, we may now be in a position

10. The relationship between 'shutting down' techniques and a class of topic types is no exception. For while 'shutting down' may be specially usable with the topic type 'making arrangements', and that topic type may be closing-relevant, it is not by virtue of the latter feature of 'making arrangements' that 'shutting down' is specially usable to end it.

11. The earlier noted attributions of brusqueness, anger, pique, etc. can now be appreciated as alternative possible warrants for closing attempts, when a closing initiation has not availed itself of the sequentially organized possibilities for warrants.

to examine other kinds of pre-closings and the kinds of warrants they may invoke for initiating the beginning of a closing section. To provide a contrast with the ensuing discussion, let us make one further observation on the kind of pre-closing we have just been discussing. The floor-offering-exchange device is one which can be initiated by any party to a conversation. In contrast to this, there are some possible pre-closing devices whose use is restricted to particular parties. The terms in which such parties may be formulated varies with conversational context.[12] For now, we can offer some observations about telephone contacts, where the formulation of the parties can be specified in terms of the specific conversation, i.e. caller–called.[13] What we find is that there are, so to speak, 'caller's techniques' and 'called's techniques' for inviting the initiation of closing sections. Before detailing these, we may make the general point (in pursuit of the claim at the beginning of this paper about the relationship of closings to overall structural organization) that it is of interest that closing sections of such conversations may be produced in ways which specifically employ, as relevant, features of their beginnings (namely, who initiated them), thus giving support to the proposal that the unit 'a single conversation' is one to which participants orient *throughout* its course.

While there are specific components whose use may be restricted to callers or called parties in inviting the initiation of conversational closings, we may note one feature that many of them have in common, namely, that they employ as their warrant for initiating the closing at some 'here' the interests of the other party. It is in the specification of those interests that the techniques become assigned to one or another party. Thus, the following invitation to a closing is caller-specific and makes reference to the interests of the other.

A discussion about a possible luncheon has been proceeding:

A Uhm livers 'n an gizzards 'n stuff like that makes it real yummy. Makes it too rich for *me* but makes it yummy.
B *Well* I'll letchu go. I don't wanna tie up your phone.

And, on the other hand, there are such called-specific techniques, also making reference to the other's interests, as

A This is costing you a lot of money.

There are, of course, devices usable by either party which do not make reference to the other's interests, most familiarly, 'I gotta go.'

12. For explication of the problem this sentence alludes to see Sacks (1972a) and Schegloff (1972).
13. For justification, see Schegloff (in press, ch. 2).

One feature common to the possible pre-closings so far discussed is that they make no reference to the particulars of the conversation in which they occur. While some of them retain and employ some elements of the conversation's beginning, such as who called, no conversationally developed materials are referred to in warranting the closing of the conversation. There are, in addition, devices which *do* make use of conversationally developed materials. Near the beginning of the conversation we will cite, the called (the receiver of the call) says:

B Are you watching Dakta:ri/
A No:no
B Oh my gosh Officer Henry is ul-locked in the cage wi- (0.4) wi' the lion, hheh.

And several minutes later, the caller initiates the closing with

A Okay, I letcha go back tuh watch yer Daktari.

Such devices again reinforce our understanding of the orientation of conversationalists to 'a single conversation' as a unit, and to '*this* single conversation' as an instance, in which *its* development to some point may be employed as a resource in accomplishing its further development as a specific, particularized occurrence. Such materials can be picked up any place in a conversation and seemingly be preserved for use in the conversation's closing. One place they systematically can occur is in the beginnings of conversations (not only in the beginnings of telephone conversations but in face-to-face interactions as well). The 'routine' questions employed at the beginnings of conversations, for example, 'What are you doing?', 'Where are you going?', 'How are you feeling?', etc., can elicit those kinds of materials which will have a use at the ending of the conversation in warranting its closing, e.g., 'Well, I'll let you get back to your books', 'Why don't you lie down and take a nap?', etc.[14] By contrast with our earlier discussion of such possible pre-closings as '*O*.K.' or 'we-ell', which may be said to accomplish or embody a warrant for closing, these may be said to announce it. That they do so may be related to the possible places in which they may be used.

In so far as the possible pre-closings which announce a warrant for closing draw upon materials particular to the conversations in which they occur, it is not feasible to specify exhaustively their privileges of occurrence. One technique which announces its warrant, but does not make reference to materials derived from the conversation, and which is generally usable (i.e. not re-

14. Such a use of materials gathered earlier in the conversation need not be restricted to materials about the other's circumstances or interests. An initiator of a conversation may insert at its beginning materials for his own use at its closing, for example, 'I'm just leaving to see the doctor, but I wanted to ask you. . . .' This technique may also allow the caller to provide for a conversation's monotopicality when, for the conversationalists involved, it would not otherwise be expectable.

stricted to particular users) can be briefly discussed, namely, 'I gotta go' (and its variants and expansions, such as 'The baby is crying, I gotta go', 'I gotta go, my dinner is burning', etc.).

We noted before that the possible pre-closings which accomplish a warrant without announcing it are placed after the close, or the closing down, of a topic (indeed, such placement may be required for their recognition as possible pre-closings). The overt announcement which we are now considering can be used to interrupt a topic. While exchanges such as '*O*.K.; O.K.' respect in their placement certain local orders of organization, such as the organization of talk on a topic or adjacency pairs (the first '*O*.K.' not being placed after the first part of an adjacency pair, or not being recognizable as a possible pre-closing if it is), the overt announcement, 'I gotta go' need not respect such boundaries, and can even interrupt not-yet-possibly-completed utterances. That is not to say that 'I gotta go' may not be placed with a respect for such local organization. It can be placed after a topic close, and we can speculate on reasons for its being used at such a place in preference to the '*O*.K.' which could also be used there. While 'I gotta go' cannot prohibit further talk, while others may insert an unmentioned mentionable after it, it does not specifically invite such a sequel, as '*O*.K.' does. For the initiation of a closing section in a way that discourages the specific alternatives of re-opening topic talk, this pre-closing may be more effective.

One implication of the preceding discussion which we can but hint at now is that from the inventory of possible pre-closing devices, one criterion of selection may be the placement that the item is to be given. That is, the availability of alternative mechanisms for accomplishing as a piece of work the invitation or initiation of a closing section allows us (as analysts) as an interesting problem how some actually employed mechanism or component can be selected. Investigation of such a problem can be expected to show that such a selected item operates not only to initiate or invite the initiation of the closing of a conversation (which any of the other available components might do also, and which therefore will not account for the use of the particular component employed), but accomplishes other interactionally relevant activities as well. What we have suggested above is that one such consideration in the selection among components to invite or initiate the closing section is the placement it will be given in terms of the local (utterance-to-utterance) and topical organization.

Another implication should be noted. It is the import of some of the preceding discussion that there are slots in conversation 'ripe' for the initiation of closing, such that utterances inserted there may be inspected for their closing relevance. To cite an earlier used example, 'why don't you lie down and take a nap' properly placed will be heard as an initiation of a closing section, not as a question to be answered with a 'because . . .' (although, of course, a co-participant can seek to decline the closing offering by treating it as a question). To cite actual data:

B has called to invite C, but has been told C is going out to dinner:

B Yeah. Well get on your clothes and get out and collect some of that free food and we'll make it some other time Judy then.
C Okay then Jack
B Bye bye
C Bye bye.

While B's initial utterance in this excerpt might be grammatically characterized as an imperative or a command, and C's 'O.K.' as a submission or accession to it, in no sense but a technical syntactic one would those be anything but whimsical characterizations. While B's utterance has certain imperative aspects in its language form, those are not ones that count; his utterance is a closing initiation; and C's utterance agrees not to a command to get dressed (nor would she be inconsistent if she failed to get dressed after the conversation), but to an invitation to close the conversation. The point is that no analysis, grammatical, semantic, pragmatic, etc., of these utterances taken singly and out of sequence, will yield their import in use, will show what co-participants might make of them and do about them. That B's utterance here accomplishes a form of closing initiation, and C's accepts the closing form and not what seems to be proposed in it, turns on the placement of these utterances in the conversation. Investigations which fail to attend to such considerations are bound to be misled.

VI. We have been considering the problem of the placement of the initiation of closing sections, and have found that this problem and the selection of a technique to accomplish initiation of the closing are related to the issue of warranting the initiation of a conversation's closing. That issue, it may be recalled, concerned how to warrant undertaking, at some 'here and now' in a conversation, a procedure that would achieve a solution to the problem of coordinating a stop to the relevance of the transition rule and that would at the same time respect the respective interests of the parties in getting their mentionables into the conversation. One such warrant could be found when the specific alternative to closing – re-opening topic talk – had no interest displayed in it by any of the participants. It should be noted that the use of a possible pre-closing of the form 'O.K.', or 'we-ell' can set up 'proceeding to close' as the central possibility, and the use of unmentioned mentionables by co-participants as specific alternatives. That is to say, the alternatives made relevant by an utterance of that form are not symmetrical. Closing is the central possibility, further talk is alternative to it; the reverse is not the case (an asymmetry hopefully captured by the term 'possible pre-closing';

'possible topic re-opener' would not do). Unless the alternative is invoked, the central possibility is to be realized.

There is another form of the warranting problem, with concomitant contrasts in placement and utterance type, which reverses this asymmetry. We will refer to it as 'pre-topic closing offerings'. We have in mind data such as the following:

1.
A Allo
B Did I wake you?
A Who's it.
B Nancy
A Oh hi
B → Hi, did I wake you
A Uh no no, not all hh//h
B ( ) hh after a while it started ringin I kept thinkin maybe I should hang up (but I) you know hh
A No no, no, it's O.K. // I was just uh rushing a little that's all hh
B Oh good.
B hh Umm don't bring any sausage because . . . etc.

2.
A Hello/
B Good morning.
A Oh hi // how are you hhh
B Lisa
B → Fine. Did I wake you up/
A No no no, I was reading . . . etc.

3.
A Buh nobody fought with huh like *I* fought with huh.
  (1.4)
A Uhh-uh fer example, uh d-oh about two weeks before she uh died I hh I don' know what possessed me. I really don't. I found myself in my car, driving ovuh tuh see her *alone*.
  (1.3)
A An' I uh ::: it *koo- took* me about oh I don't know how long t' find a parking space in that area there,
  (0.4)
B yeah
A → About a *half* hour. Are yih busy?
B Uh *no*. My liddle gran'daughter is here.
A Oh. Oh so it's hard f'you to //uh,
B That's *al*right
A – to uh::, to listen. Then uh, look, enjoy yer gran'daughter, hh
B I'll be taking her home soon,
A An' I'll try to uh::: uh to see you // on –

B Yeah, it could be – would // be (nice).
A – on Thursday. (etc. to closing)

4.

B Hello
A Vera/
B Ye:s
A Well you know, I had a little difficulty getting you.
  ((short discussion of the difficulty))
A → Am I taking you away from yer dinner/
B No::, no, I haven't even started tuh get it yet.
A Oh, you (h)have//n't.
B hhheh heh
A Well I – I never am certain, I didn't know whether I'd be too early or too late //
  or ri- etc.

5.

A ... (Karen Sweet)
B Well, howarya(h)
A Fine, how are you.
B Well just fine.
A → Were you eating,
  (1.0)
B Some grapes, ehh// heh heh
A heh, I was just looking at mine.

Such questions as 'Did I wake you', 'Are you busy', 'Am I taking you away from your dinner', and others (e.g., 'Is this long distance?', 'Are you in the middle of something?', etc.) are placed not at the analysable close of some unit, such as a topic, but at, or near, the beginning of one. One consequence of this is that, instead of some activity such as topic talk being a specific alternative to the closing they otherwise prefigure, the central possibility is an undertaking, or continuation, of the unit at the beginning of which they are placed (be it a 'topic', a 'conversation', or a 'silence' as when about to 'hold' in a telephone conversation), and closing is the specific alternative to that. When such pre-topic closing offerings are declined, then the offering or some component of the declining utterance may be topically elaborated in their own right, or the offering becomes a pre-sequence for the offerer's topic talk. If the pre-topic closing offering is accepted, there follows a closing section, one component of which routinely is making arrangements for resumption of the conversation (as in the data from 3 above).[15]

  15. These features of pre-topic closing offerings seem to be related in their capacity not only to prefigure the undertaking of some conversational unit in the absence of a reason to the contrary, but also to project a certain contour or length for the unit, such that, if the offer to close is not accepted on the occasion of the offering, no opportunity to close will soon present itself which respects the organization of that unit (for example, it may require an interruption).

Of special interest here are what might be called 'pre-first-topic closing-offerings', of which all but one of the data citations above are instances (the exception being the data from 3). These are not simply special cases of pre-topic closing offerings, specifying the 'topic' to 'first topic'. Rather, by virtue of the special status of 'first topic' discussed earlier, inquiries such as 'Are you busy?', 'Are you eating?' etc., placed before first topic are more importantly seen as placed before 'the conversation'. The bases for the insertion of such inquiries before 'first topic' cannot be discussed at length here, but two may be briefly indicated. First, such inquiries may be heard (by participants) to be warranted (i.e. to have the 'why that now' explained) by features of the contact to that point (for example by the 'number of rings before answering', as in the data from 1 above) or by assumedly mutually oriented-to features of the interaction such as its time and place [on the mutual orientation to the time and place of a conversation by participants, see Schegloff (1971)],[16] for example the orientation to the social time of day displayed by 'Am I taking you away from your dinner', in the data above. Secondly, such inquiries may be heard as attentive to the 'priorities assessment' that may be relevant in initiating a conversation. Where the initiator of a conversation is unable to assess the comparative priorities of possibly ongoing activities of the other and the prospective conversation [for a fuller discussion of this issue concerning openings, see Schegloff (1972), ch. 2)], as when first coming upon the scene (for example, knocking at the door) or calling on the telephone, an inquiry concerning possibly ongoing priority activities may be introduced, as a way of finding whether an initiated conversation shall be prosecuted. Since the subject of the inquiry is thus selected as one which might have priority over the proposed conversation, an affirmative answer may have the consequence of accepting what turns out to be a closing offering.

Pre-first-topic closing offerings have been introduced here to suggest that, just as possible pre-closings do not foreclose the possibility of further topic talk in the conversation (i.e. raising the possibility of closing does not ensure it), so does the opening of a conversation not preclude the possibility of immediately closing it. When the latter possibility is actualized, although by reference to the basic features discussed at the beginning of this paper, 'conversation' may technically be said to have taken place, the participants may find that 'no conversation occurred'. The possibilities for both conversa-

16. These alternatives may shade into each other. 'Did I wake you?' may be heard as displaying its speaker's orientation to the time of the conversation if asked at a time the speaker might know the other to have possibly been sleeping; i.e. it can be heard as referring to time if it is the right time for such a question. If not, it can be heard as picking up on a feature of the interaction to that point, for example, number of rings before answering, voice quality leading to talk about 'colds', etc. . . . .

tional continuation and for conversational closing are thus present, if appropriate techniques are used, from the very beginning of a conversation to its end.

VII. Having initially formulated the closing problem for conversation in terms of the suspension of the transition property of utterance completions, a technique was described which is used to come to terms with that problem – the terminal exchange. It was found that that exchange by itself was insufficient and that an adequate description of closing would have to provide for the proper placement of terminal exchanges which do not have unrestricted privileges of occurrence. The needed supplement was found to consist in properly initiated closing sections, and we described a variety of techniques for properly initiating closing sections, their placement, and the warrant they establish for closing a conversation.

A O.K.
B O.K.
A Bye Bye
B Bye.

Closing sections may, however, include much more. There is a collection of possible component parts for closing sections which we cannot describe in the space available here. Among others, closings may include 'making arrangements', with varieties such as giving directions, arranging later meetings, invitations, and the like; re-invocation of certain sorts of materials talked of earlier in the conversation, in particular, re-invocations of earlier-made arrangements (for example, 'See you Wednesday') and re-invocations of the reason for initiating the conversation (for example, 'Well, I just wanted to find out how Bob was'), not to repeat here the earlier discussion of materials from earlier parts of the conversation to do possible pre-closings; and components that seem to give a 'signature' of sorts to the type of conversation, using the closing section as a place where recognition of the type of conversation can be displayed (for example, 'Thank you'). Collections of these and other components can be combined to yield extended closing sections, of which the following is but a modest example:

B Well that's why I *said* 'I'm not gonna say anything, I'm not making *any* comments // about anybody'
C Hmh
C Ehyeah
B Yeah

C Yeah
B *Al*righty. Well *I'll* give you a call before we decide to come down. O.K.?
C O.K.
B *Al*righty
C O.K.
B We'll see you then
C O.K.
B *Bye* bye
C Bye.

However extensive the collection of components that are introduced, the two crucial components (*for the achievement of proper closing*; other components may be important for other reasons, but not for closing *per se*) are the terminal exchange which achieves the collaborative termination of the transition rule, and the proper initiation of the closing section which warrants the undertaking of the routine whose termination in the terminal exchange properly closes the conversation. It should be noted again, however, that at any point in the development of the collection of components which may occur between a proper initiation of a closing up to and including the terminal exchange, and even the moments immediately following it, there are procedures for re-opening the conversation to topic talk. It is by a necessarily brief description of some procedures for doing so that it may be appreciated why we have referred to this conversational part as a closing *section*, thereby ascribing to it the status of an oriented-to conversational unit.

One way topic talk may be re-opened at any point has already been discussed in another context. We noted earlier that some possible pre-closings specifically invite the insertion of unmentioned mentionables and if that invitation is accepted by a co-participant, then considerable topic talk may ensue, since other participants may find in the talk about the newly introduced mentionable, occasions for the natural fitting of a topic of their own. The same procedure of fitting, of topics 'naturally' coming up, can arise from any of the proper components of closing sections. If one component of a closing section can be re-invocation of earlier talked-about materials, then on any occasion of such an invocation, occasions for fitting new topics to that re-invocation may arise. The same is true for other components of closings, each of which may 'lead to' some fitted other topic 'coming up naturally'. Since most closing components have their roots in the body of the conversation, it appears that 'new' topics can enter into a closing section only by their fit to, or their coming up 'naturally' from, 'old' materials. This character of closing sections as 'not a place for new things to come up' is consistent with techniques for initiating them such as possible pre-closings, whose warrant (when their closing options are accepted) is that none of the parties has further mentionables to introduce.

The suggestion above that there are procedures at any point in a closing section for re-opening topic talk was not, however, intended primarily to refer to this process whereby new materials are introduced by 'hooking' them onto old materials properly appearing as re-invocations. There are also ways in which new materials may be introduced, so to speak, 'in their own right', and these reflect the sectional character of closings. When such new materials are inserted into a closing, they are specially 'marked'; we can here discuss only two forms of such marking.

One form of marking, used elsewhere in conversation and not only in closings, we can refer to as 'misplacement marking'. Classes of utterances or activities which have a proper place in a conversation but are to be done in some particular conversation in other than their proper place, or an utterance (type) which has no particular proper place but is none the less 'out of place' where it is to be done, may have their occurrence misplacement marked. As an example of the former: 'introductions' are properly done at or near the beginnings of conversations. On occasion, however, they may not occur until well into the conversation, as may happen in conversations between adjacently seated passengers in an airplane or train. Such introductions may be prefaced with a misplacement marker, for example, 'By the way, my name is . . .'. As an example of the latter sort of occasion alluded to above, we may note that interruptions of an organizational unit for utterances, such as an adjacency pair, may be similarly misplacement marked. Thus, an utterance inserted after a question has been asked but before it has been answered may begin with 'By the way . . .'.

Misplacement markers, thus, display an orientation by their user to the proper sequential-organizational character of a particular place in a conversation, and a recognition that an utterance that is thereby prefaced may not fit, and that recipient should not attempt to use this placement in understanding their occurrence. The display of such orientation and recognition apparently entitles the user to place an item outside its proper place. In the case of closings, we find that utterances introducing new materials may be misplacement marked when those utterances do not occur between the parts of an adjacency pair and do not accomplish an activity which has a proper place elsewhere in the conversation. That such utterances, but not ones which use proper closing components, are misplacement marked suggests an orientation by conversationalists to the status of 'closings' as an organizational unit – what we have referred to as a 'section' – with a proper character with which the misplacement marked utterance is not consistent.

Caller° You don'know w– uh what that would be, how much it costs.
Crandall I would think probably, about twunty five dollars.
Caller° Oh boy, hehh hhh!
Caller° Okay, thank you.

Crandall Okay dear.

Caller° OH BY THE WAY. I'd just like tuh say thet uh, I *DO* like the new programming. I've been listening, it's uh //

( )

Crandall *Good girl*!

Crandall Hey listen do me a favour wouldja write Mister Fairchild 'n tell im that, I think that'll s-shi-break up his whole day for im.

Caller° ehhh heh heh hhh!

Crandall Okay?

Caller° Okay,

Crandall ⌜Thank you
Caller° ⌞bye bye,

Crandall Mm buh(h) bye.

A second form of marking which displays an orientation to a closing section as 'not a place for new materials' we may refer to as 'contrast marking'. It is best discussed in connection with data: A, who is visiting the city, and B, who lives there, have been engaged in an extensive making of arrangements to see each other.

A I mean b'cause I – eh you're going to this meeting at twelve thirty, en I don't want to uh inconvenience *you*,

B Well, even if you get here et abayout eh ten thirty, or eleven uh' clock, we still have en hour en a hahf,

A *O*.K., *Al*right,

B Fine. We'd have a bite, en // (talk),

A Yeh. Weh – *No*! No, *don't* prepare any//thing.

B And uh – I'm not gunnah prep*are*, we'll juz whatever it'll // be, we'll ( ).

A *NO*! No. I don' meant that. I min – because uh, *she* en I'll prob'ly uh be spending the day togethuh, so uh::: we'll go out tuh lunch, or something like that. hh So I mean if you:: have a cuppa cawfee or something, I mean // thatuh that'll be fine. But // uh –

B Yeah

B Fine.

A *Ot*huh th'n that don't //uh

B Fine.

A Don't bothuh with anything else. I-uh:::

(1.2)

A I – uh::: I *did* wanna tell you, en I didn' wanna tell you uh:: last night. Uh because you had entert-uh, company. I – I – I had something – *ter*rible t'tell you. So//uh

B How terrible *is* it.

A Uh, tuh – as worse it could *be*.

(0.8)

B W – y'mean Ada?

A Uh yah

B Whad' she do, die?
A Mm::hm.

The data of particular interest here are in A's seventh utterance in the segment, 'I *did* wanna tell you.' While there are various interesting issues raised by this data, we want briefly only to indicate one of them. The accent (as well as the verb form employed which allows the accent) accomplishes one half a contrast whose other half is not explicit (the rest of the utterance does not supply it), and whose paraphrase might be, 'There *is* something else I wanted to tell you.' An accent on the second part of a contrast pair whose first part is not explicit can none the less serve to display the relevance of the first part. Thus, to cite another example, a particularly clear display of what is 'going through someone's mind' though it is not spoken or gesturally, etc., conveyed, is provided by a person waiting to take an elevator down, who is told upon its arrival that the elevator is going up, pauses a moment, and then says, 'I guess I *will* wait.' The contrast accent displays his prior, now abandoned, decision to 'go along for the ride'. In the case of 'I *did* wanna tell you', the presumptive character of closing sections as 'not the place for new materials' can be seen to be here prospectively overruled by new materials, which however are specially marked.

The insertion of misplacement marked new materials into closing sections, it may be added, marks the new materials themselves in a distinctive way. While in the case of the data just discussed, this appears to be 'deferred bad news', regularly the placing of new materials in closing sections is a way of achieving for them the status of 'after-thoughts'.

Having offered some suggestions about the status of closings as sectional units, it is in point to suggest several virtues of a sectional solution to the problems we have formulated as the problems of closing.

One aspect of the problem of closing, formulated by reference to the organization of speaker turns, it may be recalled, was that that organization generates an indefinitely extendable, but internally undifferentiated, string of turns. We noted earlier the importance of having a marked place for a problem whose focus was coordination in terminating the transition rules, and described the contribution that a terminal exchange, employing adjacency pair organization, made to the solution of that problem. That contribution was limited, however, by the placement problem for terminal exchanges, i.e. the impropriety of a closing produced by an 'unprepared terminal exchange. That placement problem is solved by the use of properly initiated closing sections. It is the closing section which, through its terminal exchange, marks a place at which collaboration on termination of the transition rule can be located. An important part of the solution to the closing problem thus involves locating the solution to the initial problem we formulated not so much in the conversation as a whole, but in a closing section; one can close a conversation by closing a section which has as its business closing a conversation. When an initiated closing is aborted by re-opening topic talk, a next effort to close does not proceed by simple insertion of a terminal exchange, but by the initiation of another closing section, again providing a unit within which the terminal exchange can be located.

A second virtue of a sectional solution can be mentioned again here briefly. Given the feature of closing sections as 'porous', i.e. the availability at any point of procedures for reopening topic talk, sectional solution has the virtue of possibly providing multiple opportunities for the introduction of unmentioned mentionables, a virtue whose importance *vis-a-vis* this conversational system's topical organization should be evident from the earlier discussion.

One final virtue of a sectional solution to the closing problem may be suggested, concerning the articulation of conversations (i.e. the unit 'a single conversation') with the interaction episodes, occasions, or streams of behavior in which they occur. One order of relevance termination can have, and one basis for the importance of the clarity of terminal exchanges, is that other actions by the participants may be geared to, or properly occasioned by, the occurrence of conversational termination. In telephone conversations, hanging up and breaking the communication medium properly awaits termination, and properly follows its occurrence. In face-to-face interaction, a whole range of physical doings and positionings, ruled out by the proprieties of maintaining a show of attention and interest (cf. Goffman, 1961, 1963, 1967), become available and/or required upon termination, for example, those related to leave-taking. In so far as the actions that may be occasioned by termination of the conversation require preparation, there is use for a place *in* the conversation to prepare for actions that should follow its termination in close order. Closing sections, in foreshadowing the imminent occurrence of termination, allow such a possibility. Indeed, topics may be improvised for insertion into a closing sequence to extend the time available for such preparations, as when visitors gather their belongings before departure (thus yielding a derivative problem when such improvised topics assume a 'life of their own' and cannot easily be brought to a close when the preparations they were to accommodate have been completed). The sectional organization of closings thus provides a resource for managing the articulation between the conversation and the interaction occasion in which it occurs.

The source of many of these virtues resides in the potential for re-opening topic talk at any point in the course of a closing section. This invites our understanding that to capture the phenomenon of closings, one cannot treat it as the natural history of some particular conversation; one cannot treat it as a routine to be run through, inevitable in its course once initiated. Rather, it must be viewed, as must conversation as a whole, as a set of prospective possibilities opening up at various points in the conversation's course; there are possibilities throughout a closing, including the moments after a 'final' good-bye, for re-opening the conversation.[17] Getting to a termination, therefore, involves work at various points in the conversation's, and the closing section's, course; it requires accomplishing. For the analyst, it requires a description of the prospects and possibilities available at the various points, how they work, what the resources are, etc., from which the participants produce what turns out to be the finally accomplished closing.

VIII. A few concluding remarks will be in point to try to specify the domain for which our analysis is relevant. What we are really dealing with is the problem of closing a conversation that ends a state of talk. It does not hold for members of a household in their living room, employees who share an office, passengers together in an automobile, etc., that is, persons who could be said to be in a 'continuing state of incipient talk'. In such circumstances, there can be lapses of the operation of what we earlier called the basic features; for example, there can be silence after a speaker's utterance which is neither an attributable silence nor a termination, which is seen as neither the suspension nor the violation of the basic features. These are adjournments, and seem to be done in a manner different from closings. Persons in such a continuing state of incipient talk need not begin new segments of conversation with exchanges of greetings, need not close segments with closing sections and terminal exchanges. Much else would appear to be different in their conversational circumstances as compared to those in which a conversation is specifically 'started-up', which we cannot detail here.

17. To cite but one example of this possibility:
B So uh, gimme a ring sometime
A yeah. A*l*right.
B Whatchu c'n do.
A Yeah
B Tch! '*Kay?*
A OK
B A'right. Bye bye
   (1.0)
A Mnnuh He*llo?*
B Yeah?
   (1.0)
A Uhm:::
   (1.8)
A Tch! hhehh hhh I didn't have anything in pu*r*icular tuh say I – I jus' fer a sekin' didn't feel like hanging up.
   etc.

These considerations suggest that how a conversation is done in its course is sensitive to the placement of the conversation in an interaction episode or occasion, and that how an upcoming lapse in the operation of the basic features is attended and dealt with by participants is sensitive to, and/or can accomplish, the placement of the conversation in its occasion. As the problem of closing a conversation has been proposed to be shifted to ending its closing section, so ending an occasion (or interaction) can be seen to be located in some conversational episode. That participants attend as a task or as a piece of business that the conversation be brought to a close may have less to do with the character, organization, structure, etc., of conversation *per se*, than with that of occasions or interactions; or, rather, it has to do with the organization of conversation as a constituent part of an occasion or interaction.

This kind of consideration can be overlooked if much of the data one is looking at is, as it is in the case of this paper, made up of telephone conversations, because there especially the occasion is more or less coterminous with the conversation; the occasion is constructed to contain the conversation and is shaped by its contingencies. Since, typically, the occasion ends when the conversation does, it appears that it is the conversation's closing that one is dealing with. But even in telephone conversations, in those cases in which the occasion has an extension beyond a single conversation, one may find that only that conversation which ends the occasion is brought to a close with the forms we have described (we have in mind situations in which a caller talks seriatim to several members of a family, for example).[18]

If these observations are correct and in point, then the observations we offered earlier about the articulation between conversation and ensuing actions, i.e. the preparation of actions which are geared to termination, are not passing observations. That there are geared actions required, and the possible need for preparing them, has to do with the *occasion's* ending, and that it is as a part of conversation that the occasion's endings may be done. It is by way of the use of closing the conversation for ending the occasion that the use of a section to end the conversation may be appreciated, in a way similar to our appreciation of the use of a snack to end an evening or a get-together.

18. A simple distinction between face-to-face and telephone interaction will not do. We do not yet have any adequate technical account of these notions, which would specify the analytic dimensions of significant distinction. A variety of intuitive, plausible distinctions do not hold up. It should not be taken, from the text, that whereas face-to-face conversation can be either continuously sustained or have the character of a continuing state of incipient talk, telephone conversation invariably has the former character. That does not appear to be the case. And even if it were, it would be the distinction between these two modes, rather than that between face-to-face and telephonic, which would be relevant.

References

ALBERT, E. (1965), ' "Rhetoric", "logic", and "poetics" in Burundi: culture patterning of speech behavior', *American Anthropologist*, vol. 66, pp. 40–41.

GARFINKEL, H., and SACKS, H. (1970), 'On formal structures of practical actions', in J. C. McKinney and E. A. Tiryakian (eds.), *Theoretical Sociology: Perspectives and Developments*, Appleton-Century-Crofts.

GOFFMAN, E. (1961), *Encounters*, Bobbs-Merrill.

GOFFMAN, E. (1963), *Behavior in Public Places*, Free Press.

GOFFMAN, E. (1967), *Interaction Ritual*, Anchor Books.

JEFFERSON, G. (1972), 'Side sequences', in D. N. Sudnow (ed.), *Studies in Social Interaction*, Free Press.

MOERMAN, M. (1967), 'Being Lue: uses and abuses of ethnic identication', *Proceedings of Spring 1967 Meetings*, American Ethnological Society.

MOERMAN, M. (1970), 'Analysis of Lue conversation, I and II', mimeo.

SACKS, H. (1972a), 'An initial investigation of the usability of conversational materials for doing sociology', in D. N. Sudnow (ed.), *Studies in Social Interaction*, Free Press.

SACKS, H. (1972b), 'On the analyzability of stories by children', in J. J. Gumperz and D. H. Hymes (eds.), *Directions in Sociolinguistics*, Holt, Rinehart & Winston.

SACKS, H. (in press), *Aspects of the Sequential Organization of Conversation*, Prentice-Hall.

SCHEGLOFF, E. A. (1967), 'The first five seconds: the order of conversational openings', Ph.D. dissertation, University of California, Berkeley.

SCHEGLOFF, E. A. (1968), 'Sequencing in conversational openings', *American Anthropologist*, vol 70, pp. 1075–95.

SCHEGLOFF, E. A. (1972), 'Notes on a conversational practice: formulating place', in D. N. Sudnow (ed.), *Studies in Social Interaction*, Free Press.

SCHEGLOFF, E. A. (in press), *The Social Organization of Conversational Openings*, University of Pennsylvania Press.

SCHENKEIN, J. (1972), 'Toward an analysis of natural conversation and the sense of "heheh"', *Semiotica*, vol. 6, pp. 344–77.

SMITH, B. H. (1968), *Poetic Closure: A Study of How Poems End*, University of Chicago Press.

SUDNOW, D. N. (ed.) (1972), *Studies in Social Interaction*, Free Press.

19 A. Lincoln Ryave and James N. Schenkein

Notes on the Art of Walking

First published in this volume.

It can be observed that the transportation of our bodies is a commonplace feature of our everyday experience of the world; to be sure, when such is not the case, we have certain warrant for noting those details of our circumstances rendering bodily transportation unlikely. While we of course have a variety of devices to achieve our transportation (automobiles, tricycles, elevators, donkeys, and so on), the body itself is regularly used for its own self-transportation. Using the body in this way can take many forms, and some of these can be pointed to with readily understood glosses in our native discourses: crawling, hopping, running, cartwheeling, jumping, skipping, walking, and so on.

The substantive focus of this discussion shall be the phenomenon of 'doing walking'. We use the verb 'doing' to underscore a conception of walking as the concerted accomplishment of members of the community involved as a matter of course in its production and recognition. We hope to indicate that these members rely upon an elaborated collection of methodic practices in the conduct of doing walking, and we want to sketch out one sort of analytic technology to gain access to the details of these methodic practices. In treating this commonplace phenomenon as the problematic achievement of members, we hope to build towards a greater understanding of social phenomena as on-going situated accomplishments. It is, after all, these methodic practices that make the phenomenon of doing walking so utterly unnoteworthy at first glance to both lay and professional social analysts alike; indeed, it is through these methodic practices that the commonplace presents itself to us as ordinary, and the exotic as extraordinary.

On the issue of data

For the purposes of inquiring into the phenomenon of doing walking, two eight-minute segments of videotape were filmed on a public pavement travelled primarily by students. In order to capture a number of instances of the phenomenon, and in order to observe a variety of situations that confront walkers negotiating their progress among other walkers, we filmed at a time when students are routinely negotiating their ways from class to class. The setting was additionally selected for the sorts of 'natural boundaries' within which walkers on this pavement must conduct their progress: on one side walkers are confronted with an eight-foot high concrete wall, and on the other with a continuous row of parked cars; along the length of kerb were also typically spaced telephone poles and parking regulation signs.

It is worth noting, although it will not be greatly developed, that the sense in which we speak of the environment as constituted by 'natural boundaries' is itself a members' on-going accomplishment. While the constraint of 'natural boundaries' may be an omnipresent contingency realized and realizable on occasions of doing walking, the content of those boundaries is both varied and variable within a single setting and across different settings. So the 'natural boundaries' members cooperate to maintain while doing walking include not merely the physical conditions of the scene, but also the encircling space accompanying other walkers as they conduct themselves along their respective paths, their trajectories, the space between those seen as walking together, and the like. We will later offer some remarks on the way in which altering or violating some 'natural boundary' will unavoidably suggest 'something special'; but for now, let us observe that walking on the tops of parked cars, down the middle of the street, or through a hand-holding couple becomes the extraordinary event it does in contrast to the ordinary concerted maintenance of those boundaries seen as constituting the environment.

One last comment on the collection of the data with videotape seems appropriate. It is plain enough that the use of videotape affords us the opportunity to review a given instance of the phenomenon innumerable times without relying on a single observation of an essentially transitory phenomenon. In addition, since a key focus of our inquiry is how an instance of the phenomenon presents itself, we require intimate study of actual instances of walking and cannot be satisfied with the study of reports *on* those instances. So while we seek to study the issue of producing and recognizing instances of doing walking, we want our inquiry to be based on data representing actual instances of doing walking, and not second-order reports which are distinct from the thing we want to treat as problematic.

The navigational problem

The ways in which doing walking is an on-going members' accomplishment can be initially appreciated by considering what we shall refer to as the 'navigational problem'. We take it that our data captures utterly routine occasions of walking under circumstances of heavy walking traffic, and that there occur in our data no instances of bumping into one another is no freak happening. The avoidance of collision is a basic index to the accomplished character of walking: that participants to the setting 'manage' not to collide with one another or with some other (e.g. physical) natural boundary is to be viewed as the product of concerted work on the part of those co-participants.

This concerted work is not a particularly troublesome matter for participants. The conduct of walking is not experienced as an activity of worry, requires no exotic forethought for its successful management, and can be achieved without viewing the prospect of collision as some likely yet prescribable happening; indeed, the converse of any of these observations provides members reasonable evidence for their 'trouble' in now having to attend to such matters.

There is, none the less, a treatment of this accomplishment as a navigational problem that recommends our attention to the structures relied upon and manipulated by participant walkers as they 'solve' their navigational problem routinely in the normal conduct of their walking. The 'problem' to which we shall address ourselves is an analytic one: what is the nature of the work executed routinely by participant walkers? An articulation of this work will represent a description of the members' solution to what is analytically treatable as the 'navigational problem' of walking.

Toward describing the members' solution

A further focus of our investigation is provided by the observation that members have the ability to distinguish between 'walking-together' and 'walking-alone'. In the course of this discussion we hope to provide a foundation for a disciplined investigation of the social-interactional relevance this distinction has for members' achieved solutions to the navigational problem. Our interests will involve us in an examination of members' methods for the *production* and *recognition* of walking-alone and of walking-together as on-going situated accomplishments. The notions of 'production' and 'recognition' are invoked to take note of the fact that doing 'walking-together' involves setting co-participants both in doing the activity (production) and in observing the activity (recognition).

We shall begin and guide our investigation by addressing the matter of how it is that we, as members, are able to do 'recognizing walking-together'; it is this recognition that provides co-participant walkers a basic constituent of their achieved solution to the navigational problem.

Our interest in the production and recognition of walking-together and walking-alone is informed by the fact that members, in the conduct of their walking, attend to this dimension of the phenomenon; that attention, or lack of it, has interactional consequences for the navigational problem. For a lone walker, the noticing of some collection of approaching walkers decidedly walking-together has particular navigational relevance: (a) without some alteration of the opposing trajectories, collision would recognizably occur, and (b) for the culture we are describing, it is expected, it is proper, for the lone walker to do walking-around those decidedly doing walking-together. This constraint seems also to be operative in cases where a lone walker (or a series of lone walkers) is confronted by a collection of walkers decidedly walking-together in the same direction but at a slower pace: the constraint is upon the lone walker, again, not to walk-between but to walk-around.

We must be clear about the nature of what we mean by 'constraint'. It is not that someone cannot walk between an on-going group walking-together when that group is met head on or employs too slow a pace in the same direction, but that to do so has definite social consequences and meanings. For example, a way of being demonstrably 'rude' is by violating the above mentioned constraint, a way young male adults have of 'choosing off' is by violating the constraint, a way one comes to build a reputation for 'absent-mindedness' is by preferring absorption in one's books over attention to one's navigational responsibilities while walking, and so on.

The constraint we mention is also properly attended to by those walkers party to a large group that is walking-together, where, in order not to prevent others from walking-around them, they will break up into smaller groups of two-abreast instead of four-abreast, for example, lest approaching or following others be forced to walk-between their ranks. The sorts of interactional possibilities occasioned by the routine two-by-two formation of walkers instead of a four-abreast formation surely deserve additional investigation. It is, of course, well known that maintaining a large group walking-together (and thereby forcing other walkers either to step aside or break the ranks of the approaching ensemble) is a classic street challenge. The point is: both those walking-together and those walking-alone can and do orient to this dimension of the phenomenon of doing walking.

Production and recognition

To put the matter another way, an integral feature of the achieved members' solution to the navigational problem is the production and recognition of walking-together and walking-alone. That is to say, contained in our noticing of the interactional relevances of walking-alone and walking-together is an implicit claim to the members' capacities and practices in both producing and recognizing, as a matter of course, that aspect of the conduct of walking. Let us now treat that aspect problematically in an effort to indicate the sort of investigation into members' solutions that is here recommended for the study of walking. We shall, of course, be devoting ourselves to an inquiry into the procedures out of which both the production and recognition of walking-alone and walking-together are fashioned.

The task of determining the procedures by which members can decide who is walking with whom in some setting was initiated by the observation that we were able, when relevant to do so, in various degrees of agreement, to come to determinations about the matter. It became apparent that what was essentially involved was some membership ability to distinguish between 'alone' and 'together'. If these are then available and situationally relevant categorization devices for members, the primary concern becomes discovering the procedures for applying these categories by member observers.

Our task then becomes one of demonstrating some attributes of what might be called 'togetherings' and 'alonings'; that is, we now could focus upon combinations of setting and activities of which a constituent feature is 'togetherness' and 'aloneness'; the procedures we may uncover in an analysis of how members achieve their observations of walking-alone and walking-together then, have particular use in later studies of parties, restaurants, movies, libraries, and other settings where the dimension revealed by the categories 'alone' and 'together' is prominent. For now, however, this more general phenomenon shall be approached with special focus on the togethering displayed in doing walking-together and on the aloning displayed in doing walking-alone.

Naturally, the application of these categories by members is a double task involving both (a) production work on the part of those members doing the walking-together or doing the walking-alone, and (b) recognition work on the part of those members observing the distribution of those categories among walkers. Let us now turn to a consideration of these two reflexive features of the phenomenon.

Recognition work

A togethering, for example doing walking-together, is a settinged activity. By that we mean the propriety and relevance of a togethering is a function of such factors as time, place, and participants: there are, clearly, proper and/ or expectable occasions for a togethering. This observation is rather fundamental in a consideration of recognition work for such factors as time, place, and participants are invoked by members to see, notice, and account for some others *as a togethering* without having to approach them to determine by interview if such is, in fact, the case. Plainly, walking-together cannot be properly done anytime, anywhere, with anybody. What are some features that are provided by a setting and invoked by members in order to recognize the propriety of, for example, walking-together?

A pervasive feature of the culture we are dealing with is the use of members' identification categories (e.g. family, stranger, friend, Bill, Oriental, boy, etc.) as mechanisms for the establishment of who can expectably be engaging in a togethering, or whatever. It can be noted that members attend to the fact that certain category relations obligate the occasion of a togethering, as with the walking-together that might be occasioned on the meeting of a friend who is going in the same direction. The obligatory status of certain category relations can be noted by the consequent availabilities of such things as 'making excuses', 'begging-off', 'changing direction of one's body movement', 'apologies', and other avoidance or circumventing arrangements to an expected walking-together. Similarly, the constraints of certain category relations provide for the impropriety of walking-together as when 'strangers' find themselves 'following one another' or 'walking side by side'; here the consequences of 'rudeness', 'picking-up', 'misidentifications', 'spying', and suspicions of other pretexts become relevant.

That there is work involved in prescribing the propriety of both the when and who of a togethering, then, provides one important basis from which members devise and invoke recognition procedures. These are attentive to what might be called proper 'togethering sets'; for example, that some people can be seen as walking-together may turn on their identifiability as a proper togethering. A child walking ten feet ahead of an adult woman may be seeable as mother-and-child, and they thereby can be taken as walking-together, whereas a uniformed policeman and teenage girl walking in a similar arrangement may present us with no recognizable togethering set, and each thereby can be taken as walking-alone.

So, recognition work can inhere in the settinged character of walking-together, which provides for the recognizability of a togethering on the basis of availability, relevance, or properness of some togetherness set. Again, this is not a matter in which one has to interrogate in order to find out if such is the case; rather one takes-it-for-granted until 'informed' otherwise.

In order to provide a more complete picture of some of the features of recognition work we need to anticipate our discussion of production work, for part and parcel of recognition is the participant's knowledge and reliance upon the accomplishment of walking-alone and walking-together. For example, members who can be seen as involved in the maintenance of spatial proximity can properly be seen as walking-together. Our data instance two members observed walking in spatial proximity, approaching a disrupting obstacle (a telephone pole) which upsets the on-going maintenance of co-present spatial proximity; when they re-establish their former co-presence after the obstacle has been passed, the sense of seeing them as a togethering was secured. Another illustration from our data is an instance in which three members were observed walking-together while making a left turn from the street-crossing onto the pavement; in that each adjusted his pace so as to make the turning non-disruptive of the established spatial proximity, the sense of seeing them as a togethering was secured.

Relatedly, those members who can be seen as involved in some togethering-bound-activity can properly be seen as walking-together. For example, in two instances from our data the sense of seeing walking-together was secured by the observations that, in the first, two members were holding hands and exchanging sustained reciprocal glances while, in the second, two members maintained an extended interchange of verbal remarks. The fact of producing walking-together provides for the propriety or relevance of certain social activities, and the recognizability of these activities will inform on the status of walkers as alone or together.

These rough examples are intended to suggest the delicacy with which our recognition work operates. The noticing of potential category relations among persons distributed along the pavement, the noticing of spatial patterns not merely as features of the scene but as patterns re-established by walkers after passing some obstacle, the noticing of paces being adjusted to achieve a harmonious collective turning while walking, the noticing of various degrees of body contact among those walking, and the noticing of various activities walkers are engaged in besides their walking – all of these involve rather fine attentions to the progressively revealed and changing setting in which the walking and its recognition occur. We are recommending here that an analysis of doing walking must be prominently energetic in its treatment of these attentions by members. And we are recommending as well that topics such as the identification of collectivities, features of being together and of being alone, the normative and moral constitution of social phenomena, and so on, can be richly generated by detailed study of members' mundane activities (such as walking). Perhaps this will become more clear in a consideration of the production work of walking-together and walking-alone.

Production work

We have noted that walking-together can be recognized on the basis of various cues by an observer (pace, direction, spatial proximity, physical contact, talking, greetings and partings, head direction, etc.). It is evident that these 'cues' must be continually produced by the parties to the togetherings in order to make the activity continually available and accountable. Being together, as a fact, provides constraints and instructs a programme of actions, which in turn provides the basis for the doing and seeing, the producing and recognizing, of a togethering such as walking-together. It takes some effort, for example, to 'keep up' or to manage to 'take the right turn', and it takes some attention to the doing of a parting upon dissolution of walking-together, and so on. How then do members go about producing walking-together?

The on-going production of walking-together involves the participants in at least maintaining spatial proximity in some recognizable pattern. By this we intend to take note of the fact that definitive to walking-together is some physical co-presence, and that one who claims to be walking-together with someone who is absent is considered to suffer from some kind of longing or some kind of madness. The requirement of spatial proximity is illustrated by the observations that (a) participants who have lost some proximity will engage in repair work ranging from hurrying or slowing to calling out or later explaining the separation, (b) relatedly, violation of the maintenance of spatial proximity fundamentally undermines the enterprise of walking-together and can be seen as a serious interactional breach, and (c) similarly related, spatial proximity is a requisite for the production of some of the togethering-bound-activities like body contact and verbal exchanges. These observations deserve some explication.

Two features related to the maintenance of proximity in walking-together are direction and pace. Clearly, as direction and/or pace of those walking-together vary, the maintenance of spatial proximity becomes problematic for the participants. The strength of maintaining spatial proximity and, thereby, physical co-presence as non-problematic features of walking-together can be seen in such things as the propriety of announced changes in direction or pace. To do such body movements unannounced provides members with, and constrains members to see, such activities as 'showing disapproval', 'cold-shouldering', 'humorous disappearance', etc. It regularly occurs that before members engage in the activity of walking-together they will formulate those problems of direction, pace, destination, etc., that can be potentially problematic for the anticipated enterprise; of course, such a matter might interestingly differ if one joins a walk-in-progress where direction and pace are already in action.

As we have noted, part and parcel of the production of the activity of walking-together and contingent upon the maintenance of spatial proximity, are certain walking-together-bound-activities. In walking-together, for example, such activities as conversing, being available for conversation, touching, laughing, offering of offerables such as cigarettes or sweets, parting, and so on, are made relevant, and expectable, by the sheer fact of walking-together. That is, the fact of walking-together provides for the propriety and expectation of these activities. They are both cause and consequence (again, the phenomenon of reflexivity) of the production of the walking-together. These observations are demonstrable, in part, by taking note of the fact that members can excuse themselves from doing walking-together with accounts that, for example, they don't want to or cannot talk right now; indeed when someone joins a walk-in-progress, he can be informed that he has intruded by not being engaged in any walking-together-bounded-activities.

The production procedures prescribing the how of walking-together, provide the basis or resource by which members accomplish the fact of recognizing that some other members are doing walking-together. That some members can be seen as walking-together turns on their appearance as producing that particular togethering.

It should be perfectly well understood that walking-alone is likewise through and through a member's achievement – both in its production and in its recognition. For example, the relevance of the dimension of spatial proximity in doing walking-alone is dramatically illustrated in our data when a lone walker embarks on a passing of some other walker: direction, pace, and body attitude were all mobilized to ensure that the moment when the passer was in precise physical co-presence with the one he was passing would only be a fleeting one; and we have previously taken note of the work a lone walker must do in avoiding 'following', 'joining', or in other ways violating others in the street. We might also mention that members who are in fact alone can sometimes affect behaviour to suggest that they are 'with' someone when, for example, their unattached status makes them open to unwanted interactions. But the thrust of these observations is to suggest that doing walking-alone and doing walking-together are both the achievements of members engaged in producing their enterprises.

Concluding remarks

This discussion should of course be treated as only a sketch of one sort of analytic technology for gaining access to the methodic practices of members engaged in doing walking. It may be useful now to review briefly the thread of the discussion.

1. Beginning with a treatment of doing walking as the problematic accomplishment of members, we first took note of the relevance for members of achieving a solution to the 'navigational problem' occasioned by doing walking – repeated observations of the data revealed that members managed to avoid collisions under circumstances of heavy two-way walking traffic.

2. In attempting to gain access to some salient details of the members' solution, our observations of the data revealed that determinations of who was walking with whom appeared relevant for the accomplishment of such things as who and when and where to pass, how and why to adjust pace or bodily attitude, with whom which activities besides doing walking might be additionally engaged in, and the like – the fact of walking-alone and of walking-together provided members both a constraint and a resource in navigating their progress while doing walking.

3. We then took note of the reflexive character of producing and recognizing the accomplishments of walking-alone and of walking-together – our observations of the data provided us with some prominent features of both the 'recognition work' of member observers and of the 'production work' of members engaged in achieving walking-alone or walking-together.

We are now at the point of suggesting that these methodic practices of the 'art of walking' are indeed accessible to disciplined investigation. It would be no injustice to this report to say that we have taken the phenomenon of doing walking as an occasion to explore the interestingness of findings generated by a particular analytic framework that might well be applied to any commonplace activity of everyday life.

So while the substantive focus has been on the phenomenon of doing walking, we have not been concerned here with descriptively detailing this activity. Rather, our aim has been to recommend the fruitfulness of investigating the ordinary activities of everyday life under the auspices of an analytic apparatus treating those activities as the problematic accomplishments of members. We hope to have pointed to a treatment of doing walking that will expose and take as its central topic the methodic practices of members engaged as a matter of course in its production and recognition. But in the end, the promise of researches such as this is not merely that they may make accessible to rigorous inquiry the accomplished character of the mundane activities of everyday life; for the promise also resides in the fact that such researches treat as their topic of inquiry those features of social life taken for granted by lay and professional social analysts alike.

Further Reading

E. Bittner, 'Radicalism and the organization of radical movements', *American Sociological Review*, vol. 28, 1963.

E. Bittner, 'Police discretion in emergency apprehension of mentally ill persons', *Social Problems*, vol. 14, 1967.

E. Bittner, 'The police on Skid-Row: a study of peace keeping', *American Sociological Review*, vol. 32, 1967.

A. F. Blum, 'Theorizing', in J. Douglas (ed.), *Understanding Everyday Life*, Aldine Press, 1970.

A. F. Blum, 'The sociology of mental illness', in J. Douglas (ed.), *Deviance and Respectability: The Social Construction of Moral Meanings*, Basic Books, 1970.

A. F. Blum, 'The corpus of knowledge as a normative order', in M. F. D. Young (ed.), *Knowledge and Control*, Collier-Macmillan, 1971.

A. F. Blum and P. McHugh, 'The social ascription of motives', *American Sociological Review*, vol. 36, 1971.

L. Churchill, 'Ethnomethodology and measurement', *Social Forces*, vol. 50, 1971.

A. V. Cicourel, *Method and Measurement in Sociology*, Free Press, 1964.

A. V. Cicourel, 'Fertility, family planning and the social organization of family life: some methodological issues', *Journal of Social Issues*, vol. 23, 1967.

A. V. Cicourel, 'Kinship, marriage, and divorce in comparative family law, *Law and Society Review*, vol. 1 no. 2, June 1967.

A. V. Cicourel, *The Social Organization of Juvenile Justice*, Wiley, 1968.

A. V. Cicourel, 'Language as a variable in social research', *Sociological Focus*, vol. 3, 1969.

A. V. Cicourel, 'The acquisition of social structure: toward a developmental sociology of language and meaning', in J. Douglas (ed.), *Understanding Everyday Life*, Aldine Press, 1970.

A. V. Cicourel, 'Basic and normative rules in the negotiation of status and role', in D. Sudnow (ed.), *Studies in Social Interaction*, Free Press, 1972.

A. V. Cicourel, *Cognitive Sociology,* Penguin, 1973.

A. V. Cicourel and R. J. Boese, 'Sign language acquisition and the teaching of deaf children', in D. Hymes *et al.* (eds.), *The Functions of Language in the Classroom*, New York Teachers College Press, 1971.

A. V. Cicourel and J. Kitsuse, *The Educational Decision Makers*, Bobbs-Merrill, 1964.

J. Douglas, *The Social Meaning of Suicide*, Princeton University Press, 1967.

J. Douglas (ed.), *Understanding Everyday Life*, Aldine Press, 1970.

H. Garfinkel, 'Some sociological concepts and methods for psychiatrists', *Psychiatric Research Reports*, vol. 6, 1956.

H. Garfinkel, 'Conditions of successful degradation ceremonies', *American Journal of Sociology*, vol. 61, 1956.

H. Garfinkel, 'Aspects of the problem of common-sense knowledge of social structure', *Transactions of the Fourth World Congress of Sociology*, vol. 4, Milan and Stresa, 1959.

H. Garfinkel, 'A conception of, and experiments with, "trust" as a condition of stable concerted actions', in O. J. Harvey (ed.), *Motivation and Social Interaction*, Ronald Press, 1963.

H. Garfinkel, *Studies in Ethnomethodology*, Prentice-Hall, 1967.

H. Garfinkel, 'Remarks on ethnomethodology', in J. Gumperz and D. Hymes (eds.), *Directions in Sociolinguistics: The Ethnography of Communication*, Holt, Rinehart & Winston, 1972.

H. Garfinkel and H. Sacks, 'On formal structures of practical actions', in J. C. McKinney and E. A. Tiryakian (eds.), *Theoretical Sociology: Perspectives and Development*, Appleton-Century-Crofts, 1970.

G. Jefferson, 'Side sequences', in D. Sudnow (ed.), *Studies in Social Interaction*, Free Press, 1972.

J. Kitsuse and A. V. Cicourel, 'A note on the uses of official statistics', *Social Problems*, vol. 11, 1963.

P. McHugh, *Defining the Situation*, Bobbs-Merrill, 1968.

P. McHugh, 'On the failure of positivism', in J. Douglas (ed.), *Understanding Everyday Life*, Aldine Press, 1970.

P. McHugh, 'A common-sense perception of deviance', in H. P. Dreitzel (ed.), *Recent Sociology*, vol. 2, Macmillan Co., 1970.

M. Moerman, 'A Little knowledge', in S. Tyler (ed.), *Cognitive Anthropology*, Holt, Rinehart & Winston, 1969.

M. Moerman, 'Analysis of Lue conversation: providing accounts, finding breaches, and taking sides', in D. Sudnow (ed.), *Studies in Social Interaction*, Free Press, 1972.

H. Sacks, 'Sociological description', *Berkeley Journal of Sociology*, vol. 8, 1963.

H. Sacks, 'The search for help: no one to turn to', in E. S. Shneidman (ed.), *Essays in Self-Destruction*, Science House Inc., 1967.

H. Sacks, 'An initial investigation of the usability of conversational data for doing sociology', in D. Sudnow (ed.), *Studies in Social Interaction*, Free Press, 1972.

H. Sacks, 'Notes on police assessment of moral character', in D. Sudnow (ed.), *Studies in Social Interaction*, Free Press, 1972.

E. Schegloff, 'Sequencing in conversational openings', *American Anthropologist*, vol. 70, 1968.

E. Schegloff, 'Notes on a conversational practice: formulating place', in D. Sudnow (ed.), *Studies in Social Interaction*, Free Press, 1972.

J. Schenkein, 'Towards an analysis of natural conversation and the sense of "heheh"', *Semiotica,* vol. 6, 1972, pp. 344–77.

M. B. Scott and S. M. Lyman, 'Accounts', *American Sociological Review*, vol. 33, 1968.

M. Speier, 'The everyday world of the child', in J. Douglas (ed.), *Understanding Everyday Life*, Aldine Press, 1970.

M. Speier, 'Some conversational problems for interactional analysis', in D. Sudnow (ed.), *Studies in Social Interaction*, Free Press, 1972.

D. Sudnow, 'Normal crimes: sociological features of the penal code in a public defender's office', *Social Problems*, vol. 12, 1965.

D. Sudnow, *Passing On: The Social Organization of Dying*, Prentice-Hall, 1967.

D. Sudnow, 'Temporal parameters of interpersonal observation', in D. Sudnow (ed.), *Studies in Social Interaction*, Free Press, 1972.

R. Turner, 'The ethnography of experiment', *American Behavioral Scientist*, April, 1967.

R. Turner, 'Some formal properties of therapy talk', in D. Sudnow (ed.), *Studies in Social Interaction*, Free Press, 1972.

S. Twer, 'Tactics for determining persons' resources for depicting, contriving, and describing behavioral episodes', in D. Sudnow (ed.), *Studies in Social Interaction*, Free Press, 1972.

D. L. Wieder, 'On meaning by rule', in J. Douglas (ed.), *Understanding Everyday Life*, Aldine Press, 1970.

T. P. Wilson, 'Normative and interpretive paradigms in sociology', in J. Douglas (ed.), *Understanding Everyday Life*, Aldine Press, 1970.

D. H. Zimmerman, 'Tasks and troubles: the practical bases of work activities in a public assistance organization', in D. A. Hansen (ed.), *Explorations in Sociology and Counselling*, Houghton Mifflin, 1969.

D. H. Zimmerman, 'The practicalities of rule use', in J. Douglas (ed.), *Understanding Everyday Life*, Aldine Press, 1970.

D. H. Zimmerman and M. Pollner, 'The everyday world as a phenomenon', in J. Douglas (ed.), *Understanding Everyday Life*, Aldine Press, 1970.

Commentary and Criticism

American Sociological Review Symposium of H. Garfinkel's *Studies in Ethnomethodology*, Reviews by G. Swanson, A. F. C. Wallace and J. Coleman, *American Sociological Review*, vol. 33, 1968.

N. K. Denzin, 'Symbolic interactionism and ethnomethodology: a proposed synthesis', in J. Douglas (ed.), *Understanding Everyday Life*, Aldine Press, 1970.

M. Israel, 'Comment on James Coleman's review of Harold Garfinkel's *Studies in Ethnomethodology*', *American Sociologist*, vol. 4, 1969.

P. Filmer, D. Walsh, M. Philipson and D. Silverman, *New Directions in Sociological Theory*, Collier-Macmillan, 1972.

D. H. Zimmerman and D. L. Wieder, 'Ethnomethodology and the problem of order: comment on Denzin', in J. Douglas (ed.), *Understanding Everyday Life*, Aldine Press, 1970.

Acknowledgements

For permission to reproduce the Readings in this volume,
acknowledgement is made to the following:

1 Institute for Study of Social Change, Purdue University
3 Melvin Pollner
4 Dorothy E. Smith
6 University of Washington Press
7 *Social Research*
8 A. V. Cicourel
9 Prentice-Hall Inc.
10 Prentice-Hall Inc.
11 Prentice-Hall Inc.
12 Basic Books Inc.
13 Mouton & Co.
15 Robert MacKay
16 Routledge & Kegan Paul Ltd & Aldine Publishing Co.
17 CBS Education International
18 Mouton & Co.

Author Index

Albert, E. 236
Angell, A. 51
Ariès, P. 184
Austin, J. L. 197–203, 207, 213

Bales, R. 15, 164, 181
Barnard, C. 80
Becker, H. S. 20, 27–35, 40
Berger, P. 39
Berreman, G. 57
Bittner, E. 20, 84, 157
Blau, P. 69
Blum, A. 9, 180, 197
Brim, O. G. 180, 181
Broom, L. 181
Burke, K. 79
Burling, R. 54

Caton, C. E. 8–9
Castaneda, C. 190
Chappell, V. C. 213
Charlsworth, M. J. 72
Chomsky, N. 183
Cicourel, A. V. 12, 30, 84, 180–89
Clausen J. 181
Clemmer, D. 171
Colby, B. 24
Cooley, C. 69
Crowle, A. 204
Curphey, T. J. 96

Dalton, M. 80
Dickson, W. J. 80
Dingle, H. 23
Durkheim, E. 120, 149, 151

Elkin, F. 181
Elliot, H. 8–9
Engels, F. 41
Etzioni, A. 69
Evans-Pritchard, E. E. 48–50

Farberow, N. L. 96
Freeman, H. D. 212
Fischer, A. 223, 226
Fischer, J. 223, 226

Garfinkel, H. 7, 12, 14–15, 25–32, 39,
    75, 84, 129, 157, 160–66, 171,
    180–86, 190, 197, 209, 234
Gerth, H. 72
Gibbs, J. 33
Gill, H. 171
Goffman, E. 77, 211–12, 261
Goodenough, W. 64
Gurwitsch, A. 31, 162

Hall, E. T. 184
Haire, M. 74
Harrah, D. 119
Henderson, A. M. 72
Hickey, G. C. 54
Holt, J. 183
Homans, G. C. 9–10
Horton, P. B. 181
Hughes, J. 24
Hunt, C. L. 181
Husserl, E. 69
Hymes, D. H. 235

Inkeles, A. 181–2

Jefferson, G. 233

de Kadt, E. 51
Kaufman, F. 73
Kramer, M. 109
Kuhn, T. S. 23
Kuno, B. E. 113

Labov, W. 183–4
La Raw, M. 55

Leach, E. 54
Le Bar, F. M. 54
Lehman, F. K. 54–5
Lewis, B. N. 70
Litman, R. E. 96
Luckmann, T. 39

McHugh, P. 166
Mackay, R. 183
Mannheim, K. 123, 160
Marshall, A. 72
Marx, K. 41–3
Maurer, D. 173
Mayer, C. L. 186
Maxwell, K. 70
Mead, G. H. 32
Meehl, P. E. 119
Mehan, H. 184
Mendlovitz, S. 15
Merleau-Ponty, M. 31, 39, 182, 190
Mills, C. W. 72
Moerman, M. 9–10, 20, 50, 54, 62, 64,
     197n, 233, 235
Moore, G. E. 69
Musgrave, J. K. 54

Nadel, S. F. 57
Nagel, E. 21–5
Naroll, R. 65
Neill, A. S. 183

Opie, I. 184
Opie, P. 184

Pareto, V. 69
Parsons, T. 43, 69, 72, 181
Persky, S. 210
Pines, M. 183
Plump, J. H. 184
Pollner, M. 20, 34, 39, 161, 171, 181
Polsky, N. 174

Rajadhon, P. A. 63
Rheinstein, M. 72
Roethlisberger, F. J. 80

Roth, D. 184
Rouse, W. H. D. 188
Russell, B. 72
Ryave, A. L. 196
Ryle, G. 213

Sacks, H. 11–12, 32, 161, 164, 184,
     196–8, 208–9, 216, 219, 233, 235–6,
     249
Schegloff, E. 12, 196, 208, 210–11,
     233, 249, 255
Schenkein, J. N. 196, 233
Schuessler, K. F. 15
Schutz, A. 25, 29, 74, 183, 185
Scott, W. R. 69
Selznick, P. 70–71, 77–8, 80, 181
Service, E. 54
Sharrock, W. 12
Shils, E. 72
Shneidman, E. S. 96
Simmons, O. G. 212
Smith, D. 20
Socrates 188
Speier, M. 184, 209
Spicer, E. M. 64
Spiegelberg, H. 164
Stebbing, L. S. 24
Steward, J. 64
Strodtbeck, F. 15
Sudnow, D. 11, 18, 84
Sutherland, E. 173
Sykes, G. 173

Tönnies, F. 69

Weber, M. 71–5
Whitrow, G. J. 70
Wieder, D. L. 157
Wilson, T. P. 180
Wittgenstein, L. 213

Zetterberg, H. 20, 41–3
Zimmerman, D. H. 12, 84, 128–34,
     157, 161, 171, 181

Subject Index

Accomplishments 8, 27, 174
  managed 25
  practical 196
  problematic 274
  situated 265, 267
Accounts 17, 35, 88, 95, 97, 99, 117,
    119, 121, 125–6, 128, 130–39, 142,
    156, 161, 164, 171, 183, 187, 211, 272
  adequacy of 16, 135
  factual 131–2
  formulated 123–4
  giving 212–13
  indexicality of 129
  occasioned 143
  -of-social-action 172
  philosophy of science 8, 21, 26
  reflexivity of 129
  societal members' 20
  warranted 200
Activity 37, 86, 88, 91–9, 108–9, 144,
    118–19, 127, 143–51, 156, 158,
    174–5, 178, 197–8, 200–207, 214,
    216, 218, 226–8, 233, 241, 254–5,
    258, 267, 270, 273
  category-bound, 221–5
  category-generated 211
  clinic 119, 123
  concerted 9, 12, 69, 196
  constituent 198–9, 213
  conversational 235
  day-to-day 85
  folk 182
  judgemental 32
  members' 10, 45–52
  mundane 271, 274
  ordinary 135, 274
  organizational 189
  police 90
  practical 12
  recreational 165
  research 126–7

  routine 92, 94–5
  settinged 84, 269
  signalizing 147
  social 271
  togethering-bound- 270, 272
Adequate causal analysis 149
Ad hoc 125
  -ing practices 157
  rules 94
Adjacency pair 238–45, 251, 258
Adult–child interaction 180–82, 184,
    190
Appearances, normal 86
Argot 173–9
Attention, psychological notion of 31
Attitude of everyday life 74

Bureaucracy, Weber's theory of 72–4

Categorical identification 211–12
Ceteris paribus clause 73
Closing section 242, 245–9, 251–7,
    259–64
Closings 233–5, 237, 242–9, 257–63
  pre- 249–57
Code
  accounts 161, 164
  convict 144, 160–61, 169–71
  -relevant 155
  telling the 144, 149–54, 156–65, 169–72
  open, flexible structure of 157
Cognitive system 62, 66
Collectivity 9, 45–52, 271
Collusion 73
Common sense 9, 16, 20–26, 28, 30,
    46–7, 85, 175, 190, 206, 209
  actor 29, 32
  attitude 29
  concept 70
  conceptions 46, 181
  construct 74, 78

Common sense – *continued*
 construction 75
 division of the discipline 214
 grounds 95
 knowledge 16, 18, 39, 182, 207
 meanings 75
 models 27, 40
 notion 70
 orientation 73
 outlook 75
 perspective 70
 position 180
 practice 47
 presuppositions 74–6
 reasoners 38
 situations of choice 96
 talk 39
 typifications 74
 understanding 37
 world 181–2, 186
Complaints 206–12
Compliance, gambit of 77
Conditional relevance 208
Constancy hypothesis 31
Contract 119–26
Convention(s), 69, 201
'Correction-invitation device' 178
Corroborative reference 79–80
Counting 11, 22, 84, 102–8
Course of action 85, 94, 101, 124, 139,
 140–42, 158–9
Culture 45–6, 64–6, 106, 181, 218, 267,
 269
 (adult) 180
 change 60–61
 children's 184, 190
 common 54, 57
 contact 10
 national 63
 prison 171
 sub- 173

Death 96–8, 100–108, 154
Definition of the situation 149, 160
Deviance 27–35, 37–40, 181
Deviant behavior 144–9

Distribution of speaker's rights 209
Documental representation 123,
 126
Documentary
 method 160–66, 170
 representation 123
'Doing describing' 216

Etcetera clause 157, 168
Ethnomethodology 7, 11–18, 27, 75
Ethnoscience 15, 64
Explication 9, 71, 100, 153, 173,
 180–81, 205, 214, 231, 234, 272
Explicative acts 38
Expressions
 indexical 161–2
 objective 122–3
 occasional 121–3
 ordinary, stock use of 213

Facts 130, 137, 145, 156
 as a practical accomplishment 128
 brute 203
 domain of 75
 gathering 161
 of the matter 129
 plain 132–5, 142
 self-evident 84
 social 27, 77, 149, 151, 213
Features
 constituent 17, 35–7, 97, 269
 formal 29, 182
 reflexive 269
Folk
 activity 182
 -beliefs 61
 discipline 182
 science 10
 typifications 85
For all practical purposes, 25, 96–101,
 137–8
Force
 of an utterance 206
 performative 202
Former mental patients 205–12
Free variation 164

Gestalt-contexture 161–3, 170
Gloss 17, 32, 35, 37, 180–81, 265
Greetings 208–11, 227–8, 238–9, 263, 271

Heroin 147, 173–9
Hypothesis testing 97, 177–8

Ideology 41–5
Indexicality 65, 129, 161–2
Indifference 173, 181, 208
Information 84–92, 94, 97, 109–18, 121–6, 128–34, 138, 141, 175
 'core' 116
 factual 136–7
Informational
 imbalance 89
 value 209
Interpretive
 approach 180
 competencies 182–90
 device 161, 168
 perspective 182–4
 procedures 186–7
Intersubjectivity 180, 190

Knowledge 12, 15–16, 21, 89, 158, 270
 common-sense 16, 18, 39, 182, 207
 corpus of 45–52
 inside 95
 members' 18, 204–10, 216, 218
 ordered 17
 shared 51, 208
 socialized 205
 stock of 85
 tacit 85

Labelling 27, 29–34, 37–40, 62, 65, 94
Leave-taking 261
Located phenomenon 201
Logic-in-use 94

Management of relationships 210
Marking
 contract 259
 misplacement 258

Maxim 30, 145–50, 157, 160–61, 165–70
 hearer's 219–26
 labelling 31
 viewer's 225–60
Membership categorization devices 218–22
Mentionables 242–8, 252, 257
Motivated
 act 288
 refusal 211
Motivation 65, 88, 115–16, 135, 140, 143, 149–53, 164–8
Motivationally transparent 135
Multi-consequential 153
Multi-formulative 153–4

Natural boundaries 266
Navigational problem 266–8, 273
Neopraxiology 18
Normative approach 180
 perspective 181–2

Observable–reportable 17
Occasioned corpus 161, 171
'Oral tradition' 151
Order 119, 122
 moral 144, 161, 170
 normative 144, 150–51, 170–72
 ontological 182
 problem of 43
 social 11, 84, 114, 172, 214
Ordinary language philosophy 8
Organization(s) 11, 20, 70–77, 84, 86, 126, 134–5, 137, 143, 162, 176, 189
 close order 241
 correctional 149
 formal 69, 71–80
 of closings 261–2
 of conversation 263–4
 of speaker turns 260
 of talk 196, 247
 orders of 235, 251
 overall structural 239, 249
  of conversation 233, 235
 rehabilitative 144

Organization(s) – *continued*
  sequential 233, 258
  social 43, 153
  work 131
Ownership 49–52

Paper work 116
Participant observation 66–7, 144
  covert 174
Passing 174, 179, 210
Performatives 197–8, 204, 207
  conventional supports of 202
  explicit 201
  implicit 199–202
  primitive 199–202
Perspective 45
  common-sense 70
  interpretive 182–4
  labelling 27
  normative 181–2
  of the actor 74–5
  reciprocity of 187
Phenomenological method 164
Police 30, 34–7, 84–7, 89–95, 146
Practical reasoning 7–11, 18, 20, 84
Prediction 150, 167–8, 212, 221
Programmatic constructions 70
Properties
  formal 60, 84, 170
  invariant 207
  stable 75
Proverbs 9–10, 95, 100

Quantification 10

Records 99, 117, 121–9, 134–43
  actuarial 119–26
  'bad' 113–14, 119
  bureaucratic 132
  clinic 109, 113–14, 119–21
  official 84–5, 92, 94, 133
  organizational 84, 94, 132
  police 84, 93
Reflexive 37, 152, 159, 164, 183, 185,
  269, 273
Reflexivity 129, 272

Relevant absences 208
Rules 28, 33, 39, 54–5, 70, 75–80, 84,
  98, 100, 114, 117–18, 146–9,
  164–71, 174, 177, 221
  ad hoc 94
  chaining 229
  coding 122
  consistency 219
    corollary 220, 224
  conversation 235
  decision 97
  economy 219
  explicit 90
  formal 78
  grammatical 122
  implicit 66
  -in-common 67
  in use 157
  interpretive 183
  kinship 46
  legal 95
  normal 85
  of adjacency pair operation 239
  of application 219
  of conduct 77
  of inductive and deductive inference
    97
  of practice 114
  of rational decision-making 97
  organizational 85
  procedural 94
  reference satisfactoriness 219
  relevance 219, 225, 228
  schematic 77
  sequencing 229
  social 68
  substantive 94
  surface 183, 185
  transition 252, 257
  violation 30–6
  working 43
Rule – governed 117, 149

Schema
  interpretive 9
  ordering 125

self-elaborating 161
tentative 161
Scheme of interpretation 76, 125, 149, 161, 170, 185–8
Science 21–6, 171, 197
  accredited 8, 23
  folk 10
  normal 23
  proto- 9
Scientific explanation 170
Sequential
  implicativeness 239
  ordering 226
  organization 233, 258
  placement 242
  properties 210
Signs 43, 106
Slots 210, 228, 251
Small groups 15
Socialization 180–84
Sociolinguistics 197
Speaker–hearer 11
Speech act 201
Stigma 212
Story 59, 100, 117, 129–30, 134, 142, 155, 158, 177, 216, 226–32
Structural–functional analysis 71
Subanun 17
Subjectivism 216
Suicide 11, 84, 96–101

Taxonomy 156
Telephone
  call 210, 223
  contacts 249
  conversations 250, 260–63
Theorizing 8–9, 20, 41, 72, 180–81
  actors' 74
  practical 95
  psychological 31
Theory, theories 7–9, 20, 74, 85, 88, 94, 180–84, 204, 213
  actors' 85
  construction 41

deductive 170–71
labelling 20, 31–4
  of action 94
  of decision-making 97
  of interests 169–70
  of the convict code 169
'Ticket' 231–2
Tokens 123
Topic
  bounding 248
  close 251
  first 242–8, 255
  improvised 261
  initiating a 210
  of a conversation 158
  selection 210
  structure 245–6
  talk 210, 246–8, 251–8, 262
    organization of 233, 242–3
  type 248
Total speech situation 201, 206–14
Transformational grammar 213
Transition
  property 256
  relevance 236–41
  rule 252, 257
Trans-situationality 150
Tribe 54, 57, 62–5
Troubles 107, 115–19, 123, 134, 151, 208, 211, 231, 267
  general methodological 113
  normal, natural 113–15
  structurally normal 119
Turns 246
  at talking 214
  speaker 233, 235–6, 260

Walking 196, 267–70, 272
  doing 265–6, 271, 273–4
Work 11, 153, 263, 267
  accounting 169
  production 269–71, 273
  recognition 269–71, 273
World view 45